FEAR OF BLACK
CONSCIOUSNESS

FEAR OF BLACK CONSCIOUSNESS

LEWIS R. GORDON

FARRAR, STRAUS AND GIROUX

NEW YORK

Farrar, Straus and Giroux
120 Broadway, New York 10271

Grateful acknowledgment is made for permission to reprint the following
previously published material:
Lines from Chandramohan Sathyanathan, *Love After Babel and Other Poems*
(Daraja Press, 2020), used with permission.
Excerpt from James Davis III, "Law, Prison, and Double-Double
Consciousness: A Phenomenological View of the Black Prisoner's Experience,"
The Yale Law Journal Forum 28 (April 2019), used with permission.
Lines from Richard Jones, "Negro Please," in *A Hill in Lunenburg: New Poems*
(American Star Books, 2014), used with permission.

Library of Congress Cataloging-in-Publication Data
Names: Gordon, Lewis R. (Lewis Ricardo), 1962– author.
Title: Fear of black consciousness / Lewis R. Gordon.
Description: First edition. | New York : Farrar, Straus and Giroux, 2022. | Includes
    bibliographical references and index.
Identifiers: LCCN 2021038616 | ISBN 9780374159023 (hardcover)
Subjects: LCSH: Blacks—Race identity. | Race awareness. | Racism. | Anti-racism.
Classification: LCC HT1575 .G67 2022 | DDC 305.896/073—dc23/eng/20211020
LC record available at https://lccn.loc.gov/2021038616

Our books may be purchased in bulk for promotional, educational, or business
use. Please contact your local bookseller or the Macmillan Corporate and
Premium Sales Department at 1-800-221-7945, extension 5442, or by email at
MacmillanSpecialMarkets@macmillan.com.

www.fsgbooks.com
www.twitter.com/fsgbooks • www.facebook.com/fsgbooks

10 9 8 7 6 5 4 3 2 1

To Hank Aaron, Colin Abel, Samir Amin, Hugh Becca,

Chadwick Boseman, Ray Bottass, Kamau Brathwaite,

Sarah (Waterloo) Broadie, James Cone, Elijah Cummings,

Anani Dzidzienyo, Ruth Bader Ginsburg, Sheila Grant,

Kwame Gyekye, Wilson Harris, F. Abiola Irele, Colin Krikler,

Shirley Levy, Alanna Lockwood, María Lugones, Joseph

Margolis, John Mascolo, Jill Mehler, Denise Dawn Elaine

Mitchell, Minoweh Ikidowin (aka Donna Edmonds Mitchell),

Milton Mitchell, Aubrey Maitshwe Mokoape, Richard Wayne

Penniman (aka Little Richard), Ghjuvan'Teramu Rocchi,

Emile Michael Solomon, Lorenzo ("Uncle Sonny") Solomon,

Walter South, and Wamba dia Wamba, who joined the

ancestors during the composition and completion of this book

CONTENTS

FEAR OF BLACK
CONSCIOUSNESS

PROLOGUE

Looking within
At times a failure to see
In the face of limitations

Looking within
Grows—intensifles
Implodes

Falling within
Is the heaviest descent,
Physicists tell us

Ask any black hole
—from, of course,
a distance

    —Author's poem

I was not born with a black consciousness. I very much doubt anyone could be. The same applies to a brown, red, white, yellow, or any
other kind of racialized consciousness. We could go down a long list of
identities without which we are born. Yet we eventually learn, and at
times are forced into them.

I was born in the island country of Jamaica in 1962, a few months before its legal independence from the British Empire. That meant I was afforded the privilege of a childhood of prime ministers who were all brown or black—or at least of color. Yet we children had no reason to think of them in those terms. They were simply the highest leadership of our country. Similar people were found on our printed currency, and it was not unusual for us to meet a dentist, lawyer, or schoolteacher who looked like most of us. The same applied to journalists and entertainers on television. The people who produced our music were the same, and although we would see very light-skinned people at the beaches or at tourist sites, nothing in them represented limits in us. After all, "we" were there in all walks of life. From the elite to the working class to the mountain or "country" folks, all were "us." We were Jamaicans. That ordinary form of belonging is something many blacks who live in predominantly white countries don't experience. When I woke each morning, my aim wasn't to leave the country of my birth, and as far as I knew and expected, life was about being part of a world that preceded everyone I knew and would continue well after we are gone. We were, in other words, ordinary.

All my childhood images of authority, beauty, and love were of people who, in the contexts of North America and Europe, crossed color lines. The greatest image of authority in my family was my maternal great-grandfather, Uriah Ewan, whom we simply called "Grandfather." Grandfather was a six-foot-ten, dark-skinned Panamanian-Liberian man in his nineties. Having lost his battle with glaucoma, he was also blind. His words were full of wisdom, and his touch—he had to touch us with his fingers or hold us with his big hands in order to "see" us—was always loving and tender. My other images of authority were my maternal great-grandmother, Beatrice Norton Ewan ("Granny Bea"), who was a Jewish woman of Irish, Scottish, and Tamil descent; my paternal grandmother, Gertrude Stoddart, Chinese and Scottish; and my many aunts, of many hues. My main image of beauty was my mother, Yvonne Patricia Solomon, who was a dark-skinned woman of Jewish ancestry on both sides, as her maternal Irish Jewish lineage was met with her paternal Palestinian Jewish one. Family, for me, was colorful. It still is.

This is not to say that I was not aware of Jamaica's complexion aristocracy. As the island had become an independent country a few months after my birth, vestiges of British colonialism remained. Light-skinned people were called "beautiful," "decent," and "smart." Dark-skinned people were often called "ugly," "indecent," and "stupid"—even "*renk*" (a patois term for smelly). This posed many contradictions, since my dark-skinned mother received compliments for her beauty and brains wherever she went. There was also that high regard in which we held Grandfather, and nearly every one of my actual encounters with beauty, kindness, and wisdom was from dark-skinned relatives and friends. Yet it was clear that Jamaican society favored light-skinned people. The overwhelming nonwhite professionals were brown and lighter. Despite so much of Jamaican society being on the side of those light-skinned people, it always struck me that pale people were never satisfied. There was always something bothering them.

One dark-color incident stood out to me far above the rest. There was a dark-skinned boy in the junior school I attended when I was six. Some older children constantly teased him and called him "Paul Bogle." The historic Bogle's handsome face is on Jamaica's two-dollar bill. Bogle was one of the country's national heroes. He was hanged for rebelling against the British. Imagine a child in the United States being teased for resembling Nathan Hale, who famously regretted having only one life to give for his country. That little boy should have been proud to look like Bogle, and the others should have been marveling at his resemblance. Yet they teased him, because for them, as it turned out, the dominating feature of Bogle, like that of the boy, was the darkness of his skin. Despite that abuse, no one, including his abusers, took the position that that boy wasn't Jamaican or, even more, of a different "race."

I left the island of Jamaica in 1971, with the aid of two aunts, to reunite with my mother, who had migrated to New York City with only five U.S. dollars in her pocket when she left my stepfather. Her story and what her three boys faced are now familiar narratives, as stories of undocumented migrants and refugees facing hardship are now well known across the globe. My excitement from being in the city of a country often shown in movies was quickly transformed by the reality of the dirt, grit, and violence of the Bronx, where I would live for nearly twenty years. It was there that I developed a racialized black consciousness.

My first experience of black consciousness was in elementary school. I was seated next to a little white boy named Tommy. I was very enthusiastic about being in school. I read everything and was eager to answer questions when the teacher called upon us. During the second week, Tommy turned to me and asked, with a smirk, "How's it going, nigger?"

Odd as it sounds, I didn't know what the word "nigger" meant. What made me suspicious was his smirk. It was clear he was taking advantage of my ignorance and was enjoying doing so. When I asked him what the word meant, he laughed and refused to explain. So during an exercise in breakout groups, I asked other students to explain. They were brown and darker Puerto Ricans and, in today's parlance, African Americans. The look on their faces made it clear something was awry. They had some difficulty explaining it until one finally said, "It's a bad name for black people. It means being dirty, stupid—black."

I went back to my seat.

Tommy smiled. "So, what'd you learn, nigger?"

I grabbed his throat and threw him to the ground and stomped on his face. The teacher pulled me off of him.

Later, in the principal's office, my teacher—a tall, blond Italian woman whose style was straight out of the late 1960s television series *Mod Squad*—came to talk to me. She said, "You seem like such a nice boy. I didn't expect that of you."

I didn't say anything.

She sighed. "You've been so nice. And smart. I really didn't expect that."

"Why?" I asked her. "Why aren't you talking to Tommy about what you expect of him?"

When school was dismissed and we were all heading home, I saw Tommy. He was with a group of white boys. He pointed to me. As they walked up to me with their fists clenched, I broke through them and toppled Tommy over. As his friends descended upon me, I pushed them to the side. Tommy broke free and ran, and I ran after him. His friends stood frozen at what for them was apparently unthinkable. I soon learned that the image of a white boy running away from a black boy was rare in that part of the Bronx—and for that matter, anywhere in the United States. Our school was where the Italian neighborhood on the one hand and the black and Puerto Rican one on the other met as a central point from which each group was to go separate ways. I had not yet learned to see the Italian, Irish, and European Jewish children as white. They resembled some of my relatives back in Jamaica, none of whom identified as white.

I have had many experiences of being called "nigger" over the years. Not tolerating it—even when doing so meant receiving abuse—made it clear to me that the valorization of nonviolence and tolerance I heard throughout my subsequent adolescent years was profoundly mistaken. It's a recipe for cultivating in black people nothing short of an inferiority complex. Standing up against white degradation, even when we lose, is, frankly, healthy. Deep down, most white people know this. They wouldn't do otherwise if the situations were reversed. Fighting against humiliation and disrespect enables us to live with ourselves. I spent two grades with Tommy in that elementary school. Not once after that incident did he or any other white student utter the word "nigger" in class. Did they hold that insult in thought? Most likely. But their hesitation to hurl it at us marked a diminution of their power.

Unfortunately, this peace was not the same among the black and the Puerto Rican students. Too many fights attested to the myriad of abasements among us, and in my case—since I was at times taken for Puerto Rican—the experience went across antiblackness, anti–Puerto Ricanness, and anti-nearly-everything-else. For instance, experiencing my first winter, I realized that holding my bag against my chest kept me warm. As I walked down the street, a boy ran up to me yelling, "Look at the fag, carrying his books like a girl!"

Yet despite all those conflicts, many of the white children and those of color in those classes became friends, or at least friendly. As friends do, black children would visit each other's apartments. None of our families owned homes. An Italian boy by the name of Johnny and I became friends, and we would walk through the Italian neighborhood near Arthur Avenue, where the famous scene from the movie *The Godfather*, of Michael Corleone shooting the corrupt Irish cop and the Turkish gang rival, takes place. In fact, come to think of it, Johnny resembled Al Pacino, the actor who played Michael Corleone. Things were fine until we realized that heading to hang out at his home was not a good idea. A wonderful person though he was, his family was another story. That was the end of our friendship.

The years that followed included everything from being spat on and getting attacked by whites with baseball bats to witnessing blood flowing across sidewalks as crowds of whites attacked black students in my middle school, and, of course, the litany of ways in which white children were and continue to be singled out for advancement and black and brown children were—as many continue to be—weeded out. Three decades later, black people knew fully well what President George W. Bush's No Child Left Behind policy meant. No *white* child left behind.

As of the writing of this prologue, people all over the globe are besieged by a deadly pandemic exacerbated by the incompetence on the one hand and the malfeasance on the other of leadership in some countries nostalgic for times in which black people standing up for themselves would lead to their corpses dangling from the nearest trees. Yet, as the gun replaced the rope for white vigilantes against a black man jogging in Atlanta and a police officer's knee functioned as the same for nine minutes and twenty-nine seconds in Minneapolis, people took to the streets in 2020 under the realization of what it means to cry "I can't breathe."

I learned something from my childhood experience of coming into black consciousness: it's a rude awakening.

INTRODUCTION: STRUGGLING TO BREATHE

In early 2020, I went on an errand to New York City. The day after I returned, I felt lower back pains that I attributed to getting too old for the drive back and forth from northern Connecticut. Then I began to experience chills. I was struck down a few days later with full-blown COVID-19. The affliction became my plight as a "long hauler" into the succeeding year.

A few months in, a friend asked me what it was like. I told him I felt like I had been thrown into a pit of biting Komodo dragons, and after managing to climb out, I rolled over onto shards of glass and found that a relief. At the height of the illness, I opened my "death file." High fevers brought on hallucinations that included visits from deceased loved ones. I found their visits comforting despite being aware it was my subconscious at work. We would have wonderful conversations, humorous even, about their afterlife. Then I remembered that when I used to dream about deceased relatives, mentioning their death had always led to their departure. This time, they weren't leaving. I began to wonder if I had already taken my last breath. I was fortunately mistaken. It wasn't my time.

I refused to go to the hospital. Having seen how blacks are treated by medical professionals in emergency rooms, I concluded: black people go in, but most of us don't get out—at least alive. The terrible demographics of casualties from the disease supported my conclusion. Even where black people may have equal access, it doesn't follow that there is no racism involved in the administering of medical services to us. I have spoken to other black and South Asian men who avoided hospitals when they realized they were afflicted. They reasoned that they are alive because they'd nursed themselves at home. I understand, however, that it would be ill-advised to avoid life-saving vaccines and caring health professionals.

I lost friends, students, relatives, and I am in touch with so many who lost loved ones as the pandemic raged on. Their survivors struggle with the fact of not having been able to be with their loved ones in those final moments and the process of their interment or cremation. A good friend in Paris is still in sorrow over a loved one's dying alone because no one had been permitted to visit him in the hospital. She and his relatives were permitted only to stand outside at distances in front of the crematorium. As an Orthodox Jew who survived the Shoah (Holocaust), she experienced multiple levels of trauma while watching the smoke rise into the air as his corpse turned to ash.

I think often of what my maternal grandmother used to say from her late eighties onward when I telephoned her. "How're you doing, young lady?" I would ask her.

Her response: "Still here."

Not all of us understand the significance of being able to say those words. For some starting to feel better, the high from the initial rush of oxygen led them to leap recklessly back into the outside world, not understanding that feeling better is not identical with actually being so. The wreckage on their insides makes racing back out into the world a dangerous thing to do. Many of them report being "reinfected," when they are most likely suffering from a relapse or simply have damaged themselves by interrupting their bodies' effort to mend from the inside out.

I'm still here. History never waits for anyone. There's still so much to do. With humility—because there are so many things greater than us—some of us press on. Being alive, we face the continued opportunity and, as expressed in Judaism, *mitzvah* of living.

The COVID-19 pandemic arrived amid other ongoing pandemics. They include antiblack racism, rapacious capitalism, disguised colonialism, neofascism, and dehumanizing social policies of structured inequality. This book was written during the convergence of those pandemics—ongoing antidemocratic efforts to effect global disempowerment of all but a small set of elites under the guise of "liberal democracy." A name for this is neoliberalism, whose mantra is "privatization." Under that rubric, it valorizes abstract and moralistic notions of "the individual" as though each person is an individual god capable of determining the conditions of their needs by themselves. As human beings depend on one another for our survival, the isolation born from privatization renders most of us vulnerable, as access and institutional support recede from the majority of human beings into the hands of a few global elites. This decline in social services continues the production of vulnerability. This precarious situation inevitably creates, as witnessed throughout the North American spring of 2020, a crisis of legitimacy. Promises of privatized arrangements ultimately benefiting "all" are clearly false; a search for the sources of the misery, ranging from the pandemic to surges in unemployment, follows. The neoliberal response of more privatization, more capitalism, and more deregulation is, at minimum, mystifying.

Another response comes from neoconservatism. The neoconservative response to the crises of neoliberalism is to look back instead of forward. Forward thinking tends toward notions of the "social," such as democratic socialism in one form and social democracies in another. Democratic socialism involves democratic management of a socialist society. Social democracy involves democratic means of achieving socialism, which makes the achievement somewhere between capitalism and socialism. Rejecting anything with the word "social" in it, neoconservatives focus on the "liberal" in liberal democracy. Eliminating that, however, means exploring what should remain. If what is left is "democracy" by itself, the question is: What kind?

For neoconservatives, what is to be done depends on diagnosing the sources of the crises. For them, the causes are disorder and the *international* reach of the global. The task, as they see it, is to recede into an ordered and contained society. This means propping up institutions of law and order, with the latter as the source of legitimacy. Devoting attention to order requires the elimination of sources of disorder, which neoconservatives regard as dissent and difference. Thus, groups and ideas that they consider disorderly become targets for containment and elimination. These groups invariably are outsiders and whomever they consider undesirable foreigners. The turn to xenophobia has its bedfellows of racism, misogyny, homophobia, and hatred of all those who are considered outsiders. This reactionary turn rejects the idea of countries such as Brazil, India, the United Kingdom, and the United States as citizens of the world and replaces it with nationalism premised on cherry-picked values from each country's past under the aegis of "tradition." Premised on anti-difference, this appeal expresses notions of purity. The search for the "pure" nation, inevitably racist, means also that, unlike neoliberalism, neoconservatism focuses on groups. The search for the pure nation in a country such as the United States means "white"—specifically, white Anglo-Saxon Protestant—and, as the world saw in Donald Trump's 2016 presidential campaign and subsequent presidency, gives that white-dominated past a coveted adjective, "great," for which some were willing to storm the U.S. Capitol building in January 2021 as Congress certified his November 2020 loss and successor Joseph Biden's victory.

Despite their common agenda of radicalized privatization of power, global economic elites are split between the neoliberals and the neoconservatives. Their shared wealth, however, means they can each invest in the global spread of their agenda. The neoconservative wing does so through investing in authoritarianism and the erosion of government services. This radicalizes inequalities wherever they take hold. The increased crises they generate create more mystification, and as with the neoliberal demand for more privatization and capitalism, the neoconservative element demands *more elimination of difference and services that protect it.* Conservatism and neoconservatism, radicalized, inevitably lead to fascism; however, this form of extremism is no longer willing to admit what it is. Its current adherents prefer terms such as "alt-right" and "white nationalism" or, as stated in India, "Hindu nationalism" or "Brahmanism." In sites of power, they use all the old mechanisms of fascism: misinformation and disinformation, militarization and the use of force to erode the public sphere, racial scapegoating, valorized masculinity, and the perpetuation of insecurity to legitimate the need for security through militarization and policing.

Racism is already evident in the paths of neoliberalism through neoconservatism and fascism. Neoliberal racism doesn't at first appear racist. After all, neoliberals claim to defend civil liberties and rights, and there are neoliberal politicians of color. The problem is that they recognize only *individuals* as bearing such rights. This is of little help for people who are objects of racial discrimination. No black or Indigenous person is discriminated against *as an individual*. Antiblack racism is against *blacks*. Anti-Indigenous racism is against *Indigenous peoples*. Neoliberalism thus nurtures racism by undermining the conditions of addressing it. It is, in short, reckless.

Neoconservatism and fascism do not defend the individual over groups. They recognize groups. Their racism is direct. They deem other groups "dangerous" and target them for incarceration or, worse, elimination. This is why so-called militias, the military, and police gather to fight Black Lives Matter protestors marching for the rights of black and Indigenous peoples but stand to the side and at times assist white supremacist groups marching with weapons in full view and, as witnessed in the attack on the U.S. Capitol, injuring and killing police, despite having once chanted that blue—that is, police—lives matter.[1]

As neoliberalism, neoconservatism, and fascism are promoted by people with extraordinary economic capital, their reach is global, as seen in countries ranging from Brazil to Hungary to India. And their negative effects are one and the same. They are, in a word, pandemics.

Social dimensions of pandemics have been evident since Christopher Columbus landed in the Bahamas in 1492. Not only did he and his crew bring biological diseases from Europe, but they also inaugurated Euromodern colonialism, which includes the production of vulnerabilities through which those contagions could be easily spread. This development—Euromodern colonialism—infected the world and was thus a social pandemic. It set the stage for precarious conditions through which all subsequent pandemics found fertile soil. Its cruelty was, as far as the metropoles or colonial centers were concerned, quarantined. For those suffering from its symptoms—enslavement, genocide, high mortality rates, ongoing poverty, everyday violence, degradation of spirit—this meant invisibility as an experience of their quarantined suffering. Then, as now, such people were for the most part kept out of sight from those who profited from their misery. There were occasional moments of exposure, such as when the Sharpe Rebellion in Jamaica (1831–1832) led to the British outlawing the enslavement and trade of kidnapped human beings across the Atlantic Ocean. Because the British Empire was at that time global, this was interpreted as the outlawing of slavery on the high seas. Yet enslavement continues.[2] So, too, do the other social symptoms, which nearly eliminated the Indigenous peoples of North and South America and Australia. The descendants of those people, encountering the COVID-19 pandemic, conclude the obvious: its symptoms of injustice are nothing new.

Black people endure some additional symptoms. Wherever enslavement was outlawed, investments in its maintenance continued. Thus, as W.E.B. Du Bois and many others showed in the U.S. context, policing's focus on black people in effect deputized whites.[3] Curtailment of the movement of black people led to the near ubiquitous tagging of crime onto us, which in turn led to the well-known, racially marked system of incarceration and its accompanying economy—the prison-industrial complex. This logic was, and continues to be, the quarantining of black people. In addition to imprisonment, its mechanisms included lynching, economic deprivation, segregation of housing, and a complex propaganda campaign in which degradation of black people was premised on the elevation of white people through misinformation and disinformation of history and other forms of human science ranging from economics to human biology to psychology to sociology to medicine. From birth to grave, this meant for all Americans, from black through white, learning how to evade anything that would expose the contradictions of a system that alleges that black people are the problem, instead of people who face problems imposed upon us by a racist, unjust society.

Black people never took all this without a fight. After all, how can one breathe under such circumstances? This concern with breathing is one of the hallmarks of black consciousness. How could this not be so when lynching was one of the technologies of black subordination? Frantz Fanon—the great philosopher, psychiatrist, and revolutionary from the Caribbean island of Martinique—wrote of "breath" and "breathing" so many times in his writings that it was inevitable for him to point out how the colonial conditions that placed black people in that situation imposed the same on colonized people in Southeast Asia: "It is not because the Indo-Chinese have discovered their own culture that they revolt. It is because 'quite simply' it was, in more than one way, becoming impossible for them to breathe."[4]

This theme of having to revolt because of the threat of asphyxiation continues into the twenty-first century. Recall Eric Garner's final words when he was in Staten Island police officer Daniel Pantaleo's choke hold: "I can't breathe!" These were also the dying words of George Floyd, uttered as his neck was under the knee of the police officer Derek Chauvin in Minneapolis.

The collective struggle to breathe, which is the mark of all black rebellions from the Haitian Revolution through to the anti-colonial struggles in Africa and the revolts in North America and South America, was hardly a concern of whites beyond the conservative logic of their own protection *from* such revolts. The pandemic, however, offers a rude awakening into the perspective of black consciousness, which for now I will just call black peoples' points of view. Despite all the efforts of white power, SARS-CoV-2 (the novel coronavirus) doesn't "see" national borders, race, or any other boundary. It responds only to openings or, more accurately, "preexisting conditions." The preexisting pandemics of neoliberalism, neoconservatism, fascism, and their accompanying racism created social sites of vulnerability that spread the virus more efficiently in countries such as the United States, the United Kingdom, India, and Brazil despite the technological and economic resources at their disposal. The virus's devastation is most evident among the populations on which those societies devote their technologies of disempowerment—blacks in all four, along with Indigenous peoples in Brazil, India, and the United States. There are many other countries with similar effects, but the hegemonic status of the United

States and the United Kingdom, especially as imperial countries and architects of neoliberalism and neoconservatism, makes them graphic exemplars. Brazil and India follow through their national leaderships' adoption of such policies.

The experience of the pandemic is one in which quarantining also has the effect of mystification. Neoliberalism and neoconservatism see no difference between social distance and physical distance. Because neoliberalism isolates individuals to the point of denying their connection to others, given its disdain for collectives, it marks social reality as its enemy. It thus makes sense that neoliberal governments prescribe *social* distance. The virus is, however, transmitted physically, which means the recommendation should be for *physical distance*. One could be physically close but socially distant and vice versa. Social closeness continues in various forms, though it's primarily through communication technologies such as FaceTime, Skype, Google Meet, Microsoft Teams, Webex, and Zoom. Those who manifest full-blown COVID-19, however, are both socially and physically distant. Quarantined, they are out of sight. When afflicted to the point of being unable to communicate or unconscious, they are also socially distant. Many cannot speak, and when placed in COVID-19 wards of hospitals, they are wrapped up in sanitary materials, sedated, and able to breathe only through ventilator tubes. What are they but passive objects of medical attention? Their humanity is erased in a vast network of radical quarantining. Tucked away, they are invisible, as many succumb to the culminating effect of the disease—ceasing to breathe.

For those who don't treat the pandemic as a hoax, the looming threat of breathlessness makes those without infection or symptoms appear more like survivors or those who are blessed. This view regards the afflicted as marked or, worse, condemned. Old moralistic rationalizations against the contaminated are more easily achieved when the majority of them are among historically outcast and neglected peoples. The invisibility of the disease is also shared by those it marks. Not having it brought into plain sight encourages disbelief in its reality. This is more easily concluded among many on the ideological right because they are already primed with the logic of their invulnerability—whether with the belief that a divine force such as Jesus is on their side or with the presumption of the system offering them a "right" to whatever they want, including their survival. This thus took absurd forms in spring 2020 in the United States when right-wing protestors did not take preventive measures against infection for the luxury of haircuts and other nonessential activities and through the election season when they attended large, superspreading events such as Trump rallies. As those among them who became infected and passed away fell into the logic of quarantined deaths, they were not seen and thus their demise was not perceived as real as far as their fellow fanatics were concerned. The people of the United States, as history has already shown under Jair Bolsonaro's presidency in Brazil and others marked by retrograde and racist policies, are not the lone sufferers of the consequences of malevolent and incompetent leadership.[5]

The guiding theme of these pandemics—antidemocracy, colonialism, racism, and a disease—is invisibility. As pandemics of invisibility, they are nurtured by the insistence, whether psychological or ideological, against the appearance of their symptoms. I recall how angry some people would get at me for even mentioning my suffering from my long-term illness. It's as if much of humanity reverted to the childhood response of covering their heads under blankets when they perceive a bogeyman in their bedrooms. What's the bogeyman to do? Leave because rendered impotent by a *blanket*? There are, of course, psychoanalytical elements at work in such activities. Closing one's eyes or covering one's face is a secret admission of projection. There is a form of responsibility present in all denials. The history of the United States and many other countries marked by white supremacy is a long tale of covering national memory with blankets with regard to colonialism, racism, and the attempted, sometimes successful, genocide of Indigenous peoples. That denial is among the foundations of such countries. So as the death count mounted, and investments in bad science misinformed and disinformed the public—and many people embraced, like a blanket, that misinformation and disinformation—more energy was required to dissociate from, repress, and suppress truth. The alternatives became implosion or explosion.

George Floyd's murder was not quarantined. Witnessed all over the world, it brought to the fore the reality of asphyxiation. If the people witnessing it had acted like deputies responding to an illegal and immoral activity—attempted murder—and overpowered the police, Floyd would be alive. As only whites have the de facto right to commit citizens' arrest in the United States, this was not to be. Everyone knows the intervening bystanders would have been arrested for assaulting police officers or, worse, killed by the police. Because of Darnella Frazier, then seventeen years old, recording the horrible event despite police threats to her, many across the globe became witnesses to an incident permitted by structural complicity, political impotence, injustice, and social ill-health.[6] Floyd's murder is emblematic of a failure to address these converging pandemics. The police, many have come to see, are structurally agents of social asphyxiation. Humanity existed for nearly three hundred thousand years without police forces, and the truth of the matter is—beyond the fantasies of cinema, television, and literary fiction—that most people are rarely in need of police for anything other than directing traffic or filing reports after car accidents or burglaries.[7] *Protecting* people is rare, and investigating and bringing to justice those who perpetrate crime even rarer. Surely humanity can find a better way to live together than to divert so much of our economy to forces that, in defending the need for such investments, produce violence and, in addition, crime as de facto managers of them. As the violence of the police reminds us of what it means not to be able to breathe, it becomes emblematic of these converging pandemics. The masked people who have taken to the streets against them bring to the fore the significance of breath; their protests are social masks against a contagion.

Although black consciousness is a rude awakening, another type of consciousness can grow out of that awareness: the need to become actional, to fight against oppression. This kind of consciousness, Black consciousness, is distinct from (lowercase) black consciousness; it is a political consciousness that addresses the choking contradictions of antiblack societies. For fear of seeing their negative reflection, these antiblack societies often attempt to break their mirrors. To suppress this consciousness requires suppressing not only black possibility but also political life. Antiblack societies are therefore fundamentally antipolitical and antidemocratic—because they are devoted to blocking black people's access to citizenship—and thus fight also against their own members who fight against black disempowerment. This struggle reveals a feared truth of black empowerment: the fight against antiblack racism is ultimately a fight *for* democracy.

Humanity must continue fighting against antidemocratic forces because, from the assaults on the environment to those on the services by which human beings could live in a humane world, everyone needs to breathe. Fighting against them requires an unwavering struggle for democracy. Brought out into the open, such an effort is a desperate reach for air, what Fanon so aptly phrased as "the oxygen that invents a new humanity."[8] This is true. Provided, of course, there remains a humanity to invent.

This book is an exploration of black consciousness and *Black* consciousness. Briefly, black consciousness is mostly affected and sometimes immobile; Black consciousness is effective and always active. Both are feared in antiblack societies, although the second is more so than the first. This fear ultimately leads to disrespect for truth, and antipathy to the ethical and political implications of admitting that truth, which is the realization of what is actually revealed about claims of white supremacy and black inferiority when seen through the eyes of Blacks. That revelation is the set of lies on which the avowed legitimacy of antiblack societies is built. That all antiblack societies today claim to be democracies makes this hypocrisy stark. Those lies include the societies' avowed celebration of freedom while waging war against it through blocking actual democracy.

I will show that there is a movement from a suffering black consciousness to a liberatory Black consciousness in which revelation of the dirty laundry and fraud of white supremacy and black inferiority is a dreaded truth. In a world premised on having the moral high ground for political legitimacy, this makes many whites who have governed a good portion of the planet over the past few hundred years morally and ultimately politically bankrupt. A retreat into individualized moral redemption is what many accused of this failure seek. This effort, I argue, is one in which a fear of Black consciousness is also a flight from reality and political responsibility.

The path I take will be first working through the mist of white narcissism and the varieties of consciousness it perpetuates. I will then move on to the study of specifically racial consciousness, racism, and the kinds of invisibility they produce. That analysis will be followed by discussions of the many ways in which antiblack racist societies try to evade political responsibility for antiblack racism. I will conclude with a meditation on political and creative responses of Black consciousness that does not apologize for black and Black lives having value.

One may wonder what intellectual reflection and political responsibility offer for the struggle against antiblack racism, which requires taking on the task of building a humane world of dignity, freedom, and respect.

Many years ago I found myself in a dispute with a community activist who learned I was a doctoral student of philosophy. My activist friend declared: "I have no time for abstractions. I work with the concrete."

"You do know 'the concrete' is an abstraction, don't you?" I replied.

My point to that friend from long ago was that communicating, reflecting, and thinking play important roles in struggles, and they require appropriate forms of generalizing. Although there is a slippery slope from generalizing to *overgeneralizing*, one must nevertheless generalize in order for something to be understood by those other than oneself. If the ideas that follow are useful, they of necessity must reach beyond *me* to the general *you*.

Generalizations will always have their limits. I will use many examples from the news, history, and even popular culture (films and music) to transcend those limitations.

Another caveat: despite my efforts, some readers may not see themselves in this book and, worse, may even be angered at what I say and reveal. What we come to see in others may serve as a mirror to help us see ourselves with some clarity and, if we dare admit, the liberating force of truth and fresh air.

So stated, let us continue this journey together across, and for many at times under, these dark, perilous waters.

PART I

BOUND

Well, children, where there is so much racket
there must be something out of kilter.

–Sojourner Truth[1]

1

FEARED

Consider the following tale from colonial times in the British Caribbean. An Anglican minister of education was sent to inspect one of the colonies' schools. Wanting to see how they were being run, he decided to arrive unannounced at one of the secondary schools. As he approached the gate, a black boy of perhaps eleven years of age was hurrying in. The minister stopped the boy in the hopes of gauging some of the benefits of a good colonial education. He placed his hand on the boy's shoulder.

"Young man."

"Yes, sir," the boy responded, nervous at being stopped by the white gentleman.

"Could you please tell me who knocked down the Walls of Jericho?"

The boy looked at the rather imposing white English representative of the empire. He immediately knew what to say. "Not me."

The minister was flabbergasted. He grabbed the boy by the arm. "Come with me." Entering the school, he demanded to see the headmaster. He was taken to an Afro-Caribbean man. Let us call that official Mr. Smith.

"Are you the headmaster?"

"Yes, sir. I am Mr. Smith."

"Good. I am the minister of education. I am here to inspect your school. I just asked this young man who knocked down the Walls of Jericho, and you know what he told me?"

"What did he tell you, sir?"

"He said he didn't do it!"

Mr. Smith looked at the frightened boy and then at the upset minister. He took off his glasses. Poor Mr. Smith had worked his way up through the demeaning colonial education system. He managed to secure sufficient training to become a schoolteacher and subsequently, through great effort, earned the title of headmaster. He made sure to hire a top staff and was proud of the many graduates who went on for better things than offered by the villages from which they came. After a sigh, he replied, "Sir, I have known this boy for a long time. If he said he didn't do it, I assure you he didn't do it."

Outraged, the minister eventually got the governor general's office on the line.

"What is it?" asked an official.

"I am at the Anglican school. I just asked both a student and the headmaster about who knocked down the Walls of Jericho, and you know what both of them told me?"

"What did they tell you, sir?"

"They said the boy didn't do it!"

After a pause, the official responded, "I think you have the wrong department. Wait a minute, and I will put you in touch with Building and Waterworks."

Talking about black and Black consciousness requires an exploration of miscommunication, misunderstanding, and missed opportunities, as well as all kinds of misses and missives that they occasion: anxiety, despair, dread, and fear. Thus, talking about them often leads to talking around them or, worse, about anything else but them.

The irony of avoiding a subject is that doing so may make it more present. The elephant in the room is the familiar metaphor. The effort it takes to avoid what is in plain sight requires identifying it while skillfully evading it. The motivation here is the discomfort, perhaps fear, the denied or evaded subject stimulates. In some cases, what is feared is what one may learn about oneself, the image of oneself that might emerge.

I recently spoke with a friend who was reading a book of reflections by white women intellectuals on how women see themselves. I asked her whether those authors' perspectives on women and men were in fact specifically white. I explained I was reading writings of African and Indigenous American women who argued that much influential literature about the lives of women and men—about the lives of human beings—was about white people, and in fact white points of view and experiences supposedly stood for "human nature," or "everyone." Much of what is taken to be the way women and men behave is about how white women and men tend to behave. My friend, who, like me, is of African descent, was at first dubious of my claim, until I asked her to read the Mayo Clinic's description of narcissistic personality disorder (also known as malignant narcissism). According to the Mayo Clinic, malignant narcissists have "an exaggerated sense of self-importance," a "sense of entitlement" requiring "constant, excessive admiration," an expectation of having "to be recognized as superior even without achievements that warrant it," an inflated sense of their achievements and talents, a preoccupation with "fantasies about success, power, brilliance, beauty or the perfect mate," a belief that they "can only associate with equally special people," and a penchant for monopolizing conversations and belittling people they claim to be inferior. The clinic adds that people with narcissistic disorder expect "special favors and unquestioning compliance with their expectations"; often take advantage of others to secure their goals; ignore or are unwilling to recognize the needs and feelings of others; envy others and are convinced others envy them; are arrogant, boastful, conceited, and pretentious; and insist on having the best of everything such as "the best car or office." Despite postures of self-importance, such people cannot handle receiving criticism. They become "impatient or angry when they don't receive special treatment." They're oversensitive, and they react with rage and contempt and try to belittle others "to make themselves appear superior." They suffer emotional difficulty and stress from a constant sense of their imperfection—in spite of insisting they are better than others—which reveal "secret feelings of insecurity, shame, vulnerability and humiliation."[1]

The reader can guess where this was going. I asked my friend to describe white people—not what describes *every* individual white person, but what many people, especially people of color (black, brown, red, etc.), think of when we imagine what it means to be white.

She laughed. The list of pathologies was the same.

Whiteness, understood here as a consciousness imposed on the world in which to be normal is to be white, is basically a group that crashes someone else's birthday party and whose members tell everyone that not only are they amazing and are doing everyone a favor by crashing the party, but further that the celebration ought to be in their honor.

Such people have a well-orchestrated story of "superiority." They belittle everyone else, consume the most, and get angry at not receiving special treatment for whatever they desire. Yet at the same time they are highly sensitive to receiving criticism and often hide what such behavior suggests—namely, profound insecurity. Such people are always the victims, even when they control the conditions of what affects everyone else. And where they do not claim to be victims, they rationalize their behavior as "human nature." Supposedly everyone is like them. Their response is simply to prove the point through paradoxical denial of its applying specifically to white people. The irony is that this, too, confirms their whiteness in everyone being able to recognize it.

Why does such behavior flourish even in the face of its denial? In part, it persists because it is seductive. Many people, even among those dominated, want white supremacy to be what it claims to be because that would give some meaning to their suffering through making white domination seem just. They cannot, in other words, face its truth, which is, in fact, its lie. It is a set of beliefs and institutions handed down across generations saturated with bad faith.

White narcissism forces negative and false images of the self onto others. Beyond those, there are also special kinds of consciousness it produces:

1. There is the consciousness of being a "race," which the white world produced, and which many people across all racial and ethnic groups have come to believe in, over the past few hundred years.
2. There is the set of black perspectives, often called "black experience" and understanding, of that consciousness. That is what black people produced.
3. There is the everyday life of black people when white people are not around or at least not on black people's minds. That is also what black people produced—and continue to produce.
4. And there is the active political transformation of the first, second, and third perspectives into a movement from "black" to "Black" consciousness.

Think about the world that produced the first kind of black consciousness. A world dominated by "white consciousness," white normativity, or, made plain, "white is right." Although it may not be the world as *every* individually designated white person sees it, it is recognizable to most people in white supremacist societies from childhood to grave.[2] No explanation into the production of this first kind of black consciousness would make sense without looking into the circumstances that led to the development of white consciousness, which has historically imposed negative self-images on many black people. Black people live, however, beyond negative projections of white consciousness. It's not as though when black people look into the mirror while brushing their teeth, they lament, "Still black . . . ," followed by the wail of a blues guitar, and trudge on with the burden of doing "black things," each of which is marked by a constellation of negative stereotypes of self-hatred or, worse, a profound level of ignorance, the result of which is delusional happiness.

If black people were simply what imposed negative images claim blacks to be, if we were those things whose sale in the market of flesh supposedly offered no points of view, many, perhaps most, white people would be relieved.

Yet black people do have points of view.

Most black people, though—whether as descendants of the enslaved or Indigenous colonized people—try to live their lives, come
what may. Many did not survive. A remarkable number managed to
persevere. Black life, whether that of plain old everyday folk or heroic freedom fighters—as well as sellouts, Uncle Toms, Sambos, and
hustlers—is a complicated history of beauty and ugliness, joy and
suffering, hope and despair, resilience and fatigue.

Many black people hold an extraordinary position of generosity to
white people. From the perspective of white consciousness steeped in
narcissism, the world comes down to perfection versus imperfection,
the latter of which supposedly must be eliminated. That is why many
white people, suffering from egological fragility, take accusations of
being racist so personally. Most black people, on the other hand, see
a world of imperfections, which we ascribe also to ourselves. When a
black person meets a white person, the presumption, often verified, is
that the white person has a deep-rooted belief in his or her superiority
over peoples of color, especially blacks. Discovering humility in some
comes as a pleasant surprise. For most black people, then, relationships
with white people come down to a willingness to work with, live with,
and at times simply survive white encounters. White people often hold
all the cards. Those rude white guests at the birthday party, we should
remember, also have the protection of the police, the government, and
much, if not most, of society.

If black people had no points of view, there would be no need to
look or think further. Commitments to truth, justice, and their cultivation in the quest to build a better world demand otherwise.

I had a peculiar conversation back in the early 1990s at a reception
for a university colloquium at which I was the guest speaker. Near-
ing the end of our small talk, a white professor, about two decades my
senior, asked if I had ever been in therapy. I found the question odd.
"Why do you ask?"

She answered, "You seem . . . well . . . *healthy*. That's not normal."

Her comment stuck with me for years (which is perhaps unhealthy).
In a way, a similar, tacit assumption often underlies interactions

between most whites and blacks. In a white supremacist society, the bearers of that supremacy require the normalization of pathological blackness. That colleague was saying that to belong to her world—in the sense of fitting in, to the extent that that was possible—required me to be mentally ill. To some extent, as we will later see, she was right.

That colleague was also voicing a white need. Blacks are supposedly abnormal; therefore, for me to be "normal," pathology *must* be there. She needed to see it.

Frantz Fanon observed back in the 1950s that reason took flight whenever black people entered white spaces.[3] There has been some progress since then. Now reason exits slowly.

Fanon argued that a normal black person, having grown up with a normal black family, experiences neurosis with the slightest contact with the white world.[4] There is already the conundrum. The white world is, after all, nearly everywhere. Made specific, Fanon meant the kind of direct interaction as the one I had with that white professor back in the 1990s. It's an experience of reason creeping away.

Over the years, efforts to explain why reason seems to be so unreasonable under such circumstances have produced a vast body of literature and op-eds.[5] In recent times rationalizations have homed in on the physicality of black people. Instead of referring to black persons or black people, there is a tendency, especially among black students and academics, to refer to *black bodies*.

The expression "black bodies" pops up often wherever antiblack racism raises its ugly, and at times polite, head. It is there on blogs, in news interviews, in editorials in major newspapers, in broadcast lectures, and in award-winning books ranging from Ta-Nehisi Coates's *Between the World and Me* to Ibram X. Kendi's *How to Be an Antiracist*.[6] It makes sense since racism involves a form of two-dimensional thinking in which black people supposedly lack inner lives. Fanon referred to this as "the epidermal schema." It refers to treating black people as mere surfaces, superficial physical beings without consciousness and thus a point of view—in short, only bodies. Yet in the midst of attention to black bodies, many blacks are left wondering what happened to *black people*. How has it become acceptable—indeed, even *preferable*—for black people to refer to ourselves as "bodies" instead of as "people" or as "human beings"?

It is as if many black people have surrendered to the view that we are what we are imagined to be by those who refuse to see us as human beings. It is one thing for nonblack people to look at black people from the outside, as though black people were only a surface—in a word, *things*—but for black people to do so is an extraordinary defeat. It is akin to conceding that we have no point of view. To have a perspective is to be conscious, to look onto others and, beyond them, to the world. That is what people do: people are embodied consciousnesses, "consciousness in the flesh," the "lived body," at least while we remain connected to reality.[7] And more, with the addition of thought, consciousness in this sense is embodied mind.

So what happened to black *people* under the weight of black bodies?

A focus on the body ignores the importance of embodied mind, what it means to be consciousness lived and in the flesh. Why not look at black embodied consciousness and mind? Ignoring doing so, as we will see, is seductive because black embodied-consciousness-mind offers truth in antiblack societies. From such eyes, the horrors and injustice of such societies are, in a word, naked. It is no accident that one of the rationalizations for black inferiority in white supremacist societies is the Curse of Ham, who, as the biblical tale relates, looked upon his drunken, naked father, Noah. The theme of narcissistic rage continues.

Antiblack societies sustain themselves on pleasing falsehoods for whites such as white supremacy. Their project, in a nutshell, is to expand themselves from antiblack societies to making *the world* antiblack, leaving no remaining perspective from which white contradictions can be seen, can be naked. Such a goal, reaching so far beyond itself, requires dragging a whole lot of people into it. With blackness to keep at bay, practices of purification eventually lead to the other extreme: Can anything be white enough when the goal is to place at a distance all things black—or at least dark?

Truth, however, like nature, doesn't negotiate. It need not give us what we want. White supremacy requires constant aggrandizement of whiteness, despite unpleasant realities.

We have already observed narcissism as an underlying feature of white supremacy through the example of the interlopers at the birthday party who declare their superiority to the other guests. The comedian Lewis Black once remarked that if such guests' claims were true, others at the party would eventually have to eat them so they could get a bit of their "power."[8] We already know about white fantasies of African "natives" dancing around large cauldrons in which white victims simmer. The surest signs of the illegitimacy of white supremacy are not only these tales of narcissism, marked simultaneously by desire and fear, but also their history of force.[9] Conquest, enslavement, and genocide demonstrate might, if not just chance. They lack, however, the satisfaction of being right. The failure to acknowledge the illegitimacy of white supremacy leads to the other kinds of evasion, at the expense of not only human but also many other forms of life.

Many black people look into the eyes of the death-dealing consciousness of white claims of supremacy with the question: How far will it go to sustain itself? The bloody history of lynchings, genocide, enslavement, and colonialism offers an answer. The director and screenwriter Jordan Peele allegorized this aspiration in his 2017 film *Get Out*. White supremacy wants nothing less than everything, even if that requires erasing all opposition, including its own conscience. Peele's film uses the genres of science fiction and horror to explore what it means to be conscious of reality and "stay *woke*," as the hip hop artist Childish Gambino puts it in his song "Redbone," which plays through the opening credits. Though antiblack societies fear, and are even repulsed by, what has become known as the black body, they also desire to possess it—so long as it is lived and controlled by conscious white minds. The fear, then, is of black bodies inhabited by conscious black minds. Compare this with the past-celebrated and now-maligned phenomenon of "blackface," which harkens for conscious white living minds beneath black skin. The possessed black consciousness there is offered as entertainment. Black consciousness in that instance is desirable to the extent to which whiteness is able to control and limit its possibilities.

So for whom is it desirable to see white consciousness living in black bodies, and for whom is it a source of anxiety, at times even terror, to encounter black bodies imbued with black consciousness?

Get Out's opening credits beautifully announce a provocative thesis through Michael Abels's song "Sikiliza Kwa Wahenga." The words are from Kiswahili. The translation is "Listen to your ancestors." It is hauntingly sung in the low register and whispered by a chorus beneath images of passing trees reminiscent of what past enslaved people saw as they fled from enslavement. The daylight is bright, yet the mood is cold. The scene switches from trees along a highway to urban areas. The song "Redbone" is now the leitmotif as the camera reveals black-and-white photographs first of a dark-skinned black man in black clothing holding white balloons. His face is blurred to the point of making him in effect faceless. It moves to the image of a dark-skinned black woman's exposed pregnant belly. She is wearing a white tube top. Her face, too, is hidden. An out-of-focus dark-skinned black man in a white T-shirt, his face away from the camera, is in the background, along with a black sport utility vehicle in an urban landscape. The sky is white. The next image, also in black and white, is a white pit bull leaping forth with a faceless dark-skinned black boy trying to hold him back by pulling his chain leash. There is a building in the background with three sets of windows with white shades—the first, with one three-quarters drawn and the other half drawn; the second, with both half drawn; and the third, with the only window fully drawn. The ground is bleak: dirt, stones, broken glass, and bits of scrap.

The unfolding scene changes to ordinary color. It is of the protagonist's living room, with two large black-and-white photographs. On the left, there is a lit lamppost at twilight. On the right, there is a pigeon in silhouette taking flight, wings spread, with dark sides of skyscrapers to its left and right and a white sky above. A blond dog is on a black leather couch. Another shot of the apartment is the kitchen, where there is a black-and-white photograph of a boy wearing a West African mask, but the boy's hands are white. The shot expands to reveal an open bathroom, where a dark-skinned black man—darker than all the blacks in the black-and-white photographs—is washing himself in front of the mirror. His is the only distinct black face in the opening credits' sequence.

The camera switches to a close-up of varieties of donuts and croissants in bright, vivid color. The camera moves up to a white woman relishing pastries in a case.

The camera returns to the black man in the bathroom. He is now rubbing on white shaving cream.

Back to the white woman deciding on the donuts, with Childish Gambino singing of wanting, having, and needing. She smiles.

Back to the black man, who is now shaving. He cuts himself, and the camera immediately returns to the white woman, who is now in an elevator. The doors open as Gambino counsels to stay woke.

The white woman enters the hall and turns left; the black man is now fully dressed. He is looking at black-and-white shots on his digital camera. The apartment is 208. There is a red fire extinguisher in a white casing in the hall not far from the door. Since the camera focuses on the numbers and the extinguisher, I take them as symbolic. Red, especially coloring a device needed to extinguish fire, reminds the viewer simultaneously of danger and safety. Right before the black man opens the door and smiles, Gambino warns not to close your eyes.

There it is. So much to analyze, and many interpretations abound.

We learn the white woman's name is Rose. Red roses are often offerings of love. They are, however, also appropriate for funerals. They also have thorns. We should remember the red fire extinguisher. As a device to put out fires, it's a foreboding reference to a connection to come, and, indeed, most uses of the color red in the film point to the same. Recall the blood drawn from the protagonist right before Rose steps out of the elevator. Rose, we discover, is on the hunt for Chris, whose name, we should bear in mind, means "messiah," which in turn means to be anointed. A messiah is also a savior. He is her latest effort to acquire a black body into which her father plans to save a white conscious mind from a feeble and deteriorating white body.

We also learn through the course of the film of an out-of-body hypnotic experience stimulated by the psychiatrist Missy Armitage, Rose's mother, scraping a silver spoon in a steady circle within a porcelain teacup. The hypnotic sound throws Chris into the "sunken place." It is part of a process of priming the embodied subject to be taken over by a white mind.[10] Chris, representing blacks, thus becomes a spectator of his—and in another character's case, her—embodied enslavement.

Though that is the reveal, so to speak, other elements are worth considering along the way. One is of special interest for my point about desire. Throughout *Get Out* white characters are overcome with desire, like Rose in front of the donuts, when they look at the bodies of potential black hosts.

An elderly member of the cult remarks that black is in fashion. Freed from confronting black consciousness, he could admit, at the purely aesthetic level, how his cult members and he really feel about black bodies. Instead of negrophobia, there is *negrosomatophilia*. It means a desire for "negro" bodies. We could use "Afro" and make it *afrosomatophilia*, to mean a desire for African-descended bodies. For the Negrophobe or Afrophobe—a person who fears "negroes" or African-descended people—it's not the *body* that frightens them. It's fear of a special kind of consciousness looking back at them: black consciousness.

What, however, is black consciousness without a body?

I'll return to this question later, but for now, let us just say that in a society that separates consciousness and mind from the body, it is possible to hate black people but desire black bodies.

Peele's film posits that a white consciousness looking back at the white antagonists poses no problem, even from black bodies. This is a phenomenon of which many blacks who attempt to play such a role for whites learn, though it requires so much vigilance that many blacks who play this game end up becoming spectators on their own life. The character they construct lives among whites, especially avowedly liberal ones—although there is no shortage of conservative varieties—seemingly without tension. "Look black," the message goes, but "do not *be* black."

Dean Armitage, Rose's father, reveals he voted for President Barack Obama and shortly afterward adds he would have supposedly voted for him a third time if it were permitted.

Given Obama's successor, the remark no longer requires the proverbial grain of salt.

Racism at the psychological level is a story of narcissism. The creepy Obama mantra raises the question of whether Dean Armitage saw in Obama a black body lived by a white consciousness and mind, a white reflection of himself. If so, he saw in Obama an ideal coagulant. Or worse, perhaps Obama, the film might be suggesting, is already one.

"Coagula" is the term the cult uses for the fusion of white conscious minds in black conscious bodies with suppressed minds. The cult is called the Order of the Coagula. They are also members of the Red Alchemist Society, which, in turn, is an allusion to the Knights Templar, a medieval order of which about 90 percent of its members were engaged in innovating on and developing finance instead of engaging in military combat. The red to which I alluded in discussing Rose's name connects to these knights, who wore a red cross, and, of course, the Red Alchemist Society and cult's name are connected to the coagulation of blood. Recall that Chris cut himself—lost blood— shaving while Rose was en route to his apartment.

So, Dean Armitage sees *something* when he looks at or even thinks about Obama. Given the white hysteria at Obama's election to the presidency of the United States in 2008, there was clearly fear of whether he possessed a Black consciousness. And given that the Republicans were determined to make him a one-term president and then, in his second term, went so far as refusing to give his Supreme Court nominee even a hearing in the Senate, it was clear that his possible Black consciousness was being forced into a subordinated black one. In the world of *Get Out*, another scenario could be that the Order had intercepted Obama's possible Black consciousness and trapped it in the sunken place of one of its members. If what Armitage sees only looks black but is not black, what, then, does it mean *to be* black?

To mean and to be are not the same. Meaning itself, after all, has many meanings. There is social meaning. There is intended meaning.

There is preferred meaning. There is meaning beneath meaning. Whatever black people are, what black people "mean" to those who are afraid of or who exoticize blacks is not identical with how black people live. Additionally, some black people attempt to live without a point of view, which leaves in the hands of others the question of what they are.

What it means to be black is, then, not so simple as pointing to someone on the street or, as exclaimed by a little white boy pointing at Fanon on a train in the early 1950s: "Look, a *nigger!*"[11]

One could be mistaken.

And even if one were to do that and not be mistaken, a special experience and question is raised when someone hears, pauses, and looks you in the eye.

2

BLACKENED

To no longer see mute whiteness
To no longer see death.

    –Frantz Fanon

How can a consciousness be black?

I have already begun to answer that question by addressing what it means for a consciousness to be white. There is to some extent the awareness of being designated "white" and an understanding of the connotations—historical, political, and psychological—of such an epithet.

Some years ago I read a wonderful student thesis in which the author asked, "What do whites want?"

Most whites do not think about this, but deep down they know, as do most people of color: whites want *everything*.

This desire for everything has animated the creation of white people and that of white domination. White people didn't always exist. The light-skinned ancestors of the people who became white had a different consciousness. They didn't think of themselves as white; they had no reason to do so. If by chance today's white people were to acquire a time machine and go back across the ages to inform their ancestors of their whiteness, the folly of such an effort would become apparent. If they traveled back further, they would discover, to their chagrin, that everyone would resemble the people today they call black.

Most contemporary white people forget they are white and are reminded only by context. In those rare moments of identification, they locate their whiteness not only in relation to nonwhites but also in what is at stake if they lose it. A Brazilian friend of Italian ancestry once told me that, when filling out applications, she sometimes faced a quandary over deciding which box to check under "race," since she most identified as Brazilian. She *could* categorize herself as "other" when she travels to countries such as Canada and the U.K., she admitted, but what mostly came to her mind in those situations was everything she would lose if she didn't check "white."

Pleonexia—wanting everything—requires the absence of limits. White pleonexia transforms land, living things, including other human beings, and even thoughts into property; the covetous mentality is applied to the skies, to outer space, and even to time. As Jean-Paul Sartre puts it, mistaking it as a *human* aspiration, it is the desire to be G-d.[1] This desire expands to the expectation, if not presumption, of invulnerability and absolute entitlement. Narcissism plus radical access is indicative of a white consciousness.

During the "Racism and Multiculturalism" conference at Rhodes University in South Africa in the late 1990s, the hosts took the presenters to a wildlife reserve. I hate even the idea of a safari, but I went along in the spirit of being a good guest. As the game warden and the resident veterinarian were explaining safety measures at the facility, I glimpsed one of the guests, a white Frenchman in his thirties, straying away from the group. Curious about what he was up to, I watched as he made his way over to a fence, behind which rested a lioness. Seeing him coming close, the lioness rose on all fours. The Frenchman looked at her for about a minute and then slowly extended his hand to pet her. The lioness licked her lips.

"*Stop!*" yelled the game warden.

The Frenchman paused, his hand near the fence. "Why?"

"Because she'll eat you!"

There is something many people of color, especially those of us from the Global South, know about white people *as a group* but rarely discuss with them. Although many white people despise nonwhite peoples, especially blacks, they *love* animals.[2] The love is to the point of many if not most whites seeming no longer capable of imagining animals as *wild*.

In summer 2004, my family and I traveled to Darwin, Australia. In the cab from the airport, I asked our driver about the large, ferocious saltwater crocodiles in the area.

"Any attacks?" I wanted to know.

"Yep. One just last week. A woman was eaten."

"That's awful! What happened?"

"She was a tourist. She went swimming in a billabong around midnight."

A billabong is a stagnant lake or pond, the likes of which are found all over Australia. Inky dark at night, they are all but certain to hide crocodiles, pythons, and other creatures.

"Let me guess: Was she from northern Europe?" I asked.

"How did you know?"

Whiteness encourages a perverse perception of animals. There are more tigers in people's homes in the United States than left in the wild in Asia, and one can be assured that most of the captive tigers' owners are white.[3] This fact is placed on full display in *Tiger King* (2020), the bizarre and surreal Netflix documentary series on the lives of some of the most flamboyant zoophilists. It has always been strange to me that the same white people who would call the police on a black man or woman sleeping on a park bench, bird-watching, or walking down their street would not hesitate to pet a lioness, roll with a tiger, or swim with a crocodile. It is as if, in their imagination, animals obey an un-written law: "Don't harm white people." It's the stuff of Tarzan movies and other fantasies about whites who frolic happily among animals in the wilderness.

Unsurprisingly, accounts of ill-fated encounters between whites and wild animals are in no short supply. This is not to say that there are no animal lovers among peoples of color. The late Michael Jack-son's home zoo is an example, and the association of pit bulls with urban blacks is another.[4] There is just, often, a fundamentally different attitude toward them. Viewing with a black audience "The Gal Who Got Rattled," one of the vignettes from Joel and Ethan Coen's poignant 2018 film anthology *The Ballad of Buster Scruggs*, illustrates this. The story has an annoying little dog that won't stop barking as the migrants make their way across the plains on the wagon train. Eventually, one of the trail leaders offers to put the dog down because it's attracting too much attention from wild animals and the Indigenous peoples whose country through which they are trespassing. Failing to do so eventually leads to the tragic situation in which, in an attempt to rescue the dog, the female protagonist shoots herself in the head rather than be captured by "wild" Indians. My fellow black audience members' position was resolute from the outset: get rid of the dog. White audiences would be more on the side of its owner, the ill-fated white female protagonist who cherished and protected it.

The presumption that one is entitled to everything creates a consciousness with presumed unlimited access and rights to whatever it wants. Such a consciousness treats a limitation as an intrinsic evil. Think of the outrage, the cries of "reverse discrimination," when blacks are hired in universities where the white population is often in excess of 90 percent—sometimes as high as 95 percent. This is bewildering to black faculty and blacks in other professions who often find themselves the lone person of color in the room.

In a world dominated for a half millennium by a greedy consciousness, other consciousnesses live a different story. Whereas one wants riches and unbridled liberties, the others hope for a better world with the possibility of some justice.

Several years ago, I traveled to East London, South Africa, to speak at the University of Fort Hare, a historically black institution. My hosts were quite generous; because of my epilepsy, they hired drivers to ferry me the hundred miles to and from the town then called Grahamstown, now Makhanda. On my return journey, my driver took a leisurely route along the coast. As we passed rows of large, beautiful seaside houses, I asked the driver who lived in them. Without hesitation, irony, or humor, the driver, who was black, replied, "The whites."

In countries across the world, what most people have not come to terms with is the distance between the quality of life afforded to even working-class whites and that afforded to most black and Indigenous peoples. Take the city of Boston, Massachusetts, a city not short of white resentment, where in 2017 the median net worth of white households was valued at $247,500. For the city's historic black population—and this is not a typo—the median household net worth was $8.[5]

In *The Black Tax*, the financier Shawn D. Rochester explores the disparity between white and black net worth across the United States.[6] Colonialism, enslavement, and racism resulted in the imposition of the titular tax, which saps away the fruits of black people's labor. Enslavement, Rochester argues, is a 100 percent tax on one's labor. The structure of a legal system ruled by double standards, and a civil society designated for the production of white wealth and black poverty, imposes a long chain of costs, the basic consequence of which is blacks having little and whites having a lot.

In Hispanophone and Lusophone countries of the Caribbean, Central America, and South America—such as Argentina, Brazil, Chile, Colombia, Cuba, the Dominican Republic, Ecuador, Mexico, Uruguay, Venezuela—there were *blanqueamiento* (racial whitening) policies. They took the form not only of restrictions on black procreation but also of economic incentives ranging from awarding white immigrants lands and government financial support with which to cultivate property and generate white wealth. This was not granted to the black populations, who were expected, through the promotion of eugenics, eventually to be cleansed from the national gene pool. The outcome was clear: becoming whiter became not only a racial ideal but also an economic reward.[7]

And yet many, if not most, whites want more—any gain for blacks is, in their view, their own loss. Whatever remains should be extracted. The greedy consciousness, of course, also wants justice, or at least claims to want it; the problem is that it would like "justice" and "having everything" to mean the same thing.

Black consciousness, at least with regard to black identity, is not about having everything. What, then, is it about? What do blacks want?

Over the past centuries, much has been said about blacks, but too little is of substance, and much is often false and harmful. To say something of constructive value requires time, reflection, and insight; one achieves this by respecting and valuing the subject of reflection.

Therein lies the problem.

From birth to grave, many, if not most, whites and other nonblack people learn to avoid thinking about the challenges black people face, such as exploitation, genocide, and racism. While being white connotes a right to everything, being black, from that point of view, connotes a *lack* of a right to anything.

The right to nothing also poses a form of nothingness. This raises a metaphysical problem. A twist in *Get Out*'s Coagula cult's trapping black conscious minds is a secret darkness haunting the conscious presence of light. This poses an additional problem when people admit such opacity; it cultivates, at least in the abstract, a sense of blacks lurking everywhere. Even where there are other people of color who do not ever expect to meet blacks, contemporary life demands at least a moment's reflection on what they might do should such an opportunity or a threat arise.

In the early 1990s, I taught a course at a university in the midwestern United States where many rural whites came to study. Quite a few undergraduates, especially among the first-year students, made an increasingly familiar confession: that my class was their first experience of seeing or communicating with a black person in the flesh. When they confessed their anxiety over that fact, I took their words as proof of a paradoxical, contextual comfort with their own discomfort. Their ideas about blacks came from their relatives, friends, and popular culture—sources that warned them of dangerous, subhuman creatures that haunted their imaginations. Expecting a bogeyman, they were often shocked to meet a human being.

Of course, this was not necessarily the case with all inexperienced students. Some could not bear what they saw—a human being of a *dark color*—and left the course. Others said nothing. And still others were surprised by a strange discovery: they had expectations for how they would respond when they were eventually in the presence of a black, which for them meant the same thing as *blacks*. Those who imagined being indifferent were bothered by how much the situation affected them; others were caught in the anxiety of discomfort that also stimulated fascination. The range of responses was wide.

During the 1980s, when I briefly worked as a public-school substitute teacher, I was occasionally assigned to secondary schools with mostly white, working-class students. I developed an informative exercise for those situations: I asked the students to tell me what they knew about black people. They would be reluctant at first, but eventually a student would state something presumed to be common knowledge.

"Blacks are criminals."

"OK," I would say, and then write the word "criminals" with white chalk on the blackboard.

Eventually all hands would go up, and a long list of pathologies would flow from their lips: blacks were endemically poor, diseased, dirty, lacking in sexual control, violent.

Then I would ask them if, as whites, supposedly the opposites of blacks, their lives lacked the characteristics on the list. If blacks were poor, and whites were what blacks were not, then were they themselves *rich*?

They looked at one another. No.

I would enumerate the many nefarious activities on the board: stealing, which included shoplifting; using illicit drugs; damaging property; physical assault; poor hygiene. Did none of them commit any of those offenses? Their eyes revealed what they knew about one another.

No one tried illegal substances or used legal ones in an illegal way such as underage drinking of alcohol? Did they lack sexual experience? Were they never in fights?

They were glossy-haired teenagers, many of whom identified as "Guidos" and "Guidettes," slang for party-type, working-class Italians; others were "metalheads" attired in short black leather jackets, white T-shirts, long spiked hair dyed black, and torn jeans. Were they drug-free and sexually inexperienced? *Hell no.*

The punch line never fell flat: "You must be the blackest white people I've ever met."

Of course, this would lead to a meditation on what white people were. It is not that those students were not white; it was clear that they conceived of an imagined white identity that was not their lived reality. The great comedian Richard Pryor famously recounted a story that should make many whites pause. Shortly after arriving in Africa (he did not at that time say which country), he asked one of the locals, "Which tribe do I look like?"

The man looked him over and responded, "Italian."

The white students' self-perception was blurred by a world of presumed opposites, one word for which is "Manichaeism." The term comes from the religious movement named after the Persian prophet Mani (216–274 c.e.). The main tenet of Manichaeism, the avowed "religion of light," was to purify each realm through separating them.[8] Thus light must be purified of any link to darkness. Light, Manichaeans claimed, belongs to the good, which is spiritual; darkness, to evil, which is material.

Can such a divide possibly work for human beings? We are not purely spiritual creatures, nor exclusively material ones. Wouldn't eliminating the connection between the two be our death knell?

Mani had a clear answer on whether consciousness could be black: it could not, at least not in its pure form. To consciousness, understood as spirit, which Mani interpreted as the light, blackness was entirely material, something to avoid or eliminate. It dragged consciousness down and threatened to swallow it up. The goal of Manichaeism was to liberate consciousness from the material body, which was fleeting and wicked, and which harbored blackness. A black *consciousness*, from this point of view, is oxymoronic.

Despite his name meaning "eternity" or "one who lives forever" in Persian, Mani died in prison in 274 under the reign of the Persian emperor Bahrām. His followers claim that he was crucified. His material form, at least, fell true to his thought.

When we ask, "What am I?" we often struggle with the fact that we appear as material things in the world and yet sense that we simultaneously transcend that state. We can commit ourselves so much to one over the other that we end up failing to see how we are an integration of both. And like Mani, too many of us attribute negative value to what we think is material and "dark," instead of reflecting on the flaws of what is immaterial and "light," or understanding how each contains the other—the hidden light of darkness, the secret darkness of light. This basic problem affects not only our everyday negotiations of relationships between the dark and the light but also our social scientific studies of how each is lived.

For example, I came across a problem in the early 1990s, when I was writing my first book, *Bad Faith and Antiblack Racism.* Having decided to analyze dynamics of police brutality, I perused social scientific journal articles on it and discovered that their data suggested that the phenomenon was rare. I knew this was false. I grew up in black neighborhoods of the Bronx in New York City, where police assaults were a near daily occurrence. I witnessed more instances of police illegitimate use of force than were reported in the social scientific literature I was consulting. My family experienced police cruelty; my friends; everyone I knew. Relatives who worked in city hospitals complained regularly about the brutalized suspects who arrived in handcuffs. The police were so bad that in some cases they even assaulted healthcare workers who were alarmed at the state of the accused being brought into emergency wards. How was I going to discuss the truth when authoritative scholarly sources suggested something different?

My eldest son, Mathieu, was three years old at the time. One day, while he and I were walking home in New Haven, we passed a policeman on a horse. At that age, Mathieu admired anyone in a uniform with the authority to use force. Add the horse, and the police officer must have looked like a superhero.

"Hello, Mr. Policeman!" He waved, smiling widely.

The officer looked down and smiled back. It was a pleasant encounter.

Damn, I thought as we walked away. My son's future held a terrible awakening: as he grew up, he would learn of the danger inherent to interactions between police officers and black people.

Then I had my aha moment. I returned to the library and found James P. Comer and Alvin F. Poussaint's *Black Child Care.*[9] Going straight to the index, I found what I was looking for: "police brutality." The book consisted of letters from parents seeking the two psychiatrists' advice on raising their children. The most striking element, however, were the parents' additional concerns, which included how to address alcoholism and other forms of drug addiction, rape and other crimes, and interracial environments and miscegenation.

It occurred to me then that one factor limiting data on police brutality in social scientific literature in the United States was the power of the Police Benevolent Association (PBA). Police brutality was official only when accused police officers were *convicted* of an offense. Given how low the chances of conviction for police brutality were and continue to be, especially when the victims are black, brown, or red, using conviction as the metric effectively erased reality. The effect was what could also be called police epistemic brutality—police suppressing knowledge and truth about their behavior. The testimonies of parents in *Black Child Care*, and the book's emphasis on the special caution required when raising black children, afforded a clearer look at the subject.

Although seeking data on police brutality was my initial concern, the subjects raised in *Black Child Care* offered an important social scientific reflection. For comparison, I examined some so-called generic childcare books. (Words such as "common," "dominant," "generic," and "mainstream" often mean *white*.) Those books did not offer discussions of the subjects I found in the book on black childcare. Instead, they focused on ego development and assertiveness, selecting the best schools, toilet training, and unfettered exploration—perfect for the development of a future king, queen, colonizer, or settler, at whose disposal is the world. What else were those books for but to teach those children how to be white?

Yet is that the reality lived by all white children? Or even most children? I have posed this question to white audiences across the globe, and most admit that it is not. As the many white autobiographies of traumatic childhoods attest, nearly every concern raised in the black childcare book, from alcoholism to rape, is a reality of raising children across lines of class, ethnicity, gender, race, and sexual orientation.

Consider domestic violence, mental illness, and incest: most suppos- edly ideal communities have these undersides. This shared darkness is, no doubt, one of the sources of white youths' strong identification with black music, ranging from the blues to rock 'n' roll to hip hop. Instead of Guidos and metalheads, today's secondary schools host cliques of white children attired in variations of hip blackness—acquired, in turn, from white pop-cultural displays of black cultures.

Of course, the peculiarity of police harassment and brutality sepa- rates the reality of raising black children—and, I must add, Indigenous or First Nation children—from other groups. Placing that exception to the side, which childcare books accurately depict the reality of raising children—the "universal" (for white parents) or the "particular" (for black and Indigenous parents)?

Black Child Care, whose cover had a somber black boy, was even- tually revised and renamed *Raising Black Children: Two Leading Psy- chiatrists Confront the Educational, Social and Emotional Problems Facing Black Children*, the cover of which has a black girl and boy wrapped in a moment of joy and laughter.[10] Meanwhile, it took decades for childcare books to emerge that acknowledged the particularity of what had been considered generic childcare advice. One of those is Al- ison Gopnik's *The Gardener and the Carpenter: What the New Science of Child Development Tells Us About the Relationship Between Parents and Children*.[11] The child on its cover is white and blond, but the book addresses topics such as abortion, AIDS, essentialism, and race. Police brutality, however, is still absent.

This realization is not limited to childcare books. It stands as a feature of how knowledge is offered on many matters pertaining to those who are presumed particular versus those who are supposedly universal. It took nearly three decades after my initial research efforts for publications offering a meeting of evidence and social criticism on continued police brutality and white vigilantism in the United States to come to print.[12] The art of non-seeing is at work in what many peo- ple are encouraged to think *must be so*.

Even the term "police brutality" is a problem—where force is pre- sumed legitimate, only its excess is condemned. The accurate term would be "police violence"—indicating situations in which *no use of force is legitimate.* The presumed legitimacy of the police and the illegitimacy of those they harm are the results of a permissive attitude toward criminality in law enforcement. They keep the dark from the light.

It's not only whites who find themselves in Manichaean, dark-versus-light situations around black people. And it's not only non-blacks who encounter contradictions of avowed racial knowing. Black people—say, from towns where they were the only black people they knew—also experience destabilization upon meeting blacks who are different from themselves; they feel robbed of a quintessential experience of black representation: no longer *the ones*, they experience a challenge to their authenticity. W.E.B. Du Bois reflected on the truth about this phenomenon: being born black does not entail knowing, in social scientific terms, what it means to be black.[13] It certainly does not mean knowing in advance what rigorous research has discovered. One could live without much knowledge, especially of one's self and the history of one's people, especially when trauma could discourage one from often admitting what one experiences.

The truth is that one's personal black story is *a* black story, but not all black stories are *the* black story. There are personal, historical, scientific, philosophical, poetic, mythical, and religious or sacred stories, each with its own layers of truth. In the United States, black Christians often presume "real" black people are Christian; Black Muslims offer other narratives, and even among them, there are differences according to the denomination of Islam, from Sunni to Shi'a, to which they belong. Black Jews are of many kinds, from Ashkenazi to Sephardic to Mizrachi to Hebrew-Israelite to Abayudaya to Lemba to secular. And among all these groups are those who are African, Asian, Australian, Caribbean, European, North American, and South American. And on all these continents and regions, there are those who are immigrants. Among those immigrants, there are differences across generations. Add class, and there are stories of the black poor versus the black middle class and those who are rich. Rural blacks have their stories; urban blacks, theirs. Among formally educated blacks, there are differences across the institutions through which we've achieved our education ranging from historically black colleges and universities (HBCUs) to public research universities and community colleges, to Catholic and other religious institutions, to the Ivy League and other elite private universities and liberal arts colleges. A set of differences are in the U.K., Germany, France, and other European countries along all these lines. The same in South Africa, and all countries in which there are black people. And with all these, we could add political views from right-wing to conservative to liberal to left of liberal to radical left. The generative historical story is crucial. Differences emerge even within families, where aspirations of some members challenge the values of others, as Lorraine Hansberry shows in *A Raisin in the Sun* (1959).

There were not always black people, in the way racist societies understand us; there were not always white people. Black and white, in the sense used by racist societies, are codependent. Black people were fabricated from the forces and trepidations that created white people.

There was a time when peoples of the world understood themselves primarily through the languages they spoke, their sacred sites, or their homeland. "Hebrew" and "Igbo," for example, refer to both languages and the people who speak those languages. In many languages, the word used to refer to their speakers translates roughly to "human" or "person." "Bantu," for instance, despite its negative connotations under colonialism in southern Africa, is simply the plural of *-ntu* in the constellation of languages spoken there, and it means "person" or "human." In the ancient African language Mdw Ntr, spoken by the people of the ancient African country of Kmt, the word for "person" is *anx*. The word *km* means "black." "Kmt" means the "black land," or "people of the black land" as a collective noun. Oddly enough, the word *anx* also means "sandal strap," "life," and "mirror." Written in hieroglyphs, its relationship to the word *ankh* (life) is evident. Egypt is the name ancient Greek-speaking colonizers imposed on the vast country of Kmt. It was the Greek transformation of one of the names of ancient Memphis. Its Temple, *Ha(t)-ka-ptah* (temple of the soul [or life source] of Ptah) became the Greek *Aígyptos*, which eventually became "Egypt." What in the ancient language of Mdw Ntr is at times translated as "Egyptian" is *rmT*. The word means "humankind."

Some ancient peoples named themselves after great leaders, their sacred totem, or the place of origin, but never after a color. Assuming themselves the norm, they would have no reason to do so; they differentiated themselves instead from animals, plants, the natural elements, locations, and gods. An example of location is when the *rmT* referred to people of lower Kmt as *mHw*. The word means "lower," as from a specific geographical location that is today northern Egypt. Upper Kmt was south; lower Kmt, north. This was based on the Nile River, which flows northward into the Mediterranean Sea.

It is unfortunate that the people immediately south of Kmt, the Nubians, are often contrasted as black when portrayed alongside the often cinnamon-colored people of the north. The people of Kmt called Nubia *Sty* and Nubians *Styw*. Notice the absence of the word *km* (black). An adjective for things created by *Styw* is *nHsy*. Interestingly, that word is related to a set of others referring to a variety of concepts ranging from escaping death to "eternity."

Leaping across time to the sixteenth through to the nineteenth century C.E., millions of African peoples who were born Aja, Akan, Edo, Fanti, Igbo, Tallensi, Wolof, or Yorùbá were kidnapped and suffered the horrors of a process by which they became "blacks" and so, too, the identity of their descendants.[14]

Although most popularly studied as the transatlantic slave trade and the East Indian Ocean slave trade, those historical activities have been mischaracterized.[15] "Trade" occurs where an offer can be refused. Someone offers what another wants, and the other offers something in return. Failing to make an agreement, nothing beyond the encounter is traded. Where people are hunted and snatched, trade occurs only among those who have corralled them and then negotiate with one another. Only the Arab designation is correct, since it refers to Arabs trading in the enslavement of peoples. The others should properly be called the European slave trade and the East Indian slave trade or Asian slave trade. Oceans do not trade people.

There is, however, something those who have studied this history know. Blacks, and many other groups who suffered a similar process, understood in racist terms, were *made.*

This tale of the making of blacks brings us to the development of a powerful, trauma-inducing concept: race. I use the word "trauma" because the most common response to the question of race is avoidance—a response we cannot afford.

3

ERASED; OR, "I DON'T SEE RACE"

If consciousness is associated with spirit or the light, then the prospects for blackness are at best dim.

There was a time when no one was black, white, or any of the racial epithets used today. We could say that people were seen in naked visual perception—brown, beige, pink, yellow, bone white (albino), dark. People with methemoglobinemia look blue. Even the colorblind see a spectrum.

People in the past did not "see" what many people today "see" when they categorize human beings according to color. We see through an accumulated baggage of historical, racialized material. Even if people in the past "saw" light and dark, they did not "see" race.

Some people today would say the same of themselves: "I don't see race."

"I don't see color," some might say.

Translation: "I'm not racist."

Another translation: "I *cannot be racist*, because I would first have to see race."

And another: "Because I don't see color, I cannot see race; therefore, I *am incapable of being racist*."

There is more: "I can see beyond what others see. I see that *they* see color and race; I'm better than them, because I see that what they see is wrong. And since racism relies on believing what is false, my seeing the true form of my fellow human being—no color, no race—means that I am beyond racism. I am good."

There was a time when racists didn't worry about being called "racist." This was because racism was "normal." Being racist in racist societies was *rational*, as Frantz Fanon argued in the 1950s.[1] Earlier black critics, such as the eighteenth-century American revolutionaries Lemuel Haynes and Benjamin Banneker, criticized the actions of the white Founding Fathers of the United States and their policies but didn't call them "racists."[2] This must no doubt seem odd to contemporary readers, since many of those Founding Fathers and their heirs placed a lot of effort into justifying obvious mistreatment and the resulting inequality of Indigenous peoples and kidnapped, enslaved Africans in the colonies of the "Americas" north and south. In George Washington's case, the brutality involved also prying the teeth from some of the enslaved to make his dentures and, as with Jefferson, fathering numerous children from their female "property."

The reader may wonder why I also placed quotation marks around "Americas." That's because the word is an eponym for one of the avowed "conquerors," the mapmaker Amerigo Vespucci, of that part of the world. What the people already living there called the region and its constellation of countries is a variety of names, of which Abya Yala is one. The decolonial intellectual Catherine Walsh offers the following reflection on this important reclamation:

> Abya Yala is the name that the *Kuna-Tule* people (of the lands now known as Panama and Colombia) gave to the "Americas" before the colonial invasion. It signifies "land in full maturity" or "land of vital blood." Its present-day use began to take form in 1992 when Indigenous peoples from throughout the continent came together to counter the "Discovery" celebrations, "to reflect upon 500 years of the European invasion and to formulate alternatives for a better life, in harmony with Nature and Human Dignity."[3]

I also placed quotation marks around "conquerors." This was how the people who sailed from the western shores of Iberian Christendom across the Atlantic Ocean regarded themselves. The descendants of the people who greeted them offer a more accurate term, Walsh reminds us, since these people are still fighting for their survival and freedom. They call those self-avowed conquerors "invaders."[4]

A process of global transformation of those who count as a person began in 1492 when Christopher Columbus landed in the Bahamas. That person's understanding of the self, tagged in English by the word "I," many of us have inherited as a history of Columbus's supposedly seeking a short trade route to Asia. What is often ignored is that that self quickly became the "I" who practiced genocide against Indigenous peoples and inaugurated global human trafficking.[5] That "I" could live in a world of racism without a self-ascribed racist identity. It was thus not facing, at least back during its formative years of development, such an accusation.

The terms "racism" and "racist" don't pop up until the 1930s, in French characterizations of Nazi ideology. Earlier expressions, such as "racialism" and "racialists," date back to the late nineteenth century in the British colony of South Africa. Before then, race-minded politicians, scholars, and scientists wrote of "Anglo-Saxons," "Aryans," and imagined "Teutons" as their ancestors. They spoke and wrote disparagingly of the "savage" and the "negro," which was derived from the Portuguese word for the color black. Although the French expression for the color black is *la couleur noire*, the French transformed the now racialized Portuguese word into *le nègre*, which specified the racial form of the color. By the eighteenth century, the Scottish and northern English pronunciation of the French version was "neger," which took root and was eventually transformed into "nigger." The word "nigger" was initially broad in scope. It applied not only to dark Africans but also to dark-skinned peoples of Australia, India, the island countries of Polynesia, and Abya Yala. Though "nigger" survives, it has its unfortunate public use among U.S. blacks asserting its supposed "reclamation" and "reappropriation" in "nigguh" and "nigga." Its use among whites is primarily behind closed doors or beyond the ears of blacks, except when they are assaulting or lynching them. There is no doubt that more variations of this pejorative term are to come.

Eighteenth-century colonists devised laws specifying nearly every kind of racial designation. We no longer speak of "quadroons" or "octoroons," though such legacies are sustained in some places more than in others. Brazil's 1976 census, for instance, has 136 different racial color designations, many of which are still active. Often, when people say they don't see color, they mean specifically that they don't see *black*. A good number of those 136 Brazilian racial designations are ways of avoiding identifying oneself as black, especially under the country's continued *branqueamento* (*blanqueamiento*, whitening) practices.[6] This kind of not-seeing through over-seeing requires creativity and skills of self-deception.

What's wrong with seeing oneself or another person as black? Or if not simply black—what's wrong with seeing color?

Imagine a woman and a man on a dinner date. The conversation goes well. Familiar cues of attraction unfold. She twirls her hair; he tilts his head while taking another sip of wine. After a few hours of talking and then walking under moonlight, reflecting on many aspects of each other's lives, they eventually arrive at the woman's front door. The man informs the woman he had a great time. She says the same. He then adds, seeming a bit anxious: "There's just one thing on my mind."

"What?" the woman asks.

"Well," he says. "It was so wonderful. I felt comfortable speaking with you except . . . for one thing. You're a woman. If only I could stop seeing you as a woman, I could see you with true respect. I could then have the perfect combination of respecting someone to whom I'm attracted."

There is a word for a man who, in order to respect a woman, must *not see her as a woman*. Misogyny here takes the form of gender blindness, or specifically, woman blindness.

Is it progressive, then, as the "colorblind" might imagine, to claim not to see race? If a person thinks that seeing someone as black signifies disrespect, doesn't it follow that the person thinks blacks are not worthy of respect? One could argue, drawing on the example of a man admitting his disrespect for women, that there is a line of feminist thought that is also anti-gender and anti-woman, or at least against *seeing* women or the appearance of women. Proponents of that line of feminist thought would point out, as some have, that a woman cannot be respected, even by women.[7] Many of those feminists would, however, agree that it would be misogynistic not to be able to respect a woman as a woman. The racial conclusion, then, is that it's antiblack to not be able to respect a person who appears black.

Doesn't "I don't see race" really mean "I don't want to see race"?

When one sees, one also feels a range of responses from affection to repulsion, comfort to fear. Now we enter the terrain of irony and self-denial, where one feels what one professes not to feel, denies seeing what one sees, claims to believe what one doesn't believe. There is a term for these attitudes or acts of self-denying consciousness. It's called "bad faith."[8]

The expression "bad faith" has a legal and a philosophical meaning. The legal meaning describes the attitude of a person who testifies or enters a contract with false intentions. "He signed the agreement in bad faith," a litigant might complain in court. The philosophical meaning rests on the peculiar fact that people are capable of lying to themselves. In his defense, the signatory to the agreement could claim he did not sign the contract in bad faith; he did so sincerely. Sincerity, however, from the philosophical perspective, can be in bad faith. Many racists are sincere.

To understand how sincerity can be in bad faith requires an elaboration of what it means to be in bad faith. The concept of bad faith involves the ability to lie to oneself. Lying is something one does, which means it belongs to the agent who lies. The liar and the deceived are the same. As an action, it is an expression of consciousness, but, as many readers are aware, there are conscious and unconscious actions. One could regard unconscious activity as behavior instead of action, properly understood as intentional. But that is too simple a view of consciousness, because we often come to realize something we have been doing—such as shaking our leg or saying phrases such as "I know, I know"—when someone else points it out to us. For us to say we had no control over what we were doing or said would occasion doubt, even though it would be correct to say we were unaware or didn't realize what we were doing. Consciousness, which includes awareness, must be more complicated.

Consciousness is always *of* something, whether experienced or imagined. It always involves something of which one is conscious. Without anything, consciousness disappears. There is, in other words, no such "thing" as consciousness itself. It is a relationship with reality. This relational activity is called *intentionality*. The something of which consciousness is intended is that which appears. Things of which we are not conscious come into consciousness. Such things stand out. At that point, we say they exist. This is actually what the word "existence" means, as it arises from the Latin expression *ex* (out) *sistere* (to stand). To stand out is to emerge or to appear. In French, "to exist" also means "to live."

Consciousness involves things being manifested, and manifestation is a transition from not appearing to appearing. Another word for things that appear is "phenomena." The concept has a wonderful mythic origin. It came about from the ancient Persian myth of the god Phanes (manifestor).[9] Phanes was the offspring of the god/goddess Chronos (time). Phenomena are born from time.

Consciousness requires a relationship to phenomena, to things that appear. Bad faith, meanwhile, involves attempting to take consciousness out of the relationships through which things appear, emerge, become manifest or intelligible. It's the imposition of non-relationality onto relations.

For consciousness to be *of* something, the thing must be *there* through which the relationship of being conscious of it is *here*. This here-there relationship means consciousness must be *embodied*; it must be in a space and time. Consciousness must be somewhere.

People fantasize about being outside their bodies—one of the great hopes of Manichaeism, which originated in third-century-c.e. Persia: freeing the light of consciousness from the darkness of matter. What that might entail is difficult to say. Without being somewhere, consciousness would be either nowhere or everywhere, without a *there* or *here* through which to be anywhere. This means that we could be disembodied only through denying the perspective or embodied standpoint from which we imagine disembodiment. It would be a form of bad faith.

Dimensions of bad faith are also illuminating in the French language.[10] The adjective *mauvais* means "false" or "worthless," and in the feminine *mauvaise* means "bad." *La foi*, generally translated as "faith," also means "belief," "confidence," "pledge," or "trust." Thus, *la mauvaise foi*, though often translated as "bad faith," refers to a wide range of attitudes that are not immediately apparent in its English expression. We will work with the English, however, since that is the language in which I here offer these reflections.

"Bad faith" refers to a variety of distinct yet connected conscious acts. Belief, for example, could be a manifestation of bad faith. To believe, instead of to know, requires an element of doubt. Yet there are people who offer the notion of a true, justified belief, or *perfect belief*. If the belief were perfect, however, there would be no reason for doubt, and it would thus not be a "belief." Such a vision of belief is an example of bad faith.

Imagine a group of survivors has been in an underground shelter for a decade. Their watches no longer work. They aren't sure if it is night or day outside. One believes it is sunny. A cohabitant believes otherwise. Why? It could be cloudy or perhaps night. The first stands by her belief. Her cohabitant responds, "I don't doubt that you believe it. Your belief just doesn't matter. If we go outside, we'll see. We'll know."

A bell announcing safety rings. The bunker's safety latches unlock. They go outside. It's a dark, cloudy day. Our first inhabitant responds: "It isn't sunny."

"I notice you didn't say you 'believed' it isn't sunny," her cohabitant comments. "The weather is not about belief. It's about truth and facts. Thoughts are connected to truth and facts. Yes, you *believed* it was sunny. But you were wrong."

Some people take retreat into imagination. "If I am imagining it is not sunny, wouldn't it then be a belief? Or even more, wouldn't I now be telling the truth? How can we tell right now that it's really day but not sunny and not just our imagination fooling us?"

Jean-Paul Sartre offered a famous response to people who claim there's no distinction between imagination and perception, between ideas and the experience of things.[11] He asked for these "phenomenalists," people who argue there is only appearance of things and that there is no difference between imagined and real appearance, to compare counting the columns of an imagined Parthenon with the experience of counting the columns in the presence of the actual Greek temple. The number of columns of the imagined version would be uncertain; the number of columns of the real Parthenon is specific, and others can join us in counting them. We create the image of the imagined Parthenon; the real one resists what we may wish it to be.

Simone de Beauvoir and Sartre presented a famous example of bad faith. A woman is at dinner on what is not, at least in her mind, a romantic date. In the midst of the conversation, the suitor takes her hand; in an act of bad faith, the woman continues speaking as if unaware. This is an illustration of the human capacity for *disembodiment*. Despite attempting to communicate amorous desire through holding her hand, the suitor discovers he is grasping it as nothing more than a *thing*. The woman evacuated herself from it.

Consciousness, which must reside somewhere, must be in the flesh. It is properly *lived*. The woman did something extraordinary yet also mundane: she enabled her suitor to touch her hand but *not her*—or, at least, that is what she may have believed. Her hand appeared lifeless.

It would be a mistake to read the example of the approached woman, as I will refer to her (whereas other critics call her "the coquette"), as a *moral* example. There are conditions—torture, rape, humiliation—under which one would have good reason to seek disembodiment; it's a survival tactic to think "That's not being done to *me*." The options for most women in a sexist society, even those who consider themselves exceptions, are limited. A similar problem applies to men of color in slaveocracies and racist societies, where techniques of sexual violence are used to control enslaved women and men of color.[12] The example of the approached woman suggests what Beauvoir calls "ambiguity."[13] In human or social relationships and situations only part of a story is revealed—and that depends on the varieties of meaning attached to what is experienced, done, or told.

We should also consider the suitor's experience of the hand he is holding. One can experience another's disembodiment; the suitor could *notice* that the woman evacuated her hand. There is a form of opacity despite what both see and, given the situation, may deny for the sake of courtesy. The sociality of the situation is affected. Social meaning depends on connectedness for coherence, but this couple's case is one of a physical touch that affects communication. People can make themselves believe they are things in some instances, disembodied phantoms in others. The problem is that "things"—at least non-living ones—aren't properly social; they are without points of view. To be social, there must be communicated, embodied points of view.

This is not to say that what is being discovered these days in physics about the location of photons and standpoints must be wrong. From antiquity through the present, the question of whether material reality has a point of view has been a matter of debate. Contemporary research on material reality also being perspectival—reality with a point of view—simply amounts to saying that being "things" is an ascribed attribute. It means they could also be possibilities of "here." That doesn't change the main point of the argument. Things—*as only things or beings in themselves*—aren't social.

Terms such as "sincerity" and "authenticity" are commonly equated with good faith. Thus, to be sincere, authentic, or in good faith is supposedly not to be in bad faith. These are ideas that amount to being who or what one really is or at least avows oneself to be. Yet one can make oneself believe things that are false, including things about oneself. Investments in those false beliefs often involve turning away from reality or, worse, attempting to force reality to conform to those falsehoods. What better defense than to appeal to one's sincerity, authenticity, and good faith? To address truth requires attunement to reality and facing others' freedom of judgment. The opposite of bad faith thus transcends one's sincerity and even good faith. It is a critical relationship to *evidence* and to seriousness. All evidence embodies a question and relies on the art of questioning, through which truth, including responsibility for truth, unfolds. There is thus a relationship between questioning and freedom because both are accompanied by responsibility. "Asking questions," Dena Neusner, the author of *Simply Seder* reminds us, "is a sign of freedom."[14] A critical consciousness embraces its freedom.

Bad faith works by lying to oneself, which requires eliminating one's relationship to evidence—that which clearly shows lies to be lies. To protect itself, bad faith must disarm the evidentiality of evidence—that is, its ability to appear. Rendered impotent, evidence can no longer interfere with the ability of a person or group to believe something in bad faith. For example, many people would like to believe that women are essentially women through focusing on their anatomy as the sole source of evidence instead of the meaning brought to everyone's physical appearance through the social world in which women live. Beauvoir challenged the idea that anatomy entailed destiny—whether a woman's body overdetermines what she is—by arguing that one "becomes a woman."[15] Must her anatomy require her to move through the world according to a set of expectations imposed on "women" in every society? Since Beauvoir, others, the most prominent of whom is Judith Butler, transformed this question through asking whether anyone must be any subject such as "woman" or anything else.[16] Butler asks us to explore the possibility of agency (the power to act) and freedom without the subjects we call "agents." Hers is an example of a critical feminist response to whether "woman" is an appropriate site of political practice and respect.

Before Butler and Beauvoir, Friedrich Nietzsche took up the question of subjects—what are commonly today called "identities"—by questioning the values through which they are made. Taking responsibility for these values releases them from their "spirit of seriousness," which is the attitude or belief in ideas or meanings as given from nature instead of relationships produced by human actions and for which we are responsible. The spirit of seriousness hinders freedom and is itself a form of bad faith. In a rallying cry against bad faith, Nietzsche called for a "transvaluation of values," or freely taking responsibility for bringing value to our values.[17]

The spirit of seriousness, turned onto the self, slides into *taking oneself too seriously*, which is a form of egotism. Doing so closes the door on relationships with others, and consequently social reality and love. To avoid closing oneself off, it's a good idea to "decreate" the ego. "Decreation," writes Simone Weil, means to "make something created pass into the uncreated. . . . We participate in the creation of the world by decreating ourselves."[18] There is a similar idea in Eastern thought, Keiji Nishitani explains, in which egotism is a source of evil.[19] Letting go of the ego affords radical responsibility: there is no longer a lifeline from the abyss.

For Nietzsche, resisting seriousness involves *play*, or realizing the construction of rules through which life's games or values are played. Disputes arise, in sports and games, around whether players are following the rules; therefore, since there are different ways to play a given game, the rules should be determined before the game begins. For example, the "serious" player of checkers is convinced that the rules of checkers are as fixed as those of chemistry, even though one could permit jumping backward over pieces. There could be jumping over those in which there is a space between two of them. One need not stop there. Eventually, many realize there could be three-dimensional checker games. One could jump up or down, forward or backward, and sideways. And beyond those, there could be conceptual checkers *spoken* to each player. There could be coded checkers. To argue none of those are "really" checkers because they aren't red and black round pieces or coins played on an eight-by-eight-inch flat board with beige and black squares reeks of seriousness. Explaining that this five-thousand-year-old game, also known as draughts, has been played many ways over those millennia would not mean much to the player imbued with seriousness. Such a player forgets about being a *player* because that person is no longer *playing*. Checkers, in that player's case, becomes like the meeting of two atoms of hydrogen and one atom of oxygen. If a chemical is lacking that combination of those atoms, it is incorrect to call it "water." Playing by any of those possible rules is not, for that player, checkers.

The rules of chemistry and those of board games differ in an important respect that the serious player ignores. The elements are governed by nature; board games are human-created activities determined by rules upon which players agree. Not taking ourselves too seriously entails remembering the rules through which values are produced and taking responsibility for them.[20] We not only produce values but, in so doing, also make ourselves. We become, in other words, what we do. Racism, for example, is a form of serious activity that produces racists.

In addition to reminding us that we are responsible for the rules by which we live, play has the potential for joy and laughter. The ability to laugh at oneself is a release from the bonds of seriousness.[21] A rotund comedian remarks, "I don't sleep at the beach. People keep trying to push me back to sea." Comedy brings the absurd to the ordinary through pointing out displaced humanity—in this case, theriomorphizing oneself as a beached whale. Those who fail to see or understand the displacement miss the joke. This can also occur with visual and musical humor. For example, a comical cinematic technique is to film an animal in motion with a soundtrack. Think of an alligator walking to Curtis Mayfield's soulful "Between You Baby and Me" (1979). Try B.B. King's 1969 rendition of Roy Hawkins and Rick Darnell's "The Thrill Is Gone" (1951) or Fela Kuti's "Sorrow, Tears, and Blood" (1977). Or perhaps Johann Strauss's "Blue Danube" (1866) or Richard Wagner's "Ride of the Valkyries" (1856). The cultural source will not change the comic effect. How about a recorded chant of the Hare Krishna mantra? How about a flamingo walking to the same? An ant?

Laughter is a social *gesture*. This is because it is a form of communication of recognizing something funny. Recognition and understanding are in each moment of laughter. But despite this important social role of acknowledgment, laughter also seizes us. All laughter is to some extent a loss of control. We could very well have become a species without laughter through lacking the ability to lose control.

To that extent, we would have become "tense." Becoming too tense, we could break. As we cannot in advance fit into every situation we may enter, we need adaptability and elasticity or flexibility. Released from the throes of rigidity through laughter, our body appears as, in the words of the great French philosopher Henri Bergson, "*a deformity that a normally built person could successfully imitate.*"[22] Look at family photos or those of audiences engulfed in laughter. If that were our everyday way of walking through the world, we would seem deformed.[23] The rigidity from which we are released comes to bear in the moment of laughter with a conclusion significant for our analysis: "*The attitudes, gestures and movements of the human body are laughable in exact proportion as that body reminds us of a mere machine.*"[24] Laughter frees us from seriousness as mechanism. Freedom is expressed in how we live or wear embodiment. It requires gracefulness. A human being living as human is graceful.

Some people treat the body as something they *wear.*[25] The question then becomes whether their body "fits." Can one wear a race or gender? If so, many of us should wonder if we are wearing the "right" race or gender. If we decide our race or gender doesn't fit, we face social expectations that may result in ill-treatment ranging from anger to laughter. Consider the response of laughter. Aimed at displaced gender or race, laughter is a response to seeing or understanding something that may perhaps be a form of refusal to see and understand. It could be a bad-faith form of laughter, which is a possibility that weighs down the purpose of laughing with a mechanical effect. Unlike ordinary laughter, which is a return to gracefulness through a snapped release from rigidity, laughter in bad faith demands rigidity of the self and others. There, the laughter springs not from witnessing rigidity in another but instead from the declaration of gracefulness manifested where it supposedly does not belong. It is to treat a human being in motion as a creature with an inappropriate soundtrack and force him, her, or them back into their supposed awkward place.

Racism imposes mechanism and rigidity on human life through race. It seals some of us in armor, others in shackles. The person who

claims not to fit in any racial category, or one who claims to fit another race or gender than he, she, or they received at birth, could be
a challenge to the idea of living in racial purity. Some also assert the
triumph of purity through rejecting racial purity. An appeal to purity
relies on eliminating all external relationships, which include race, as
"contaminants," and they could respond by retreating into sterile disconnectedness or nonrelations: what remains for them is a supposedly
pure self.

One could object as follows. How about having only pure relationships with pure things? One could try to achieve that, but the question
would be raised: What made such things pure in the first place? What
would make a *relationship* pure? To answer that requires explaining
impurity. That emerges when something that should not be in contact
with something else violates boundaries. If one thing has the quality of
not being another thing, how, then, could the purity of each be considered when the other is taken into account? What would be the basis of
the required separation?

The whole effort boggles the mind when posed abstractly. In ordinary life, there are things that could harm us and things we do not
like. We try not to be in a relationship with those things. We reach for
things that are otherwise. To be clean, then, is not about making sure
nothing contacts us. Yet, lacking control over something, like a board
game, is a contaminant for some people. They wish to touch without being touched, see without being seen, hear without being heard,
smell without being smelled, contact without being contacted. One
could work imaginatively to achieve some of these goals, but contact-
ing without being contacted is an unlikely one to pull off. That would
require being in no relationship with anything or anyone—possibly
including oneself.

What, however, if relationships also become a form of impurity?
That which is impure is, after all, discovered, and sometimes it is so
when it is too late. Its harm has been done. It's not long before one realizes that impurity comes from standing out.

"I don't see race; I don't see color." This declaration is against the
idea of race and color standing out.

"I don't see race" is a pleasing falsehood posed against a displeasing truth. Seeing race, seeing color, entails responsibility for what one sees. It also means realizing one lives in a society that sees people racially. In one stroke, the denial elevates the denier in rejecting responsibility for challenges posed by a world in which race matters. It's easier to be sealed in a mechanism of not seeing. That delusion was shattered for many who saw the recording of a group of police officers—one black, another Asian American, and the third white—doing nothing while their colleague pressed his knee on a handcuffed black man's neck for nine minutes and twenty-nine seconds, resulting in his death.

There is also the question of whether the issue at stake is about seeing race or not. Imagining one's perspective as vital and then absolving oneself of that responsibility offers a seductive delusion. What happens to race and racism when blindness is afforded validity?

We receive permission to try not to be connected to racial matters. Race and racism become intrusions with intrinsic illegitimacy better left ignored.

It has become fashionable in critical studies of race to call this avowed denial and blindness "epistemic ignorance"—which is oxymoronic, as "epistemic" refers to knowing. A knowing failure to know is hardly a good defense against responsibility.

This is not to say that all is made good through the acknowledgment of seeing race. Throughout the period of formal enslavement and then segregation in the United States, there were many white people who claimed to see race but denied being racists. This was also the case in apartheid South Africa. Whites in both countries had black slaves or "servants" (their often preferred term) who lived in their homes and whom they claimed to "love." These were forms of being integrated into a system of giving the masters what they preferred to see. Some interrogation into those cases would reveal an attitude to their house slaves and servants similar to the status of pets and other domesticated animals. Their "seeing" race is a form of non-seeing. The humanity of blacks never entered their house.

So, in contrast, "not seeing" race supposedly opens the door of human appearance. But wouldn't this bar blacks from entering? Instead of not seeing blacks, why not find a way to see without doing so too seriously?

There is laughter to be had at the expense of those who pretend not to know. An excited white teenage girl ran up to my youngest son, Elijah, in the hall of their high school. "I just saw the *Black Panther*!" she exclaimed. "It's amazing!"

Elijah, a multi-artist whose repertoire includes stand-up comedy, detected a form of self-indulgence in her announcement to *him*—a Black Jewish classmate. He opted for some amusement at her expense. "That's racist," he remarked. "You should say the 'African American Panther.'"

Stricken, she rushed to apologize.

PART II

RACE-MAKING AND RACISM

Unfulfilled expectations cause grief and
we have already had our share.

–Vine Deloria, Jr.

4

RACE-MAKING

There is a market in Coyoacán, in Mexico City, not far from the famed artist Frida Kahlo's house-turned-museum, where locals claim a pot of soup has been simmering for more than a thousand years. Interrupted briefly by the Spanish conquistadors, the market one day resumed, and so did that simmering pot of soup. Did the stirrers of the pot eventually—as if passing a baton in a relay race—hand over their spoon to others who did the same, in an unbroken chain, through to the soup stirrers of today? Had the primordial broth—with various new ingredients added over time, including water; new spices, meat, and vegetables from distant, invaded lands; fish and crustaceans from faraway oceans—been poured into subsequent pots? Perhaps pots ranging from clay to metal, in the ongoing effort to balance the old with the new and to prepare for what was—and for us, now is—to come?

Might not there be in a market in Africa, where humanity began, a pot of soup that started its journey in a vessel crafted out of stone or clay, then iron, then one day stainless steel?

The network of genes in our bodies is much like the ingredients in that pot of soup. Nonetheless, many have attempted to purify the soup through processes of elimination, without realizing that in doing so they would leave only boiling water—or worse, an empty pot.

Some people would like to purify the world of race; unfortunately, this often takes the form of eliminating color. This includes ridding the world of black consciousness. Getting rid of black people often follows.

Racial matters are deceivingly simple. A teenager stops to buy some candy while talking to his girlfriend on a cell phone. An adult man accosts him. The adolescent attempts to get away from the man, who approaches and lunges as if to catch a culprit; the youth fights to protect himself; the man shoots him; the boy dies. The man is eventually tried and acquitted; the jury determines that he was acting in self-defense. The acquitted man, George Zimmerman, is white, or at least considered so in relation to the young man he slayed; the deceased teenager, Trayvon Martin, is black.

Now, reverse the race of the actors: the man is black; the teenager, white. Most readers would be certain of a different outcome. Instead of an acquittal, there would likely be a conviction for first-degree murder. In the not-so-distant past, the black suspect would be less likely to make it to trial than to face a white mob and a noose around his neck at the foot of a tall, sturdy tree.

A critic may object on the grounds that one never really *knows* what would happen if counterfactual situations were realized. There is, in response, empirical evidence of how things often turn out when a black individual is accused or convicted of the homicide of a white individual—consulting the U.S. Death Penalty Information Center's annual reports would suffice.[1] Presumption of innocence has a nasty habit of stopping short when the accused is red, brown, or, especially, black.

That race is so determinative raises the question of its lived reality. The addition of racism is a factor, as it places a long chain of considerations behind what is available to whites versus other groups, especially blacks, who are, as we have seen, treated as the antithesis or opposites of whites.

As we have seen, talking about race and racism is weighed down with much baggage because, for the most part, most people—and I mean this globally—are trained from birth to avoid it. Talking about race often involves simultaneously attempting to disavow doing so, which is neurotic. A condition for the presence of race is, in those instances, its absence. This problem spills over into the behavior of those who study it. Scholars of race must in some way disavow the legitimacy of their research project in an effort to legitimize their work. This is why, among many reasons, both racism and discussions about racism are often saturated with bad faith.

Racism manifests bad faith in individuals and the institutions they create. It involves pressuring us to reject what we see, especially where our relationship to reality is at stake. People confuse racists, the individuals, with racism, the system that supports them. Unlike the Founding Fathers, who, despite facing critics ranging from Benjamin Banneker and Lemuel Haynes to Thomas Paine, lived in a world of racism that for the most part treated racists as normal or rational, we are now expected to concede racists without racism. Disempowered by the mechanisms of power bolstering a racist society, people who regard racism as the right position to hold would be at worst quacks, anomalous remnants from an unfortunate past.

Or so many would like to believe. The unfortunate developments since 2016, marked by a global reassertion, if not simply coming out into the open, of fascism, enslavement, and racism, raise the problem of institutional apparatuses of power at the disposal of fascist and racist practices of governing. The result was the increase of precarity and vulnerability through which, for example, COVID-19 quickly became a pandemic in 2020 with a pronounced effect on black and Indigenous peoples.[2]

Racism is the institutional production of nonhuman status to groups of human beings, with the consequence of a "race" or set of "races" being treated as inferior or superior to others. A race deemed inferior has limited social options. Said another way, racism requires a society to deny the humanity of certain human beings through the organization of them in categories from those intrinsically high to those endemically wretched; via regimes of power, racist society groups human beings under the category of a race in order to limit their social options and then denies them the ascription of being really human. A performative contradiction follows in which a society must first identify the abject race or races as human beings in order to deny their being human.

Racism is also an effort to evade or destroy reciprocity and equality in human relationships. Its aim is to push members of racialized
groups of people out of the sphere of social reality and into a form of
impotence akin to the film *Get Out*'s "sunken place"—a dark, ethe-
real zone where the protagonist, Chris, is trapped. Chris is not disembodying himself there; he is not in bad faith. The white cult members,
on the other hand, are aware of their victims being sunk and stratified
deep within, which means there is a form of asymmetrical condition,
with agency on one side but awareness on both. Ironically, despite
historical claims of black dependency, the film is an allegory of white
dependency on what blacks—or in this case, at least their bodies—
offer.

A powerful moment in *Get Out* is when Missy Armitage, the
mother of Chris's girlfriend, Rose, throws Chris into the sunken place
through the power of hypnosis. Chris looks up to a small opening in
which Missy looks back at him to assure he is trapped in that "there"
that is seemingly "nowhere." She must look through Chris's glazed
eyes to find an immobilized version of him. Instead of their victims
disembodying themselves, it is the members of the Coagula cult who
keep them stratified deep within the bodies they have stolen. To maintain this, they must repress or dissociate from that trapped blackness
deep within them. They must push reflection away from awareness.

Fanon observed that what he calls "the black," as understood in a
racist society, is a white construction. We could extend this observation to races and racism in general. As we saw in our second chapter,
there was no reason for the people of Africa to consider themselves
"black" but for the historical circumstances that imposed that identity
onto them and their descendants. The same applies to Indigenous peoples of Abya Yala and the South Pacific, who would not know themselves as "indigenous" but for the invasions of those who settled on
their land and imposed a "native" identity onto them.[3]

A failure to understand how invasion, colonization, enslavement,
and exploitation affected the people who suffered from these forces
also led to a false understanding of those people who inflicted that

reign of terror on them over the past five hundred years. The many ethnic groups of Africa and those of Abya Yala and Oceania were transformed into racial types, while many groups in what we now know as Europe came to be known simply as "whites." Although the initial population of invaders from Spain and Portugal were multiracial—as seen in sixteenth-century Mediterranean paintings such as *Portrait of Duke Alessandro de' Medici* by Bronzino in Florence and the famous details in *Chafariz d'el Rey* of the Alfama district of Lisbon—the quest for profit soon turned profiteers onto one another. This phenomenon required that people all over the globe come to believe that they always were as they have come to be known. Thus, the history of a once Christendom, in which the term *raza* referred to Afro-Muslim and Jewish groups across the caliphates (Muslim polities) reaching as far north as southern France from the eighth through fifteenth centuries C.E., is rewritten under white supremacy as an age of exploration by a monolithic people who carry the torch of "Western civilization" and "modernity." Elided in that story are the ways in which *raza* morphed into "race" as the foundational anthropological concept of the era, and also how "modern" was equated with that age.

The sixteenth-century lexicographer, cryptographer, and priest Sebastián de Covarrubias explained that the word *raza* originally pertained to "the caste of purebred horses, which are marked by a brand so that they can be recognized. . . . Raza in lineages is meant negatively, as in having some raza of Moor or Jew."[4] Covarrubias did not dig deeper into the origin of the word. The populations whom the Romans and then the Moors colonized in Iberia were primarily Germanic. Yet the term *raza* was not from German, Latin, or Greek, the languages that dominated the European side of the Mediterranean, but instead from Arabic, with clear connections to Amharic, Hebrew, and Mdw Ntr. As a variation of such words as *ra'* and *ras* (Arabic), *ras* (Amharic), *rosh* (Hebrew), and *ra* (Mdw Ntr), it is connected to words meaning "head" and "beginning." The most ancient, from Kmt/Egypt, refers to Ra (pronounced "ray," and at times "rea," as in the word "reason"), the sun god. Ra, we should remember, rose daily from the east. For Andalusian Iberians, this meant East Africa and West Asia. For Iberian Christians, it was the variation of a foreign word to tag foreignness to those ruling over them.

It is clear what is meant when the word *raza* is applied to human beings: it is, after all, a term meant for animals. The use of "Moor or Jew" as examples of "negative" lineage is revelatory for contemporary discussions of race. Moors were Afro-Muslims (primarily mixtures of Arabs, Berbers, Mandinka Malians, Nigerians, Numidians, and Mauritanians), and many Jews were, for the most part, indistinguishable from Moors, though both were by that point multiracial populations.[5] Now consider the reference to horses. Domestic horses evolved from their ancestral species through human intervention; thus, their "natural" form was heavily mediated or *deviated* from nature. The use of "Moor or Jew" as examples of "negative" lineage therefore suggests a belief that Moors and Jews represented a deviation from natural intentions of the divine. Their deviation exemplifies human hubris, or swaying from the natural relationship human beings should have with, for Christians, Christ. Comparing them to domesticated animals, then, also signaled the role they were expected to play in Christendom.

The Spaniards referred to the 1492 defeat of the Moors in Granada as the "reconquest." This description was clearly more of an attitude about the preferred order of power than an appeal to historical fact. The Moors had invaded and ruled over a majority-Christian Iberian peninsula, and Jews functioned as a mediating group between the mostly Christian and Muslim populations. The term "reconquest" was a way of asserting a natural order, which meant that the eight hundred years of Muslim rule was supposedly "unnatural." Since at least a fifth of the Iberian population was then made up of people who today would be considered black, one could imagine how their presence was experienced, especially since they were from the invading population, among the lighter-skinned peoples of the peninsula.

It should be borne in mind that Christendom also acquired its identity through converting the ancient Roman Empire into the Holy Roman Empire. Regarding that achievement as "conquest" would make taking back the land a second conquest. The focus on conquest reveals a fundamental feature of Iberian Christian values. In his wonderful history *The Eighth Flag*, Stanford Joines succinctly offers some added dimensions:

> Imagine a Muslim Europe ruled by Arabs and Africans.
>
> It almost happened.
>
> The Umayyad army invaded France under Abd-al-Raḥmān in 722 and plundered France at will for ten years. The Moors had become overconfident by the time Charles Martel forged an alliance of Frankish (Germanic) tribes and appeared before them on October 10, 732. Abd-al-Raḥmān did not bother to gain intelligence on this new barbarian force and completely underestimated them. Even so, the Moorish army was only narrowly defeated at the Battle of Tours when Charles' infantry, formed into phalanxes and drawn up behind trees on a steep hill, destroyed the previously unstoppable Umayyad heavy cavalry. . . . Martel unified the Franks—basically all of Europe except for England—and created the foundation for his grandson Charlemagne's empire, the first nation-state in Europe since the fall of Rome.[6]

This is a history often overlooked in absolutist accounts of white rule and avowed virtues of "Western civilization." The epoch of white supremacy under which we now live is still shorter than the period of Afro-Arab rule in what is today southern Europe. Continues Joines:

> Shortly after the defeat at Tours, the Umayyad Caliphate fell into ruin and split into petty emirates, with the Emirate of Cordoba ruling the Iberian Peninsula. The culture of Moorish Iberia was tolerant of other religions; Christians and Jews were allowed to own businesses and hold civil service positions, though registered as second-class citizens. Many Iberians, however, could never accept rule by invaders, and "Christian" Iberians fought for freedom for 780 years.

The Emirate of Cordoba lost territory to several small Christian kingdoms, and, in 1469, the marriage of Ferdinand and Isabella created the united nation of Spain. The Emirate crumbled, and on January 2, 1492, Granada, the last Moorish fortress on the Iberian Peninsula, surrendered.[7]

Our excursion into the origin of the word "race" offers a wealth of material for understanding the fluidity and scope of its contemporary use. Consider the word "Semite," which comes from the late-eighteenth-century adjective "Semitic," devised by the German historian August Ludwig von Schlözer and designed to group Northeast African and West Asian languages such as Arabic, Amharic, Aramaic, Hebrew, and Tigrinya. The term is the Latinizing of the Hebrew *Shem*, the name of one of Noah's sons—the one who wasn't cursed and whose name also means "name." Despite contemporary Jewish efforts to escape racialization, the term became locked in a reference to anti-Jewishness or hatred of people who practice Judaism. Today, the tendency is to speak of "antisemitism," coined by the Austrian Jewish scholar Moritz Steinschneider, as separate from racism.[8] We should bear in mind, however, that most people who hate Jews know nothing about Judaism; they hate Jewish people. This is indicative of a basic fact: if race is constructed, then any group can be shaped into a race and become a subject of hate. As Moors or Afro-Muslims were among the groups the initial formation of the proto-race concept in Andalusia was designed to disparage, it appears the old term has come home to roost in varieties of contemporary hatred against Muslim peoples, despite the religion's reach across different, conventionally conceived races.[9]

Another concept demanding illumination in the study of race is "modern." The term is so equated with being European and white that it is rarely defined otherwise. "Modern" derives from the French transformation of the Latin *modo* ("just now" or "present"), which, as a noun, refers to a person belonging to the present. Clearly, this is not a quality unique to the people whom we now know as European and white. Though the expression dates back to the sixteenth century, European intellectual historians point to the seventeenth-century French philosopher and mathematician René Descartes as inaugurating modern thought. Others, such as the Argentine philosopher and historian Enrique Dussel, consider the invasion of Abya Yala in the fifteenth century as the beginning of the modern age. Whereas Descartes argued, "I think, therefore I am," in fact rephrasing Saint Augustine's "If I'm mistaken, I am," Dussel insists that the true statement, reflecting the practices inherited from Iberian Christian understanding of reconquest, was "I conquer, therefore I am."[10]

If, however, the modern belongs to now or the present, how, then, could those moments of the past belong to the present? Shouldn't they be, in relation to us, ancient?

No people have reason to question their belonging to the present unless their legitimacy is challenged, as by conquest or colonization. There could also be moments of different groups meeting or changing through ongoing processes of trade. In such encounters, the question of embodying the direction in which humanity is headed, the future, rises. If a group is promised no future, its present is jeopardized, and belonging becomes a feature of its past. Think here of the Latin term *primitivus* ("first of its kind"—for example, *prime*), which was transformed from a way of referring to one's ancestors to what we now think of as being *primitive*.

Being modern means being linked to where humanity is going. Before the fifteenth century's Christian invasions and colonization of Abya Yala and eventually most of the planet, debates on the direction in which peoples were headed, what they were and ought to become, were premised on ways of life (customs, laws, language), which could lead to living mixtures with other peoples or the creolization of societies.[11] Crucial for creolization, however, is that the invaded and colonized have the potential to become members of the colonizing group, by not only adapting their customs but also influencing them. In ancient Rome, the impact of the colonized was such that the philosopher and statesman Seneca protested Romans' adoption of Jewish customs, such as the Judean Sabbath: "The customs of this most base people have so prevailed that they are adopted in all the world, and the conquered have given their laws to the conquerors."[12]

The rise of Christianity was violent. The Vandals, destroyers of not only Rome but also most of classical antiquity, from temples to libraries, were Christians. As Catherine Nixey recounts:

> This was no time for a philosopher to be philosophical. 'The tyrant' [Christianity], as the philosophers put it, was in charge and had many alarming habits. In [the philosopher] Damascius's own time [early sixth century], houses were entered and searched for books and objects deemed unacceptable. If any were found they would be removed and burned in triumphant bonfires in town squares. Discussion of religious matters in public had been branded a 'damnable audacity' and forbidden by law. Anyone who made sacrifices to the old gods could, the law said, be executed. Across the empire, ancient and beautiful temples had been attacked, their roofs stripped, their treasures melted down, their statues smashed. To ensure that their rules were kept, the government started to employ spies, officials and informers to report back on what went on in the streets and marketplaces of cities and behind closed doors in private homes. As one influential Christian speaker put it, his congregation should hunt down sinners and drive them into the way of salvation as relentlessly as a hunter pursues his prey into nets.[13]

The aim, Nixey revealed, was not simply Christian domination; it was the annihilation of all things not Christian:

> The attacks didn't stop at culture. Everything from the food on one's plate (which should be plain and certainly not involve spices), through to what one got up to in bed (which should be likewise plain, and unspicy) began, for the first time, to come under the control of religion. Male homosexuality was

outlawed; hair-plucking was despised, as too were make-up, music, suggestive dancing, rich food, purple bedsheets, silk clothes . . . The list went on.[14]

Amusingly, most of the restrictions here meet nearly every stereotype of cultural whiteness: preference for bland food, sexual repression, aversion to colorful homes, and so on. Wed this agonistic and ascetic mentality to the spread of commerce over the Atlantic Ocean and onto the Pacific Ocean, and we begin to see how the medieval concept of *raza* turned into the secular concept of race. As one of the foundations of the emerging anthropology of capitalism, race made European Christians *white* and modernity *European*. The result was *Euro*modernity.

Unique forms of melancholia arose as people indigenous to the epoch of Euromodernity found themselves, by virtue of supposedly not belonging to the future, in a present to which they were illegitimate and thus did not belong. It is melancholic in the psychoanalytical sense of a suffered loss fundamental also to becoming a self. It is also political in that it has a consequence of properly having a voice and power—crucial elements for political practice—in a presumed primeval past. But even that is contradictory, since their illegitimacy moves back retroactively. The eventual inference is that *such people should never have existed.*

This movement, of a monolithic future that erases present legitimacy and eventually delegitimizes the past, also applies to other elements of human life. A world with multiple economies and many markets was transformed into one governed by an abstraction we now know as "the market." That model, capitalism, has ascended to the status of a god—or worse, G-d.

Religion is not immune to such developments. "World religions," after all, are really indices of Christianity and its recognized antagonists: Judaism, Islam, paganism, and secularism. Many ways of living and addressing spiritual life are now placed under "religion," even though the idea of being bound by what that Latin-oriented concept meant was, and to some extent continues to be, alien to many cultures. That is why there are people who publicly practice Christianity, Judaism, and Islam only to go home to relax and place their bets—in those crucial life moments of birth, coming of age, marriage, and death—in the hands of what the so-called world religions consider heretical and pagan. Many people across the globe continue to seek the services of supposedly traditional healers and agents of divination.

That the Euromodern world challenged the humanity of many groups of people compels them to ask, "Are we human?" This leads to the question "What is a human being?" And then, "What does it mean to be human?"

These questions have clear relevance for the study of race as well as class, gender, indigeneity, sexuality, and more. Unfortunately, their study is often dominated by this history of Euromodern fantasies of conquest and cleansing, which makes mixture "impure." The result is an inherited search for so-called purity as a standard of human value and identity, an approach that has been vigorously challenged by critics of Euromodernity. Fanon, for instance, understood that a movement from an imposed identity of "the black" required historical agency in which "the Black" would be liberated as a possible positive, lived reality for and of the future, which we could characterize as "Black modernity." This means that other forms of modernity could be possible from those who have been presumed primitive or not belonging to the present.[15]

The Haitian anthropologist, jurist, philosopher, and statesman Anténor Firmin questioned the knowledge foundations of Euromodern claims; in effect, he argued that Euromodern human science was not rigorously scientific. Rigorous science attunes itself to the demands of its subject. It does not attempt to force reality into its presuppositions. Similarly, W.E.B. Du Bois observed the historiographical failures of hegemonic history and the sociological ones of putative sociology.[16] He laid the foundations for one of his intellectual heirs, Sterling Stuckey, to conclude, "White historians as a group are about as popular among Black people as white policemen."[17]

Vine Deloria, Jr. (Yankton Sioux), and Glen Coulthard (Yellow-knives Dene) affirm this sentiment with regard to white histories of Indigenous North American experience, although they would add *anthropologists*. Writes Deloria: "In a crisis situation men [and women] always attack the biggest threat to their existence. A warrior killed in battle could always go to the Happy Hunting Grounds. But where does an Indian laid low by an anthro go? To the library?"[18]

These criticisms about the roles of disciplines and their reservoirs of knowledge in an age dominated by colonialism stem from what is now known as Global Southern thought. It identifies reductionism, where the human being is denied relationships through which humanity can be made manifest. If certain peoples don't fit what the social scientists expect or are absent from their databases, the tendency is to ask what's wrong with those people. I call this denial "disciplinary decadence."[19] This disciplinary practice is what occurs when practitioners treat their disciplines as complete portraits of reality. Doing such, the task, as they see it, is to apply the methods of their discipline to every aspect of reality because their methods, as if created by a god, are supposedly complete and thus can contain or "capture" all reality. Those practitioners fetishize their method. Researching human communities, they attempt to squeeze colonized and racialized peoples into the presuppositions of the norms of disciplines centered upon the practitioners as the normal standpoints. They rail against those who do not "fit" or "obey" as "problems."[20]

To overcome disciplinary decadence, we should accept that human beings produce disciplines, which means each discipline faces human limitations when confronting reality—especially human reality. Despite our best efforts, reality always exceeds us; we thus transcend the disciplines we produce to study us. Studying human beings means studying possibilities instead of closures. It requires liberation from rigidity, and movement into the flow of communication and the elasticity of thought. It should be evident that disciplinary decadence is a spirit of seriousness or bad faith.

The decadence of which I speak involves a form of erasure of human reality through a retreat to a form of intellectual, moral, and political laziness akin to avoiding the ongoing responsibility of stirring the soup in that allegorical pot in Coyoacán. Race, as we have seen in our journey into Euromodernity, has many converging ingredients. It was brought along with a series of worldwide harbingers of death and destruction—pandemics, if we will—through which suffering overflows while life continues to fight.

5

RACISM INTERSECTED

Transcending decadent approaches to the study of race requires an understanding that race is connected to a multitude of other ways of living in the Euromodern world, including class, gender, indigeneity, and sexuality. These relations are known today as *intersectional*, an idea formed in Black feminist thought.

Intersectionality has roots in the nineteenth century, in the writings of the philosopher, social critic, and educator Anna Julia Cooper, but its explicit formulation was authored by the legal theorist Kimberlé Crenshaw.[1] Crenshaw's analysis is often misinterpreted as a layering of identities onto a single point, as in Euclidean geometry. But if this were the model, one could simply map out intersections of disadvantages ahead as fated identities. The unique ways in which people live their identities, the plethora of ways in which their identities are discovered and could be creatively transformed, would be lost. Intersectionality describes that no human being exists exclusively as a representative of one class, gender, race, sexual orientation, or other limited identity, and it is impossible, without bad faith, to see a human being as manifesting only one of these identities. How they all converge, however, affects the options available to them, including whether they are recognized as having rights before the law. To illustrate this, Crenshaw refers to colliding identities as they appear in torts, labor law, and anti-discrimination legislation. She discusses injuries that, because of how they are interpreted among jurists, are denied by the U.S. legal system of common law (code law in parts of Louisiana) when pertaining to certain groups of people. She illustrates the limitations of these interpretations through an example of a group of automobiles crashing at a four-way intersection.[2] If witnesses and the legal system interpret harm as the damage to property, the damaged cars would be their main concern. If what makes them property is them being owned by a white person, then the harm would be against the white owner. For blacks, the historical problem is that they are not historically regarded as sites of injury in white supremacist societies. This is because they embody, from this view, the meetings or intersections of a series of identities not recognized as having rights through which harm could be understood. In the case of black women, these are often gender, race, and, for most, class.

Crenshaw's argument does not ignore that whites can be harmed. Her point is that black women, especially, were not historically acknowledged as harmed subjects in the Euromodern legal system, because of a failure to see that human beings do not manifest a single category of identity. Simply referring to human beings as "man," for example, fails to acknowledge that human beings are not only men but also women; acknowledging them as "women" fails to address a particular woman's racial or sexual identity. What is missed is the lived reality of the convergence of these identities, and their social and legal implications. A black woman in an automobile collision is, for example, not just physically harmed but also injured in ways linked to the wider legal framework of the society—in other words, she is affected differently than a white woman or a black man would be. The criminalization of black women and men, for instance, would mean that though harmed in the collision, a black man or woman might face entanglement in a racist legal system that treats them as the *cause* of harm. There are many examples of black people being arrested simply for being in the proximity of harm. This is one of the reasons why many black people, even when harmed, do not seek the aid of law enforcement and other representatives of that system. For black people, summoning the police is dangerous, even in cases when they are not actually at fault in a car accident.[3] Even setting aside the discriminatory legal system, black people face many other layers of vulnerability, ranging from precarious employment to limited access to already-inadequate health services, and other aspects of a society whose ongoing models of everyday existence are premised on black exclusion. This makes pursuing those important social goods, for many black people, perilous in a society whose commitment to their exclusion treats them as not staying in their supposed place; crossing such lines increases the probability of legal entanglements in a system in which they are already, for the most part, illicit.

Crenshaw's argument is *for the legitimate appearance* of people the dominant society thinks should not appear, especially in places where having rights as full citizens and human beings is required; her work is, in other words, a study of illicit appearance—forms of appearance that violate norms of appearance. Her response is to push for the radicalization of appearance, in that we are called not only to see the identified subjects but also to see what *they* see or experience—in short, to at least understand their point of view in terms of the conditions they face.

There is also the idea of multidimensionality, which replaces "intersections" with "dimensions." Although there are overlaps between intersectionality and multidimensionality, the latter includes the concept of a matrix.[4] Matrices are similar to keys: they open or disclose realities. For example, in *The Future Evolution of Man*, the great East Indian philosopher and yogi Sri Aurobindo observed that there was no need for the transformation of energy into matter to have occurred billions of years ago (perhaps trillions if the universe or pluriverse is on one of many go-arounds), but it did, creating a universe (or pluriverse) of energy and matter.[5] That could have remained as it was, but out of matter came life, then eventually came consciousness. And that wasn't the end: out of consciousness came practices of communication, through which language and self-reflection manifested themselves in the form of the mind, all of which led to culture—the arts, science, technology, flights of imagination. One interpretation of Aurobindo's insight is that each of these evolutionary moments was simultaneously a condition for the possibility of another. That is what I mean by a key or a matrix. We live with the simultaneity and dependency of each development with what we imagine was left behind. "Dimension" is another term for these disclosed aspects of reality. We often think of dimensions spatially—which is why the concepts of intersectionality and dimensionality work together—but the idea here exceeds disclosures of space and time. In this sense, we already live in a multiverse.

Race, which is a line or dimension of how human beings now appear, leads to other forms of appearance connected to what it means to belong to the present versus the past. It is not only in legal courtrooms but also in the scientific adjudication of the human story that race comes to bear on classifications of human beings. For example, paleoanthropologists conclude that *Homo sapiens* evolved on the African continent about three hundred thousand years ago from an ancestral species—some scholars argue *Homo heidelbergensis*; others, *Homo erectus*—from which the earlier Neanderthals in Europe and West Asia, and Denisovans in East Asia, and perhaps other, unknown hominins also evolved. *Homo sapiens* eventually spread into Europe and Asia. Though conflicts may have occurred, genetic evidence shows that sexual contact prevailed between *Homo sapiens* and the other two kinds of hominins (and perhaps some unknown species), eventually resulting in "modern" human beings—that is, what we call "us."

The story suggests, however, that there are at least four types of "us": (1) human beings who never left Africa and are thus "purely" *Homo sapiens*, (2) those *Homo sapiens* who acquired some Neanderthal genes when settling in Europe or West Asia, (3) those who did the same with some Denisovans, and (4) those who have genetic material of all three, and perhaps then some, since other currently unknown species may be revealed as the study of fossil and genetic evidence advances. I placed the adverb "purely" in quotation marks because a variety of hominins formed our early *Homo sapiens* ancestors in Africa.[6] "Purity," when it comes to human beings, is a mythic dream about our origins.

White supremacists would not be happy with this account; their thinking rests on the presumption of white purity. Genetic research challenges their position by proving there is no such thing as *modern* "pure" white people. All "modern" white people are mixed—and with at least one other species of human. The closest thing to pure white-ness turns out to have been what the white supremacists would call a "primitive" species that preceded *Homo sapiens* in Eurasia, and even they weren't exclusively pale-skinned, since their relatives in West Asia were dark. Amusingly, had genetics concluded that whites were the first and "purest" while people of color were the mixed rest, we can imagine the racist gloating that would follow, including from some of the very scientists who do this research.

I have noticed that whites' realization that they carry traces of spe-cies mixture has led to an extraordinary shift in how Neanderthals are depicted in studies of human evolution; namely, an extraordinary commitment to demonstrating how "smart" they were.[7] Nearly every archaeological discovery, from a Neanderthal tooth necklace to a re-puted deer-bone flute, is celebrated as evidence of their genius, even though the archaeological evidence reveals that the dark *Homo sapi-ens* from Africa outperformed them at nearly every turn and on every level of cultural creativity. I wouldn't be surprised, as each artifact is found here and there, if an effort to grant Neanderthals posthumous PhDs were underway.

There is an additional silliness in the need for intellectually superior Neanderthals as a source of contemporary avowed white superiority: the light complexion of white *Homo sapiens* did not come from Nean-derthals. Light-skinned *Homo sapiens* came about over the past eight to ten thousand years, several thousand or more years after the last "pure" Neanderthal walked among us.[8] Not very long ago, all the in-habitants of Europe were basically dark-skinned people, which makes today's whites not much more than, in today's language, lightened black people.

Curiously, I don't see much dedication to the study of Denisovans, who lived in northeastern Asia and whose genetic presence in contem-porary East Asians and some Pacific Islanders reveals at least two waves of admixture.[9] Most race-based societies are obsessed with whiteness, which places Neanderthals at center stage, despite the white causal con-nection to them being an imagined one. For readers curious about the scientific explanation of how dark peoples of Europe became pale, it turns out genes for light-skin mutations are among sub-Saharan Africans, but they were activated through those African-descended peoples in Eurasia turning to agriculture. The reason is that plant-based diets are not as rich in vitamin D, which made light skin advantageous in the north, where there is less sunlight, which is a crucial source of that nutrient. In the south, turning to agriculture didn't lead to lighter skin because of the abundance—indeed, almost overwhelming presence—of sunlight. Returning to our earlier observation, white *Homo sapiens* are simply members of a predominantly dark-skinned species in which those members survived by virtue of light-skin mutations.[10]

Not everyone shares the increasingly rosy portrayal of Neanderthals. In opposition, and also to the extreme, is the Australian filmmaker turned pseudo–evolutionary paleoanthropologist Danny Vendramini, who argues that much recent research on Neanderthals is marred by anthropomorphism, in which paleoanthropologists project their normative prejudices about "us" onto "them."[11] Although mocked by many serious scientists, his efforts are illuminating in that he takes on the tendency to portray the hominins closest to us as white. Fossil evidence, he contends, reveals Neanderthals as stocky, squat creatures that were apelike from approximately 350,000 (most paleoanthropologists argue 430,000) years of their own evolution in an icy and unforgiving Europe and northwest Asia. Neanderthals were, in his view, vicious nocturnal predators that wreaked havoc on the early *Homo sapiens* that migrated into Europe from Africa. Up to six times stronger than the invading species, they hunted *Homo sapiens* for food and violated the females. In Vendramini's presentation, Neanderthals are rather like the Morlocks from H. G. Wells's *The Time Machine* (1895), but unlike Wells's technologically proficient, pale-skinned, blond or red-haired creatures of the night, which fed on the surface-dwelling brown or tanned Eloi, Vendramini's creatures are dark-skinned, covered with black hair from head to toe, and low in intelligence.

Vendramini's depiction of Neanderthals is strikingly similar to that of black people in D. W. Griffith's *Birth of a Nation* (1915), in which the Ku Klux Klan saves the U.S. South from blacks gone wild and raping white women during the period after the Civil War. Vendramini likewise portrays dark, lustful Neanderthals overpowering light-skinned female *Homo sapiens*.[12] Although Vendramini is explicitly antiracist in his writings, ironically the underlying racial logic of antiblackness remains. Good and smart *Homo sapiens* are white; bad and dumb Neanderthals, black. And, yes, Neanderthals are anthropophagous (human-eating) with an appetite for rape. Black male rapists are an obsession in white supremacist societies; even an otherwise good bloke such as the actor Liam Neeson infamously confessed to wanting to kill random black men because of the rape of a friend nearly half a century ago.[13] The truth is that Neeson is not alone with such urges.

Although Vendramini does not project his positive sense of self onto Neanderthals, he certainly offered his fears. Aggression is an important attribute of the Neanderthal and *Homo sapiens* tale he concocts. In Anglo-dominated countries—his is Australia—the particular brutality of life in nature is a common conception: "nasty, brutish, and short," as the English philosopher Thomas Hobbes portrayed it in his 1651 classic *Leviathan*.

After many millennia of this action of human migration had taken place in Africa and from there across Asia, Europe, and Australia, some made their way to what became the Americas. And we are left, after Euromodern colonization, with the following human types: (1) Native Americans and First Nation peoples of the Americas and South Pacific; (2) Europeans, who colonized and for a time enslaved them; (3) Africans, who were also enslaved and colonized by Europeans; (4) Asians, who, from the perspective of white supremacists, were at first sources of cheap labor and then a global intellectual and economic threat; and (5) mixtures of all these.

A cogent theory of racism requires articulating how these people make sense according to its precepts. All, ultimately, depend on (2) Europeans, read as "white." Beginning there, we see the following. This dominating, Euromodern five-part schema is semiological (governed by a logic of signs and symbols) and genealogical (about origins). From a semiological perspective, "white" is located on a line of furthest distance from its opposite. In one sense, it is normative, meaning that it is the point from which the legitimacy and illegitimacy of all others are determined. Consider the following, from which in one direction there is "over-whiteness" or whiteness beyond whiteness; and in the other, its absence:

$$(white) \longleftarrow (black \ldots$$

In this model, whiteness is a reasonable, perhaps desired distance from blackness, which is simply the absence of whiteness or the furthest point from it. Notice black has no closing right parenthesis. The location of "white" along the line moving toward the arrow-marked possibility suggests that there is a centered purpose for this normative model, which is to distance oneself from being black and to forbid going beyond whiteness. The point at which whiteness is marked is that at which blackness is absent. As an absence, blackness lacks positivity, if we interpret the movement as successions of being as positive. Whiteness appears as if out of nowhere. Or, perhaps, it simply has always been, which entails:

$$(white) \longleftarrow (white)$$

If we concede that whiteness had a beginning, then there must have been a time when whiteness did not exist. It would be like the primordial darkness in which a god declared, "Let there be light!"

In some interpretations, the first instance of moving from a blackness to whiteness would be a story akin to Aristotle's mean between extremes. Virtue, said Aristotle, requires balance. If we replace "white" with "rationality," following the presumed equation in much Euro-modern scientific study of human beings, we will find, with positive to the left and negative to the right, where the absent right parenthesis reveals the irrationality or non-rationality of going in that direction:

$$(hyper\text{-}rationality) \longleftarrow (rationality) \longleftarrow (irrationality \text{ and}$$
$$quite\ possibly\ non\text{-}rationality \ldots$$

Many racists read onto this scale a racial taxonomy of Asiatic, white, brown, and black as follows:

(Asiatic) <—— (white) <—— (brown) <—— (black . . .

At this point there are some strange rationalizations in the history of racist literature. There are some racists who argue *for* having children born of mixtures between white men and Northeast Asian women. This unveils the difficulty of examining race without accounting for its interaction with gender and other factors. Anténor Firmin criticized the French anthropologist Pierre Paul Broca for his advancement of a similar notion—that the term "mulatto" (derived from "mule") referred to the supposedly sterile offspring of a black man and a white woman, and not the fertile child produced by a white man and a woman of any color. Broca's logic mapped neatly onto the sexual ideologies of racialized enslavement, which were racially and sexually specific: sexual encounters of white women and black men must be blocked at all cost.

Some models raise the question of people designated "red." They are an anomalous group, often considered in the North American context as an offshoot of Asians, but, because placed below "white," they upset the system's logic:

(Northeast Asiatic) <—— (white)——(brown)——(black . . .
                        \
                         \
                          \
                           \
                            \
                             \
                              \
                               _____ (red)

Northeast Asians represent hyper-rationality; whites, "normal" rationality; and brown some kind of location on the way to white. Those who are browned toward blackness slide toward becoming simply blacks. The opening left parenthesis before "white" represents the maximum balanced point or mean to achieve. Going beyond it creates problems of moving toward hyper-rationality. But since even hyper-rationality at one end and blackness at the other are on the scale where whiteness represents the balanced point, the radical outsider here is "red." It is generated through an indirect whiteness as a mutation of hyper-whiteness/rationality, if the dominant academic histories of early migrations to the North American continent are to be believed. This is signified by the downward drifting backward slash heading toward "red" and the closing bottom-right parenthesis. In effect, whiteness's movement to hyper-whiteness as Northeast Asians then, if pushed further, falls from its hyper-status into red.

There is, however, another model, which, instead of settling for whiteness as a center claims whiteness as *the* aim or purpose of human evolution. What results here is a twofold schema:

$$(\text{white/European}) \longleftarrow (\text{brown}) \longrightarrow (\text{black} \ldots$$

$$(\text{yellow/Northeast Asiatic}) \longleftarrow (\text{red}) \longrightarrow (\text{black})$$

In this version, white/European and yellow/Northeast Asian stand as the aim of two discrete worlds. In some models they remain as separate but equal, and in others they simply stand so in relation to black. But in relation to each other, they are a fusion, the ideal model:

$$(\text{Eurasian}) \longleftarrow .$$

A different version is unidirectional, with whiteness as the *aim*:

$$(\text{white}) \longleftarrow (\text{black} \ldots$$

These schemas reveal the grammar through which racial terms acquire meaning. This is one of the reasons why even if the people designated by each term were to disappear, the social systems they once inhabited could very well continue to produce new inhabitants for their abandoned categories. The East Asian, black, brown, red, and white people of tomorrow—if those terms are still active—may bear no resemblance to their counterparts today. They simply have to be located somewhere along that schema, for example:

$$(\ldots) \longleftarrow (\ldots$$

This makes racist views generative not only across groups but also *within* them. For instance, in countries such as Australia, Brazil, Canada, Colombia, South Africa, and the United States, there is an unmistakable reproduction of racist differentiation in many black communities on the basis of skin color, where the opportunities available to lighter-skinned blacks are greater than those for darker-skinned blacks, as they struggle to see where they are located in the stream of dots to the right of the right opening and incomplete parenthesis.[14]

The same pattern exists in Asian communities in which the Indigenous peoples are brown or black. The Indigenous peoples of Japan (the Ainu), the Philippines (among whom include the Igorot, the Lumad, and the Mangyan), and Vietnam (among whom are the Degar, also known as the Montagnard, and the Chams) face diminution. Similar patterns are in Southwest Asian countries such as India and Pakistan, where avoidance takes the form of Untouchables—Dalits—and they receive additional pressure among South Asian immigrants across the globe.[15] What are Dalits, in this schema, but South Asian blacks? In the words of the Dalit activist intellectual V. T. Rajshekar, "The outside world hardly knows that in India there is a 3,000-year-old problem called Untouchability."[16] The story here is of a form of social and physical antiblackness—from Brahmans who claim to be descended from the same kinds of people who created Manichaeism—that preceded the concept of race and was followed, during Euromodern colonialism, by a full-fledged antiblack racism.

Among Indigenous or First Nation peoples from North America through to South America, the situation of light-skinned versus dark-skinned is similar.[17] Darker-skinned Indigenous Americans have a lower status even in many Indigenous communities than lighter-skinned members of the same communities, and the consequences, both in those communities and the dark-skinned Indigenous Americans' relation to the white and *mestizo* (mostly mixed with whites) world, are similar to those of blacks.

The light-versus-dark dynamic is also, weird as it is, among the blind, where the distinction shifts to tone, the pitch of their voices, and that familiar item of discussion across races in racist societies: their smells. Although cultural practices range from what foods one eats to what fragrances one puts on, all these are discernible with certain groups and their stigmas. The formal structure of light–dark/high–low racism persists. "Despite their physical inability to engage with race on the very visual terms that are thought to define its salience and social significance, blind people's understanding and experience with race is not unlike that of sighted individuals."[18]

The persistence of the light-versus-dark dynamic sometimes leads to contradictions. Consider the conundrum of Northeast Asiatic peoples' descendants becoming dark or "red" Indigenous peoples of the Americas. The notion of waves of people landing on the shores of Paleolithic North, Central, and South Americas, and continued influxes from the southern hemisphere, befuddles neat myths of exclusively Asiatic origins. The Brazilian anthropologist, archaeologist, and biologist Walter Neves's groundbreaking work on ancient human remains in northern Brazil defies years of conventional neat histories of migration to that part of the world.[19] These considerations posit a movement not from Asiatic to red, but instead from black and brown to red. This does not exclude the point about an Asiatic line becoming red, but it challenges the idea of an exclusively Asian-to-red transformation.

There is, as well, an important existential addition. The idea of red as a category to move *from* is premised on the centering of white, Asian, or Eurasian. It is possible for red simply to have been an end in itself:

$$\text{red} \longleftarrow .$$

Adding blackness as the origin could also suggest, as a mark of indigeneity, a possible black-red or red-black springing from a primordial African:

$$\text{red} \longleftarrow \text{African (dark)} \longrightarrow \text{black}$$

or

$$\text{black} \longleftarrow \text{African (dark)} \longrightarrow \text{red}$$

A creative semiotician (one who studies signs and symbols) could no doubt offer many other permutations. The fact of the matter, however, is that the historical contexts and the dominant academic literature leading to these reflections treat becoming white, even for East Asians, as a preordained evolutionary good—as we see in those charts that depict the transformation of the apelike hominin into *Homo sapiens* standing up tall, proud, male, and white.

This notion of the ascent to whiteness was not always the case in what can be called sciences of human classification. Over the years, I have taught a seminar called "Race in the Formation of the Human Sciences." Our readings in the first part of the course include writings from the physician François Bernier in the seventeenth century through to the philosopher Immanuel Kant in the eighteenth and then all the way through to the nineteenth-century eugenicist Francis Galton and Madison Grant, whose influence affected eugenicist policies into the twentieth. The students are often shocked at the racism they see at work in how the human sciences, at least as understood in the European academy, were formed. Much of this is because they are used to studying their intellectual heroes as gods instead of as human beings with all the imperfections of such. It is a form of what theologians call *theodicy* (god's justice). Theodicy is the kind of rationalization in which one attempts to preserve the goodness of an all-powerful and all-knowing being in a world marked by injustice. If such a being or Being is good and just, why does it not intervene? Why does it let such injustice happen?

There are many classic responses from antiquity through to recent times in which two responses dominate: (1) human finitude limits understanding the omnipotent and omniscient being or Being's ultimate plan, and (2) the love from such a being or Being entails not standing in the way of human freedom (which messes things up).[20] Both depend on the deity's omniscience and omnipotence, for they ultimately defer the main point instead of addressing it. The great Being is the one in control of everything in the first place.[21] Instead of belaboring that point, the crucial consideration is the observation that theodicean rationalizations take the prized being/Being off the hook. If we secularize it, we would see the same kinds of rationalization at work in the defense of, say, India, South Africa, the United States, and their constitutions to models of knowledge through which the degradations of excluded peoples is cultivated.[22] When it comes to the study of the writings of canonical thinkers, it is *theodicy of the text*, where canonical writings are treated as perfect works produced by gods. We should bear in mind that theodicy is also at work where such authors are demonized. In both cases, the result is the erasure of their humanity. This is not to excuse those canonical European thinkers. It is to point out that it is our responsibility to address the imperfections of thought by really reading what any author has written and doing our best to produce better alternatives. When we move to the seemingly nonracist elements of their thought, we do find some elements on which ironically their racist elements depend and, despite our intentions, some of our antiracist efforts inherit.

Here are some examples. First, there is an obsession with the "origins" of humankind in a way that leads to considering other groups of human beings as "deviations" from those origins. Second, there is the presumption that the "original" must be "pure." Third, there is concern with reproduction—or repetition—as law. All this is abstract, but much of it is familiar.

The first often presumes that the author belongs to the original or primordial group. Thus, Kant argued that human beings must have evolved in geographical and climatic conditions similar to the German/Prussian world of his day.[23] Many of those thinkers presumed that diversity was deviation and origins were pure. As many of us know today, it turns out that at least biological origins point to places of maximum genetic diversity. We know, for instance, that coffee came from Southeast Africa because of the genetic diversity of coffee beans there; potatoes evolved in South America because of its unmatched varieties of potatoes. What would "pure" mean here? If we link the term to the origin of a species, then pure human beings would be linked to where their maximal genetic diversity is. To Kant et al.'s chagrin, that turns out to be Africa.[24] Finally, my students and I noticed the obsession with reproduction for those thinkers was premised on the idea of male sources of progeny. (Remember Broca?) Thus control of female reproductive behavior was central, and this led to an obsession with blocking certain males, now racialized, from sexual procreation.[25]

In all this, we see the intimate entanglements, intersections, and multiple dimensions of how race appears. These elements offer a form of elusiveness through which racism is also at times hidden in plain sight. They include how we understand concepts such as privilege, luxury, and license in racist societies. To those, we now turn.

6

PRIVILEGE, LUXURY, LICENSE

The centering of whites in the preceding discussions suggests what Peggy McIntosh called "white privilege," in her eponymous essay.[1] Her formulation gave rise to an industry of research. Centeredness and privilege are not identical, however, and an unfortunate development of white privilege discourse, now often a component of "whiteness studies," is that the true nature of white supremacy is lost. Whiteness studies is already hegemonic, which makes "white academy" a redundant phrase. For many students of color, most required study is like a white epistemic blizzard. McIntosh, to her credit, makes visible that which is so normative in white supremacist society that it is easy to overlook, as perhaps water is to fish. As the joke goes, a fish was caught in a net and brought on deck. Gasping for air as no oxygen-rich water flowed through its gills, the fish thought it was a goner. Fortunately, it was not the kind of fish the crew was looking for, so they threw it back into the sea. Relieved, the fish swam way down deep in search of safety. Passing a school of other fish, it asked, "How is the water?" Receiving no response, it swam on. The remaining fish looked at one another. One of them finally asked, "What's water?"

Is "privilege" what is actually overlooked yet nurtured in white supremacist society? Consider the ideological function of how it is used in anti-privilege discourse. Reeking of guilt, a condition of aggression turned inward, white privilege discourse results in a call for abdication of a litany of entitlements that no human being ought to disavow, such

as being treated with respect, access to quality education, fair treatment in criminal justice systems, quality housing, food, clean water,
healthcare, employment, and low risk of death. In other words, not
all privileges are *luxuries*. The issue should not be that whites have
these goods; it's that many nonwhites, especially those who are brown,
black, and red, do not.

The anti-privilege discourse has become so prevalent that it ex-
tends beyond criticism of white men and women. I have even seen
black people who have access to a few social goods wailing about having "privilege." The lamentation borders on the pathological, since it
involves shame for having what only the depraved would reject. Who
ultimately benefits from this moralistic display? If we think of entitlements (as opposed to luxuries) as what they are—*rights*—then the
answer is apparent: those who oppose the idea of these resources being
available to everyone.

The obvious connection to what we know today as neoliberalism
and neoconservatism—both of which are marked by market funda-
mentalism, in which privatization of societies demands the deprivation of basic social goods to those whom government claims to
serve—makes evident how mistaken such a position would be. Ironically, despite good intentions of exposing complicity in injustice, there
is a form of bad faith in studies that re-center whiteness as the site
of goods associated with humanness. A form of post-whiteness, this
critical stance at times slides, like most hyphenated "post-" ideologies,
into the continuation of the original practice but obscured by shame.
The fact that neofascists and other white supremacist groups claim to
be victims of "political correctness" and "cancel culture" is an inevitable and peculiarly postmodern outcome of their nostalgia for the "old
days" when "white was right" and they could assert their whiteness,
however brash and volatile, with pride. Bear in mind that "political
correctness" is a confusing expression co-opted from the early Soviet
Union, where it simply meant toeing the Communist Party line, by the
1980s American right. Nearly every usage betrays the real target of the
phrase, which is "moral correctness." In so-called politically correct
environments in liberal democracies, accusers are often people who

confuse morality with politics. Their confusion often leads to moralism, which is a demand for a form of moral purity. Why both sides of this conflict assert their positions as political is a matter to which I will return. For now, suffice it to say that these conflicts occur in contexts where politics has become a commodity, and political identity is legitimated through testimonies of victimization instead of activities of citizenship. Thus, claims that one has been injured by "politically incorrect behavior" and that one has been harmed by "political correctness" constitute, in the imagination of both sides, their identities as harmed and thus political subjects.

White supremacists cry of victimization to the extent that they claim they are under genocidal threat from people of color. This suggests that something more than a call for reclaiming privilege is at work. Throughout the history of racial killings in the United States, whether those conducted by the police, lynchings, or other forms of white vigilante violence, the perpetrators have expected to operate with impunity, even when they pose for photographs in front of the butchered remains of their hunt. Many lynchings, after all, were advertised in local papers. On the 1934 Claude Neal lynching in Marianna, Florida, Ben Montgomery writes:

> They lashed him to a tree with tractor chains, cut him with knives, burned his flesh, and when he was dead, they turned him over to a mob of thousands, who poked him with sharpened sticks and drove their cars over his corpse before hanging him from an oak tree that still stands in front of the courthouse here, 80 years later. . . .
>
> Newspapers across the country followed the story.
>
> "Mob Holds Negro: Invitations Issued for Lynch Party," one headline read.
>
> "'All White Folks' Invited To Party," another read.[2]

Similar atrocities were committed by whites in Africa, the Caribbean, and South America. Think of the so-called Congo Free State that was in effect private property of the Belgian king Leopold II. Between

1885 and 1908, up to fifteen million of the indigenous black people were slaughtered, with cruelty ranging from mutilations to enforced production of rubber to soldiers using them for target practice.[3] Think also of Germany's genocidal activity against the indigenous black peoples of Namibia between 1904 and 1908 for resisting land grabs by German settlers.[4] How could it be appropriate to call committing such actions a "privilege"? It's a privilege to be in a position to help one's fellow human beings; many would also call that a right. It's a privilege to be in a position to defend one's country and to participate in its political institutions. It's not a privilege to degrade, maim, murder, or rape. The millions of people who, in support of Black Lives Matter, took to the streets shouting in protest in summer 2020 after witnessing the recording in which Minneapolis police officer Derek Chauvin murdered George Floyd by kneeling on his neck for nine minutes and twenty-nine seconds make it clear no such privilege exists.

The unaccountable, outrageous actions that are the hallmark of abusive whiteness should be characterized not as privilege but as forms of *license*. Defenders of license often bring up freedom and liberty as if they were synonymous. Liberty requires a lack of constraint. So-called free speech advocates tend to build their case against "political correctness" by confusing *freedom* of speech with *licensed* (limitless) speech. They ignore a basic caveat: free speech does not entail the right to be a schmuck. As the U.S. Supreme Court justice Oliver Wendell Holmes determined in *Schenck v. United States* (March 3, 1919), using words to harm others, especially where the consequence is catastrophic—such as falsely yelling "Fire!" in a crowded theater—is a violation of the freedom afforded by living in a civil society. License means being able to do whatever one wishes, regardless of harm to others and oneself. It means being "above" ethics, morality, law, and politics. In effect, it means to be a god. Freedom, however, is complicated. It involves, in a word, what many philosophers and social critics understood from antiquity to the present—namely, *maturity*, which requires not only responsibility but also an attunement to norms of evidence and living in a world with others.

License, the epitome of which is the ability to kill with impunity, exempts one from these norms. The nostalgia of white people—not only neo-Nazis and other white supremacists but any white people regarding themselves as whites under siege—is not for a day when whites were supposedly more "free." Freedom would not have required the enslavement of others and racial violence. Consider again those crowds who posed in the horrific photographs documenting what they'd done to their black, brown, red, and other nonwhite victims. Many butcher shops displayed the knuckles, kneecaps, fingers, and other relics of racial hunting not only across North America and South America but also on every continent in which Euromodern colonialism and its racist partner were practiced. Their nostalgia is for a time when being white functioned as a license to do harm without accountability.

White license was on full display in the storming of the U.S Capitol building on January 6, 2021. Instigated by lame-duck president Donald Trump, his henchman lawyer Rudolph Giuliani, senators such as Ted Cruz, Lindsey Graham, and Josh Hawley, and Representative Kevin McCarthy, among a long list of other members of the Republican Party, the overwhelmingly white mob, many of whom formerly shouted, "Blue lives matter," injured more than 150 police officers (one of whom died the next day from a stroke), and ransacked the building. One of the insurrectionists inside the Capitol carried a Confederate flag—a symbol of white supremacy in all its incarnations since 1861—while the crowd searched for the outgoing vice president Mike Pence to hang along with Representatives Nancy Pelosi and Alexandria Ocasio-Cortez. While the perpetrators took selfies and cell-phone videos, their violent spree resulted in millions of dollars of property damage, untold injuries, and even some fatalities.

Despite all this, they were able to leave under the protection of white law enforcement officers, some of whom aided them and had looked the other way as they injured black police officers. Investigators learned those insurrectionists had also planted pipe bombs in strategic sites nearby. In response, the House of Representatives issued Trump his second impeachment, leading to a "trial" in the Senate in which he was "acquitted" by a vote in which fifty-seven senators voted for conviction and forty-three for acquittal. The rules of the Senate re-

quire a two-thirds vote, which meant that sixty-seven votes for conviction were needed to find him guilty. At that point, the Senate minority
leader Mitch McConnell declared, as the basis of his vote for acquittal,
that Trump was guilty of the charges but that he was at that point a
private citizen. The clear doublespeak here is the admission of an individual being guilty but not voting for the relevant issue, which is
whether he was guilty of instigating an insurrection against a branch
of the government.

The message of this blight on justice is clear. The United States is
not a country dedicated to justice except against those who are disad-
vantaged. But more, there is a simple litmus test that everyone in and
beyond the United States knows. If President Obama had behaved at
any moment like President Trump, the hypocrisy of the Republican
members of Congress would have been evident. Additionally, we know
what would have unfolded if Black congresswomen and men had instigated such actions. White license/supremacy affords a lack of accountability for the white elected officials who were clearly guilty along with
President Trump. The message of white license in this case is loud and,
proverbially, clear.

Striking and insulting is how white right-wing media made false
equivalences between Black Lives Matter advocates who protested in
the streets the previous summer and the white mob who stormed the
Capitol. Black Lives Matter protestors were and continue to be brutalized for speech, assembly, and peaceful protest (all supposedly protected rights under the U.S. Constitution). The disparity between the
large police and military presence at Black Lives Matter protests and
their near absence at the Trump supporters' rally and then siege—
despite intelligence and social media revealing their violent intentions
when they descended on the Capitol—was a de facto demonstration of
granting the latter a license to do what they please.

Few, if any, of the white people who attacked the Capitol were disenfranchised; many, as it turns out, didn't even vote. They were fighting for the continued disenfranchisement of people of color, especially
black people. We live with the continued charade, not only in the United
States but in many countries in which right-wing populism sets root,

of a "both sides" discourse when all the evidence of an asymmetrical assault on democracy, black and Indigenous peoples, refugees, immigrants of color, and the poor is clear: taking advantage of liberal fetishizing of tolerance, right-wing forces across class lines regard all those who are not them as targets of elimination.

White supremacy affords the expectation and grace for critics to make every effort to see the humanity of treasonous whites, however violent their history. The truth of the matter is that those angry whites want the old and unfortunate game of false democracy, where their votes are expected to count *more* than everyone else's, where, even when fewer in number, they are to count more than the rest of us.

The white insurrectionists' cry of a stolen presidential election was clearly false. Everyone who votes in U.S. elections knows that each voter is afforded a single ballot on which is listed each candidate. It's thus logically not possible for other Republican candidates to have won on a ballot that didn't include Trump's name. In short, Trump lost *because the ballots were counted.* He received little more than 74 million votes while his opponent, President Joseph Biden, received 81 million. There were 159 million votes cast in the 2020 federal elections. The takeaway—presuming most, if not all, of those who attacked the U.S. Capitol supported the Republican? Those who voted were well aware their votes were counted, but they didn't like the outcome.

Bad faith—the ability to lie to oneself—is, as we saw in our third chapter, capacious. This includes suspending the force of evidence. In bad faith, one could make oneself believe what one wishes to believe. Add a full assault on evidence from Trump and his enablers about the elections results, along with their portraits of themselves and their cult leader as victims of a vast conspiracy, and the conclusion was an incendiary situation.

The care with which those violent insurrectionists have been treated throughout, even those investigated and arrested, speaks to the unjust so-called justice of a society incapable of seeing whites as anything short of innocent, and, if admitted guilty, deserving of extraordinary compassion. It is no wonder that whiteness has had a waiting list of groups anxious to join its club. Nonwhites once included Eastern

European Orthodox Christians, Southern European Catholics, and European Jews. These are groups who were once not white enough— and as European Jews often discover, are *still not white enough* in many places—but who over time, often through joining the project of identifying with the prime representatives of whiteness and, in doing so, acquiring white license, were eventually brought into the fold, often by joining the white project of dehumanizing black, brown, and red peoples.

Whereas antiblack racism places blacks beneath ethics, morality, law, and politics, white supremacy places whites above them. Consider Hitler's argument from *Mein Kampf*: How do you prove you are better than others? By making them inferior to you.[5] A group achieves whiteness by securing the license to push down other groups.

Oddly enough, the receding of this brutal logic of what could be called "white civil society" in the United States since the 1960s led to an increase in legal enforcement of its historical boundaries. When whites policed racial boundaries with violence, the task of the official police was mostly cleaning up after the fact; however, as more whites began to disapprove of such tactics (while expecting to maintain the material advantages it supplied), additional labor fell to the police. Though the conduct of the police has been racially unjust since U.S. police departments were formed in the nineteenth century, it was with this shift that their role as protectors of whiteness became more *visible*.[6] The numerous acquittals on counts of police brutality are premised on the logic of license. Simply put, they have a license to violate black people because black people supposedly don't really have rights. Derek Chauvin, the policeman who murdered George Floyd, was acting on that license and what it signified: black lives don't matter.

As with lynchings, this problem of police violence against black, brown, and red peoples exists not only in countries of North America and South America but also in many where the majority of the population is black and brown, including India, Jamaica, Kenya, Nigeria, South Africa, Uganda, and Zambia. Bob Marley and the Wailers attested to police violence in the Caribbean in their classic album

Burnin' (1973), and Fela Kuti did the same for West Africa in his poignant protest album *Sorrow, Tears, and Blood* (1977). A reality of Euromodern life is that policing focuses on black and brown people, even
when the majority of the police force is itself drawn from the same
population.

One could argue that black people have legal rights in every country across the globe, but the point of this analysis is about what is done,
not what is said or claimed. In law, this is the distinction between what
is de facto and what is de jure. There is no longer de jure (legal) white
license, but there is a de facto (actual) white license, and it's evident, in
a statistically significant way.

In a patriarchal society, men have license to do as they please in
relation to women; the elimination of this license grants women actual
and new rights. It wasn't the moral guilt of men, nor their acknowledgment of their "privilege," that led to the transformation of the lives of
women in many parts of the contemporary world. It was the political
actions of women and men committed to equality that shifted mechanisms of power sufficiently for women to access institutions that historically had excluded them.

But these developments are not always without contradictions. In
South Africa, for instance, white women acquired voting rights for the
sake of solidifying the apartheid system. The apartheidists needed a
majority to disenfranchise black males. They achieved this through
white female suffrage.[7] Many white South African women were com-
plicit with that development, and now they have the luxury of denying
that history because they are formally listed as an oppressed group under the post-apartheid constitution. Their case, in other words, is an
instance of whiteness having it all, including the status of being legally
designated among the oppressed and victimized.

Significantly, the elimination of a license is both morally practical
and coherently doable, even for those who possess it. Given a license
to kill, one could reject it as immoral *and* wage a battle for the elimination of such a license without a loss of dignity to the self. In fact,
waging such a battle could increase one's self-respect by cultivating the

dignity of others. But beyond the moral dimensions, there are objectively viable steps one might take toward eliminating licenses, given that these licenses are clearly linked to the institutions that administer and protect them. A war against such license must be waged not only morally but also *politically.*

The centering of morality avoids the challenge of offering political solutions to political problems. The moral formulation of race and racism leads to a search for a relationship between the self and a specific, individual other. But racism is a phenomenon in which only one group of people counts as "selves and others," with the attendant moral benefits. The rest are regarded in racist societies as neither selves nor other human beings, with the added vulnerability of being persons against whom all violence is permitted.[8] As they are not seen as persons or human beings, they face being charged with the crime of appearance when they assert their humanity. Their problem, then, is not one of being "the other," or, as some proponents put it, "otherization" or being "otherized." Others at least receive ethical recognition. Located outside and below even "others," according to racist hierarchical thinking, their struggle is to receive the respect afforded those who are at least others.

To make matters worse, the supposedly legitimate world imagines itself as just, which means those for whose benefit it is organized regard its eradication or transformation as an assault on justice. It's no accident that there are white people afraid of the words "liberation" and "revolution"; they see nothing in those aspirations but their own victimization and a violation of their hegemony. Simply, they see liberation and revolution as violence.

Transformation, then, must be made in terms other than the moralistic ones of that system. It demands political action.

We should bear in mind, however, that political transformation requires a different set of relations with and understanding of those in the zones of rejected humanity. Their rejection is, after all, imposed. Among each other, those living under exclusion are aware of not only their relationships with one another as selves and others but also the reality of those who hover above them as ultimately part of a misguided system that degrades the human world by presiding over it with godlike power.

The logic here is familiar. Racism and other dehumanizing practices—such as colonialism, enslavement, and untouchability—impose the Manichaean logic of contraries, where there are universal separations of positives and negatives that don't meet. The human world, however, is full of contradictions, where interactions always reveal the particularity of false universals; it is *dialectical*. This means that racism could also be understood as the project of attempting to eliminate dialectical aspects of human existence. As dialectics are relational, racism is to force human beings to be nonrelational. Human reality, as relational, is always reaching across and beyond itself. This is another way of saying that human existence is open.

The discussion I have offered thus far is not exhaustive, but it illustrates some considerations to ponder in the course of our reflections on black consciousness as the meeting of class, gender, indigeneity, race, sexuality, and the many ways in which human beings are manifested. There are resources white people have that everyone should have, and there are others that should belong to no one. As struggles for a better world continue, there are clearly more *kinds* of human beings to come as we continue to build new kinds of institutions and relationships in and through which to live.

7

TRANS BUT NOT TRANSCENDED

Trans people and the controversies faced in their efforts to negotiate their appearance with their lived experience is an example of human beings in the making. The importance of politics in the production of human possibility is familiar terrain for those who study gender and sex. Think, for example, of the usage of the word "transgender." Some critics prefer to use the word "trans."[1] They invest in the ambiguity or openness of the term and at times prefer to use the adjective as a noun. This is because such critics are often "anti-essentialists," which means they reject the notion that any human being has an "essence," or necessary quality that makes them what or who they are. Thus the word "trans" might refer to a trans woman or trans man. Others object to the inclusion of "trans" because they ascribe absolute reality to the noun being modified. Simply identifying a trans person as a "man" or a "woman," they argue, offers fidelity to the lived experience of the kinds of people in question. "She" or "he" is not a modified "she" or "he" but instead a real she or he. Similarly, those who prefer the pronoun "they" argue, in the other direction, that there is no fixed gendered or sexed noun onto which to place their identity. It's best just to call them "they."

Consider the catch-22 of what it means for an identity to be constructed and performed versus referring to it as a fixed or closed being. Some critics are, for example, anti-essentialists critical even of notions of identity.[2] For them, *any* assertion of really being subjects is problematic. They argue no one "is" whatever gender she or he says, which is one of the reasons for the preferred gender-neutral term "they." This fluidity of possibility means, then, that those who locate themselves as the "real" she or he against the trans "she" or "he" are suffering from misunderstanding, or perhaps are not being woke about what physical or biological markers mean. Put differently, anatomy need not entail destiny, and more, there is no inner meaning to our physiology but instead the constellation of rules governing the intelligibility of physical forms to come.[3]

Gender and sex, however, have not been the sole objects of study about which such arguments have been made. Other objects of study include race. In her article "In Defense of Transracialism," the philosopher Rebecca Tuvel argued that proponents of transracialism offer the same kinds of defense for their position as those who support trans identities premised on sex and gender.[4] The article predictably provoked controversy.[5] After all, she had done something indecent: she'd called out the bad faith in anti-racialists who claimed, paradoxically, also to be anti-essentialists. Although she did not call it bad faith outright, her conclusion was straightforward: If arguments supporting transracial identity, and the social and political resources for it, are formally the same as those for transgender identity, how can we legitimately support the first but not the second?

Tuvel was not claiming that transracialism *is* legitimate versus trans identities pertaining to gender and sex. She was also not arguing that gender, sex, and race are the same or that people avowing transracial identities have the same experience and specified demands for justice as individuals born from historically racialized and minoritized peoples. She was simply stating that commitment to arguments supporting one, without demonstrating the difference, entails commitment to those supporting the others, which therefore makes transracialism defensible from a logical point of view. If all are socially constructed, but are so in different ways, it would be important to explain why that difference permits creative reconstructing of the self for one but not for the others.

It is significant that Tuvel referred to "transracial*ism*" instead of, say, "transraciality"—the "ism" refers to a practiced attitude instead of the concept or notion of being transracial. Though the advocacy for one may presuppose support for the other, the task Tuvel took on involves addressing a multitude of concerns, including the ideological commitments or antipathy to a given identity.

Academic discussions of race do not always match its lived reality. It is the prevailing scholarly position that race is a social construction, and racism is its unjust parent—or offspring, depending on how one looks at it. Though experts may take different positions on the relationship of race to racism—some, for example, regard race as a manifestation of racism and thus conclude that it must be eliminated, while others argue it is possible to have race without racism—most seem to avow that race has no reality or significance beyond its meaning as a social practice.[6] It is, to repeat, a social construction.

However, too many critics fail to spell out what they mean by "social construction." How can something that students and ordinary readers "see" every day, and are able to identify with reasonable accuracy and predictability, not be "real"?

The explanation is that all meanings are socially produced and are socially real, and so the question of creating different meanings follows.[7] In other words, if race is socially generated, why couldn't a society produce different kinds of race, among other ways of being human?

Recall that *raza*, from which race was born, pertained to Jews and Afro-Muslims who, in principle, could convert to Christianity, even though their conversions were in fact held suspect.[8] Racism, which implies a hierarchy according to racial location, is haunted by the specter of conversion. The familiar script is of members of an oppressed group becoming members of the one that dominates them. In countries marked by white supremacy, the expectation is for blacks to flee blackness into the sanctuary of whiteness. Although people "becoming" white is well known—and I am not here referring to "passing"— the reverse is seldom discussed until recent times. The notion of becoming black is presumed so undesirable that such a path appears irrational, unless somehow opportunistic as portrayed in the movie *Soul Man* (1986), in which a rich white man disguises himself as black so that he can get a black-only scholarship to study law at Harvard.

Becoming black could also be interpreted as a form of "blackface" or minstrelsy, or as a threat to a paradoxically privileged status of oppression. The white person who becomes black is, ironically, especially white, if whiteness is defined as wanting to have it all—including, as we have seen, legally standing among the oppressed.

There is, however, something perverse about being the owner of oppression, an unfortunate attitude that has become a feature of political life for various reasons, one of which involves confused notions of what it means to be political. Where politics is confused with having a case to petition before the state, governing bodies, or society, political recognition is premised on injury. As individuals vie for space in a perceived zero-sum game, comparisons from more harmed to *most harmed* ensue. Individualized declarations of victimization become the basis of access to political recognition.

Friedrich Nietzsche, and the existentialists who draw upon his work, call investments in identities of victimization expressions of will-to-power marked by the vice of resentment. He argues this expresses desire for intrinsic moral superiority. Regarding oneself as legitimate only when oppressed elides an important insight: oppression is not something to own but to admit, overcome, or eliminate.

What should be said about people who are invested in black identity without fetishizing historic and continued victimization?

Identifying as black requires addressing certain political themes that identifying as white does not. In Argentina, Australia, Brazil, Canada, Colombia, New Zealand, South Africa, and the United States, members of groups not always considered white—European Jews, Greeks, Irish, Italian, and Polish, among them—have exemplified extraordinary anti-black bigotry once they achieve that status. There have also been those who rejected whiteness, and their life choices led to their having descendants who *are black* in contemporary terms. There are also people who became black not by losing a former "white" identity, but because they were always known as black. There are U.S. black people today who are discovering their light-skinned ancestors who did not share the historic path from the Middle Passage across the Atlantic Ocean to the plantations of the United States to northward or westward migration in search of freedom. This reveals a basic fact: there are black people whose origin stories reveal no original or recent African black parentage. Think also of children born of unions in which both parents were, in this sense, transracial—for example, both parents met *as blacks* but were born and at first raised as white. This is typical in some countries with Black national identities such as Barbados, Jamaica, and Trinidad. Or imagine a white couple moving to a place where they became black through habituation and socialization; how should their immediate descendants be categorized?

My relatives and many others have shared similar stories with me in a variety of contexts, some of them while I was director of the Center for Afro-Jewish Studies at Temple University, in Philadelphia. Although I met black Jews whose Jewish lineage was from the African continent, I also met quite a number who discovered that their black Jewish ancestor was an Eastern European Jewish immigrant to North America or the Caribbean. It's worth emphasizing that those European Jewish people's blackness was not brought into question by the black communities in which they lived. This is because the many cultural manifestations of living black afforded adaptability. What they shared was the conviction that racism is wrong, though they were unlikely to express that notion vigorously. Ordinary people, after all, mostly espouse ordinary ideas, and it's ordinary enough to take a negative view of black people. In short, they need not be romanticized as being down with the proverbial cause of black liberation.

Tuvel compared the respective reception of two trans coming-out stories: the *gender/sex* transition of the Olympic gold medalist and reality-show celebrity Caitlyn Jenner and the *racial* transition of the civil rights activist Rachel Dolezal. Dolezal changed her name to Nkechi Amare Diallo in 2016. The name is a shortened version of the Igbo name Nkechinyere, which means "what God has given," "gift of God," or "divine gift." A familiar equivalent in English is Mattie, which is the female version of Matthew, which is from the Greek *Matthaios*, which is in turn from the Hebrew *Mattityahu* (gift from YAHWEH). As she has declared that she will continue to use the name Dolezal for her public persona, and as that is how she is known in this controversy, I will continue referring to her as such; had she declared otherwise, I would have chosen to use Diallo.

Jenner is conservative, perhaps even right-wing, and Dolezal is liberal, perhaps even leftist. Jenner is hardly a champion for social justice; Dolezal, who also identifies as bisexual, was in the leadership of her local NAACP chapter, which makes her avowed consciousness not only black but also Black. The two trans individuals' stories offer something that supporters of trans identities may not like to hear—namely, that there may be nothing intrinsically politically progressive about trans identification. Instead, one's progressiveness or its absence may be embedded in the kind of individual set of political commitments each trans person lives.

Consider the U.S. presidential election of 2016: white conservative women voted conservative. The white conservative female vote in the United States grew in 2020.[9] The United Daughters of the Confederacy, a white female racist organization, is responsible for the erection of monuments to Confederate soldiers and the promotion of racist history textbooks in U.S. schools; there are white female members of the Ku Klux Klan, Nazi organizations, and other hate groups in the United States and similar ones in many other countries such as Australia, Brazil, Germany, South Africa, and the United Kingdom. These examples reveal there is nothing intrinsically progressive in being female. Why, then, should a white trans woman be any different?

A similar question should be posed with race. There should be nothing intrinsically progressive in being black. Black conservatives in predominantly white countries would attest to that, even though their numbers are very small.[10] Yet there is something peculiar about race and politics. It's not that there are no nonwhite sexists or racists; it's simply that nonwhites, especially black, Indigenous, and First Nation peoples, are overwhelmingly on the side of what are generally considered left-of-center political positions in white-dominated countries. Additionally, there is no black right-wing organization that has had an impact on those societies the way that white ethnic and white women right-wing ones have. Of course, neither gender nor racial designations match up neatly with politics, but the empirical evidence thus far challenges simplistic portraits based on identity. Neat formulations of human reality do not match lived manifestations of agency.[11]

We could also complicate matters by asking about a trans person who avows a different race *and* a different sex from those stated on their birth certificate. Think, for example, of a black trans woman whose birth certificate states "black" and "male" in conversation or debate with a black trans woman whose birth certificate states "white" and "male"—or a black trans man born "black female" and a black trans man born "white female." Don't these examples also raise possibilities of trans black and trans Black consciousness?[12]

It's clear that we (and by "we" I mean anyone reflecting on our living and struggling through these issues) are learning something about reality as we address questions related to transness. All kinds of reflections about the fluidity of racial identity come to the fore through thinking about transraciality. For instance, I have met many whites in North America and the Caribbean who talk about their "black grandmother"; they do not hide their black ancestry, and yet they are aware that they are white, as others around them are also aware. But why don't they call their father or mother black, since, according to the old logic, they would be considered biracial or, in fact, black?[13] How are such whites *white*? And yet they are.

White stories of lineages are nearly always about grandmothers of color, despite the American—and largely global—preoccupation with and anxiety around relationships between men of color and white women, as if such relationships were a law of physics, like gravity. But if this were always true, why are there so many white people claiming to have *grandmothers* of color? Demographers have not devoted their energy to gathering data on how many black people were designated white at birth, although my guess is the number is small. White supremacists could lament a tiny decline in the number of whites, which they no doubt will voice since they are already panicking over the minuscule number of interracial marriages with promises of mixed-race children supposedly threatening their numbers.[14]

We see here the importance of intersectional and multidimensional approaches to the study of race. Failure to see how gender, sexual reproduction, and other formations work in racial logic elides the mechanisms behind what we see and what we don't. What is actually "normal," after all, rarely requires a second look and thus is often unnoticed.

The determination to keep men of color—especially black men—away from white women hides the historical fact of white male license toward all women. The *blanqueamiento*, or whitening, policies in Latin America mentioned earlier were not simply about color. They pertained primarily to affirming white *men* as the source of whiteness, which is one of the bases of the reference to grandmothers of color across the Caribbean and Central and South America. The problematic logic includes white supremacists, who regard dilution of whiteness as occurring primarily, if not only, from white women having children with men of color. The presumption is that white men whiten races; men of color, especially black ones, dilute or weaken them. Discussion of this presumed access or license over all women is available in counter-hegemonic African diasporic scholarship from the nineteenth century through to the present.[15]

The interest in miscegenation is such that the inevitable deployment of the latest developments in genetics has been devoted to its study. This research reveals what the journalist Cara Rose DeFabio aptly summarizes: "If you're black [in North and South America], DNA ancestry results can reveal an awkward truth."[16] The "awkward truth" applies to black people not only in North America, Central America, and South America but also in Australia and many countries of the South Pacific: if you are black, brown, or Indigenous from those colonies and former colonies, the source of the genetic pool of your European ancestry is overwhelmingly male.

This is old news for antiracist activists, intellectuals, and scholars. The great Yankton Sioux philosopher, historian, theologian, and activist Vine Deloria, Jr., makes this awkward truth plain with regard to Native Americans:

> During my three years as Executive Director of the National
> Congress of American Indians it was a rare day when some

white didn't visit my office and proudly proclaim that he or
she was of Indian descent. . . . All but one [white] person I met
who claimed Indian blood claimed it on their grandmother's
side. I once did a projection backward and discovered that ev-
idently most tribes were entirely female for the first three hundred years of white occupation. No one, it seemed, wanted to
claim a male Indian as a forebear.[17]

Imagine a non-mixed black person or non-mixed Native American
who then identifies as white. At this point, there is already an appeal
to a form of racial purity that belies the situation. There are, after all,
black people who could "pass" for white, and Deloria's point is that
there are morphologically white people beseeching, as Native Americans, his recognition. If a child's parents both pass for white, and that
child identifies as white, what is the child's race? As there are whites
who are actually of black, Native American, or another nonwhite ancestry, why would identification with the ancestry be implausible?

Imagine also if many legally designated whites were to "come out"
as black. One difficulty with such a thought experiment is that we often project social conditions of the present onto the future. It doesn't
follow that the future must have the same social meanings of identity
terms as the present. A blacker world may have a different meaning
for blackness than the current one. The possibilities are many, since
the many groups in regard to whom blacks function *as black* may also
have changed, and new groups may come about. If that is so, then the
dilemmas at hand may be false ones. On one side of the dilemma is
worry about a population (formerly whites) with insignificant impact.
On the other side would be a population whose birth would mark a
world so radically different from the one we live in that our concern
may be irrelevant.

My sense is that the contemporary passionate concern with getting
physical appearance "right" is connected to the forces that are compelling a retreat into identity in the first place—namely, a decline in
people's ability (power) to have an impact on political forces (power)
affecting their lives. This is not to say that the struggle about and for

the self lacks its own existential elements; it is to say that what may be animating supporters for physical alignment with identity may also have less to do with what is lived and more to do with what is desired, although this shouldn't discount the lived experience of those who experience misalignment.

These reflections on trans identity also return us to an ongoing observation. Imposed purity compels a retreat into a specific side of binaries, whether as black/white, female/male, woman/man. After all, why must trans or any other human identity be completely one? Why couldn't there be in trans and all other identities a form of mixture through which one element of their identity enriches another?

It's possible that any human science of converging "purities" defies reality.[18] Purity obscures lived realities of mixture. Human reality, which we should remember is produced by human beings, is not one of pure being in and by itself. It's instead relations of living negations of purity—that is, *existence*, or negations of and for being. *Creolizing* would be a better way of describing human reality, as it's a radical kind of mixture—one that in effect not only manifests new forms of being but also challenges the notion of static being. The use of the present participle "creolizing" is to illustrate that mixing—especially of elements that, under a racist system, supposedly don't belong together—is not closed. It's not a closed achievement or what may today fashionably be called "an event."[19] Instead, it's an ongoing activity of the production of relations through which we come to live reality.

Purity is an ideal that can be concocted and maintained in the human world only by closing off other aspects of reality. As we saw in our discussion of paleoanthropology, even the most ancient *Homo sapiens* weren't "pure." Letting go of purity and focusing on the human potential to live in many ways suggests an additional consideration—namely, that the human being is a queer relationship with reality.[20] Ascribing absolute status to purity and straightness defies the reality of how human beings actually live.[21] Doing so requires, in effect, bad faith, because it denies the elements of reality that do not match up with lived reality and attempts to force reality to match with preferred or pleasing falsehoods instead of (for the purists) displeasing truths.

There is also the relationship between humanity and freedom. Approaching the study of dehumanization as a form of bad faith, as we have seen, raises an ironic dimension of freedom: to be free entails being free to avoid being so. What would human reality be if human beings were incapable of acting in bad faith? Could a being incapable of attempting to evade its freedom be free? Wouldn't the absence of that capability mean human beings must essentially act in so-called good faith? What, then, would happen to freedom? And if there were no freedom, would not human beings simply have a nature that poses none of the recognizable human problems because of the absence of responsibility?

Black consciousness faces the question, then, of whether it can avoid dehumanization. If not, it must confront oppression. To that concern, which makes the idea of a black consciousness becoming a Black consciousness a feared possibility for those invested in antiblack oppression, we now turn.

There is no freedom in silence.

–Steve Bantu Biko

8

FIVE KINDS OF INVISIBILITY

In this world, black bodies may be desired—but, for antiblack racists, only those without consciousness, especially black and Black consciousness. This is another way of saying that it's easier to deal with "black bodies" than black people. The formation of the Euromodern world of white supremacy and the kinds of people it produces support that conclusion.

Erasing the humanity of racialized peoples involves the production of invisibility. Although there are many kinds of invisibility in the Euromodern world, five are particularly pertinent to our reflections: (1) *racial*, (2) *indigenous*, (3) *gendered*, (4) *exoticized*, and (5) *epistemic*. Although elements of each type were formed before Euromodernity, their Euromodern manifestations will be the focus as we articulate the political dimensions of Black consciousness.

Racial invisibility involves not being seen as a human being by virtue of hyper-visibility—a state of being perceived excessively because of not belonging. It is society's obsession with the number of racialized people. Here is an example from when I was a young assistant professor at a large Midwestern public research university in the United States. There were approximately 3,500 faculty members. Fourteen of us were black; the other nonwhites numbered about seventy of Asian descent; the number of Native Americans, to my recollection, was one. She was also one of the black faculty members. It's hard to say what the number of Latinx people was because some simply identified as white, while others, especially those who were Black Latinx, identified as both Black and Latinx. The other black faculty often parked their cars close to where they taught. After teaching, holding office hours, or attending faculty meetings, they would rush straight to their vehicles and depart. I chose not to do so. Having grown up in New York City, I was excited to learn about life in the Midwest. So I organized my two classes, held with an hour's break in between, on opposite sides of the campus. I would stroll from one class to the other, greeting students, staff, and other faculty along the way.

In a short time, complaints began to pop up in the student news-paper. They included objections to affirmative action. Some expressed worries about whether it was any longer possible for white applicants to secure employment there. Others voiced concern against a supposed *deluge* of recently hired black faculty. Some felt unsafe.

I was curious at first, since I didn't see other black faculty during those strolls between classes. Then I realized the complaints were about *me*.

Imagine the point of view of the aggrieved white students and staff. When I walked by, they saw a black that day—already one too many. When I passed by on my return, they saw a *second* black. My visibility was exponential.

There are always "too many" black people. This belief, unfor-tunately, is held by black people as well as whites. Despite empirical data showing otherwise, many believe there are too many black peo-ple at play in any pathology, from crime to lack of family planning. Black women are supposedly always having too many babies. Black people are having too much sex. Sexual organs on black people are excessive—too large, too deep, too much. Black women are insatiable. Black men are overwhelmed by lust, especially for white women. Too many black people are disease-ridden; too many receive government services, despite the fact that whites disproportionately receive these benefits in every white-dominated society.

The last claim about whites is old news.[1] Indeed, the often over-looked truth about white wealth and avowed stability is the history of their cultivation. Euromodern global imperialism is marked by the extraction of material resources and labor from peoples of color for the enrichment of predominantly white populations in not only Europe but also its colonies and eventual postcolonies. The rise of the social welfare state in the twentieth century produced at first whites-only safety nets in Australia, New Zealand, South Africa, and the United States, alongside such in Central and South American countries because of their *blanqueamiento* policies and, although not always expressed as white-centered, in several, if not most, European countries. In many instances, these programs were abandoned or their resources diminished when the question of their expansion to include black populations was placed on the table. From the last quarter of the twentieth century, the notion that such social projects are ineffective has become axiomatic in centrist and right-leaning countries. Yet such claims belie the facts. White structural wealth and general physical security are the proof that social-welfare programs do indeed work.

The racist response is to argue there is something in whites and other nonblacks, such as the Chinese in China or the Japanese in Japan, that make such programs work when applied to them but fail, because of something blacks lack, when applied to blacks.[2] The argument is circular; the thing in whites and those other groups is that they are white or at least not black; the thing blacks lack is being white or at least not being black. Or, more to the point, the problem in blacks is their being black. This argument relies on denying that whites live in societies in which their humanity is not only respected but also nurtured; blacks in antiblack societies suffer from the denial of their humanity and the imposition of extraordinary conditions on their effort to live ordinary lives. Additionally, predominantly black countries struggle, in the wake of formal imperialism, to ascend in a world in which institutions of trade, information, technology, and diplomacy are affected by structural antiblack racism.

This perception of excess leads to a presumption of guilt. To appear as black is to arrive as already having done something wrong. If too many black people are supposedly committing crimes, then the fact that incarcerated populations are disproportionately black is just. W.E.B. Du Bois predicted the growth of prisons at the beginning of the twentieth century. Angela Y. Davis documented it nearly a century later.[3] Many black people are in prison for crimes they did not commit, and others are there for offenses for which whites do less or no prison time at all. White license affords non-conviction for whites whose juries even, as with Senator Mitch McConnell's admission of what the evidence reveals about former president Donald Trump, admit their guilt. No such luxury or license is available to blacks. The presumption is that even if many blacks didn't commit the crime of which they are accused, they must be guilty of something. Choose any crime except for individually enacted mass homicide, on which white men have a near monopoly, and there are too many black people involved— because there are too many black people around in the first place. The old idea that the exception proves the rule serves to disarm the reality of white mass murders. However large their number, each instance stands as an "anomaly." There are thus "individual" white mass murderers; whites as a group supposedly do not commit mass murder. Blacks, on the other hand, despite not being statistically representative in this category of mass murder, are presumed to be violence incarnate. In similar kind, despite whites making up most drivers in the United States, the U.K., and Canada and their being the most likely to drive with contraband, blacks are the most likely to be pulled over and searched for possessing illicit materials.[4] Driving while black is real. Whether as accused of violence, theft, or carrying contraband, each individual black misdeed becomes black misbehavior.

This invisibility through hyper-visibility—a state of being too much because of not belonging—is a cause of black invisibility as human beings and black melancholia, a special form of bereavement. The black, as a creation of the Euromodern world, is also indigenous to it, but that world regards itself as just, legitimate, right, whole, or complete without blacks or, worse, with their elimination; the black is thus indigenous to a world that rejects blacks. Blacks belong to non-belonging.

The yearning lyrics of the jazz musicians Abbey Lincoln and Max Roach's "Lonesome Lover" (1962), in which the singer asks to be taken back to where she belongs, refer to the African diaspora aching to belong, and the site of that belonging is imagined as Africa. One might object, however: *that* Africa is a figment of the imagination. The black subject of racialized oppression was never located there in the first place, except when many of its countries became colonies.[5]

The second form of invisibility, *indigenous*, pertains to time wedded to land. The settlers regard the Indigenous peoples as belonging to the past because their land will never be returned to them; the future is foreclosed. Lacking future legitimacy, Indigenous peoples' belonging to the present is brought into question, which retroactively delegitimizes all pasts beyond the moment of colonization. These Indigenous peoples' time of legitimacy becomes primordial, and it attaches to them as "primitives." They become "tribes." The word "tribe" is a colonial slur. It once had different political connotations, as its Latin origin, *tribus*, attests; think of the contemporary word "tribute." It also had numerological significance, where *tri* refers to "three" and *bheue* was the root of "be." The ancient Hebrew word often translated as "tribe" was actually *šēbeṭ* (literally, stick or branch, as in branch of a tree). The idea was that the great patriarch branched off into a set of patriarchs, which meant it actually referred to "clans," as in large filial membership based on patriarchal lineage. Invasion and colonization inaugurated in the fifteenth century C.E. led to the term being used for people designated as "primitive"—not, for example, for the ethnic groups and clans of Ireland and Scotland.

Because they supposedly belong to the past, Indigenous peoples of Africa, Asia, North America, South America, and the Pacific islands "haunt" the present as ghosts on their ancestral lands. Their mark of authenticity is supposedly "spiritual," and what are spirits but ghosts? This talk of "spirits," much associated with Indigenous peoples in popular culture, reflects the conclusion of settler states: that, for Indigenous and First Nation peoples, there is no reclamation. As Vine Deloria, Jr., observed in *Custer Died for Your Sins*:

> In the Ghost Dance days, messiahship came to dominate Indian thought patterns and all expectations were tinged with this other-worldly hope of salvation. Every Indian leader of today must face the question of whether or not he is a great

figure of the past reincarnated to lead his people to victory, for legends die hard among our people.[6]

In *American Indian Holocaust*, the Cherokee anthropologist and demographer Russell Thornton documents the conclusion of these ghostly reflections. Reduced to only 4 percent of their original populations in the United States by the year 1900, Native Americans have since been accompanied by death, making them into living apparitions.[7]

Women, at least as they have been understood in European and many Asian societies, are the primary focus of the third type of invisibility, *gendered*. I refer here specifically to European and Asian traditions because there are societies in Africa, the South Pacific, and Abya Yala, or the Americas, in which colonial understandings of gender were introduced and enforced. Duane Brayboy, a Tosneoc Tuscarora critic, summarizes a major cause of confusion for European settlers who could imagine only two genders fixed in nature: the fluidity of Indigenous and First Nations' conceptions simply made no sense to them and, they concluded, could not be real.[8] Indigenous African critics agree. They argue that Eurocentric conceptions of gender were imposed on African peoples through not only colonialism but also the ongoing presupposition of the universality of Euro–North American and European views on people we call "women."[9]

In societies with a history of misogyny, many women's invisibility takes the form of not having a voice. This type of invisibility as voicelessness dominates women's literature from antiquity to the present. The silent or silenced woman is a creature of myth from Heracles rescuing Alcestis from Hades to Orpheus and Eurydice facing a similar ascent in ancient Greek tragedies. Christine de Pizan wrote on this phenomenon in France in the fifteenth century, Anna Julia Cooper in the United States in the nineteenth century, and He-Yin Zhen in China at the beginning of the twentieth.[10]

More recently, the philosopher Janet L. Borgerson describes women seeking their voices not only in the company of men but also among women who subscribe to legitimate speech as belonging to males.[11] Jaspal Kaur Singh writes of the violence at the heart of silencing women in

Sikh society.[12] Carol Gilligan's classic work is *In a Different Voice*—read here as a voice not historically heard; Michelle Walker's famous essay on women doing philosophy is called "Silence and Reason: Woman's Voice in Philosophy." Kathryn Lasky's biography of the African American poet Phillis Wheatley is entitled *A Voice of Her Own*; Melissa Silverstein's book on women directors, *In Her Voice*; Miki Raver's on women in the Hebrew Bible, *Listen to Her Voice*; Judy Yung's documentary history of Chinese American women, *Unbound Voices*; Emily Honig and Gail Hershatter's book on Chinese women in the 1980s, *Personal Voices*; and the subtitle of Xinran's *The Good Women of China* is *Hidden Voices*.[13] This list can go on.

It is no wonder that the problem of speaking without being heard is a central theme of women's literature: it is connected to the question of politics, as speech is an essential element of political life. And what's the point if no one is listening?

This is an example of how gendered invisibility intersects with race, for voicelessness was imposed on black and Indigenous women and men in the expansion of Euromodernity. Colonized and enslaved people were to listen but not speak. The Haitian intellectual Anténor Firmin was barred, for instance, from speaking at the Anthropology Society of France in 1844, despite being an invited member and a diplomat. His response was to write the nearly six-hundred-page tome *The Equality of the Human Races* (1885). Many women have done the same throughout history. This is an element that links black women and men, but within black worlds it also separates them; black women often still have to fight for a voice among black men. There are, after all, majority black countries where black men are privileged—and at times, licensed—speakers.[14]

Women's search for a voice has been deeply studied by psychoanalysts. Jacques Lacan and Luce Irigaray analyzed the authority of male voices, where seeking masculine approval is part of the structure of patriarchy. Think of the Grimm brothers' 1854 "Little Snow White."[15] The Queen asks the magic mirror, "Mirror, mirror, on the wall, who is the fairest of them all?" The question is a curious one; can't she see herself in the reflection? Why does she seek validation from the voice of the mirror, instead of the image it reflects? I've asked audiences across the globe—women and men, girls and boys, and even those who reject gender self-identification—about the sex or gender of the voice answering the Queen, and the standard answer is that it's male or masculine. Despite her status, the Queen lacks a voice that can tell her she is what she values. More recently, though, I have met some women and men who imagine the mirror's response as a woman's voice. Feminist activism is having its impact.

Fanon analyzed cases of black women and men seeking validation—often verbal but at times written—from white men. He argued that this was a consequence of colonialism, enslavement, and racism, which made black women and men one with regard to their symbolic need for recognition. His counsel for escaping this dependency was political action. That there are individuals who now read "Snow White" and imagine a voice other than a man's is a consequence of such political action. Women and allied men fought to change the world, and in doing so, they began to change which voices are heard.

The fourth kind of invisibility—*exoticized*—offers itself as love and valorization. This is where whites treat blacks and other oppressed racialized groups as intrinsically good or better than they. There is a gendered form, as well, where men treat women as intrinsically ethical and smarter than men. They meet in the valorization of black women, who, from this exotic perspective, supposedly have a special "magic." Although initially advanced by black women in celebration of their often-ignored achievements, there is an underside of this logic that gender and racial exoticists would receive with enthusiasm. To be intrinsically good, all-knowing, and magical is hardly characteristic of actual human beings. Racism, we should remember, is the denial of humanity to racially designated groups of people. Whether toward black women or black men, the racial exoticist plays a bad-faith game of bestowing an intrinsic sense of superiority through being supposedly able to identify the intrinsic virtues of racially deprecated people. Exoticism is at the heart of ideas such as the "noble savage" and the romanticized spirituality projected onto Native Americans, nomadic Africans, and the supposed innocence of so-called childlike Indigenous peoples. Since many, if not most, whites hardly share this view, the racial exoticist lives a form of self-indulgence of being an exception among whites. They go beyond "I don't see race" to "I see a superior race." What, however, is the claim of a superior race but a manifestation of racism? In exoticism, the humanity of racially valorized peoples is lost. Their extolled visibility hides—renders invisible—their humanity.

The fifth kind of invisibility, *epistemic*, is knowledge-based. It combines the others by what we could describe as a movement from illicit appearance to the consequence of illegitimate knowledge. When one is supposed to be invisible, to appear is a violation of what should be seen. It would be the appearance of what should not appear. The response, from the agents of decency, is to enforce nonappearance.

This last form of invisibility has already arisen in these reflections, through a challenge to double consciousness, or the imposed, false image, born of historical misrepresentation and produced by institutions, of blacks and other people of color. If whites are the only agents of history, then only the products of whites would be historical. This is the whitewashing of history—whether cultural, intellectual, political, social, or even theological or mythical: even ancient Egyptians and Judeans, and Jesus in particular, become white. Despite the fact that the early Great Fathers of the church were mostly Africans, images of them frequently resemble Santa Claus. Nearly every great ancient philosopher, mathematician, or poet looks like some version of the large, rosy-cheeked, white-bearded elf. This is true even of Saint Nicholas, with whom Santa Claus is closely associated; born in 270 C.E. in what is today Turkey, he was brown at best. This applies as well to women of the past such as the great Egyptian mathematician and philosopher Hypatia and the Jewish Berber queen Dihya (also known as the Kahina—"seer"). The logic of this form of invisibility is that black, brown, and red people *cannot* produce knowledge. In the words of the Dalit poet Chandramohan Sathyanathan:

> I am haunted by the "lack" of history.
> My gaze trips at the troughs

Of the tidal wave of time
Lashing on the shores of my memory.

. . .

My tongue is swollen like a stuffed python
With the "baggage of imagined history."[16]

Examining all five forms of invisibility together, we see how matrices of dehumanization distribute invisibility across many people in
the Euromodern or white supremacist world. The ideas from a philosopher such as Hypatia almost disappeared in collective memory
because her books were burned after her gruesome execution in 415
C.E. at the hands of rabid Christians and her memory whitewashed
along with that of so many of her peers in Northeast Africa. Today
more people know about her martyrdom than her thought, and she is
portrayed as white in most depictions, including the biopic film *Agora*
(2009). The seventh-century Berber queen Dihya, a fearsome leader of
her people, described by the Arab invaders as "dark skinned with lots
of hair and huge eyes," is at times depicted as white with blond or red
hair.

Invisibility offers contradictions. For instance, although these five
forms of invisibility can converge in a single group or be distributed
across many others, they also require historical context. As Deloria
observed: "Because the Negro labored, he was considered a draft animal. Because the Indian occupied large areas of land, he was considered
a wild animal."[17] He argues that the elimination of legal enslavement of
nonprisoners in the United States, where those who dominated them
considered blacks useless except as beasts of burden, raised speculation that black people would become obsolete. Native Americans, in
contrast, were transformed from animal to human only when settlers
wanted their land in a system premised on property acquisition and
transaction. After a period of original or primitive accumulation vis-
à-vis exterminating "wildlife" from the land, settlers seized the homes
of those Indigenous people who remained on the land in transactions
that were, in effect, legalized theft. Those transactions could be made
only between human beings, and so Native Americans had to be ten-

tatively reinterpreted as "human"—a transformation that demanded, for whites who used themselves as the standard of what it means to be human, assimilation.

The project of whitening Native Americans was devised under the guise of legal "recognition," which was in effect a form of misrecognition: in order to be legally seen, they could only be recognized *as white* or illicitly Native. Their non-whiteness had to disappear. This is the logic of integration and assimilation. Integration places the people under governmental jurisdiction and control. Assimilation is their absorption and erasure. In Australia, Canada, and the United States, these are the principles of white Anglo-Saxon Protestant rule. The expectation is that everyone is to be ruled by this group, and to be acceptable, everyone should try to become them. This was possible for European immigrants who could transition through appearing Anglo-Saxon Protestant. The lightness of their complexion met the color criterion. For groups who refused to complete the formula with the religious criterion, they could for the most part perform the cultural and color codes to avow whiteness. And besides, their suppressed or downplayed religious differences pointed to Europe, which in those countries represented the birthplace of whiteness—even where light-skinned, Native Americans had no such genealogical marker. The paradox, then, is in a supposed acknowledgment of humanness (lightness) that erased their humanity *as Natives*.

Drawing upon Fanon's critical discussions of recognition and Patrick Wolfe's writings on settler colonialism and native elimination, Glen Coulthard raises several pitfalls of racially colonized peoples seeking white recognition.[18] In its very structure, this kind of recognition enacted asymmetrical power. To make matters worse, Coulthard and Wolfe argue, the land—the motivation behind the offer of recognition—was conceived of in two radically different ways. For the settler populations, land meant property; for the Indigenous and First Nation peoples, it meant life.

My family and I witnessed a concrete example of this distinction during our first visit to Australia, in 2004. Invited by the Koori philosopher danielle davis, who was at that time teaching and studying in

New South Wales, we had the good fortune of being hosted by other members of the various Indigenous communities there. Taking us around Sydney and other cities, our Koori hosts never failed to point out a great place at which to eat. We also took some standard tours, such as a visit to the Blue Mountains, guided by white settlers—who always made sure to tell us the price of houses in the area. Property was their central concern, even among the majestic slopes of those mountains. Given my interest in ancient art, we booked a tour of Kakadu National Park in the Northern Territory, southeast of Darwin. The park is well known for, among many things, its ancient galleries. The white settlers call them "rock art"; the Yolngu people, the Indigenous people there, refer to them as "galleries." The early-morning bus ride from Darwin was an eye-opening experience. Relaxed in a window seat, I gazed down at puddles of water as we crossed each overpass. None was without a resident crocodile. I reflected on the story we'd heard earlier about white tourists swimming in billabongs. Upon our arrival at Kakadu, we were informed that it was Picnic Day, which is a holiday celebrated by the white settlers since the 1800s. I had paid in advance for our tour, but there were no guides to take us around the park. There was one option. The manager explained that Kakadu was only part of a larger area of land that the Indigenous people had won back through a series of lawsuits. The regained land was roughly the size of a combination of New Jersey and New York States. One side became Kakadu, a national park to share with the world; the other became Arnhem, an area no outsider could visit without special permission and then only when accompanied by an Indigenous guide. As luck had it, there was a Yolngu guide by the name of Lionel who was willing to take us to see the galleries.

Lionel showed up in an old Volkswagen van. When he stepped out of the vehicle, he took everyone's breath away. He looked like a brown Brad Pitt.

It was Lionel who taught us that his community referred to the painting areas as "galleries." Driving out into Arnhem, we experienced a silence unlike any other. Life was all around but, except for the visible botanical life, neither seen nor heard. I have a wonderful picture of my daughters, Jenni and Sula, ten and five years old at the time, in each other's arms looking out into the horizon at a safe distance from a billabong.

We spent the day going from one gallery to another. Each set of paintings was exquisite—the vibrancy of the colors, the layers of paintings on top of other paintings, palimpsests going back tens of thousands of years. The earliest revealed outlines of elongated blue ancestors and creatures long extinct, with later ones of familiar birds, mammals, and reptiles. After a while, I asked Lionel, "What are the paintings about?"

"They're menus," he said.

Despite the vastness of the continent, the sustainability of life in Australia has always been precarious. The ancient peoples learned quickly that it was important to know not only what to eat but also when and how much. The menus were simultaneously dining options, history, and guides for ecological management. This is something that it took some time for the white settlers to learn, as Robert Hughes recounts in *Fatal Shores*, his history of the brutal white colonization of Australia.[19]

The revelation illuminated an ongoing concern of the country's various Indigenous peoples. Although some of our Koori hosts did not speak their Indigenous language (Awabakal) and may not have even known about the specifics of what their ancestors had inscribed in the galleries, they nevertheless maintained an important connection to their country and ancestors by always making sure we knew where to find a good meal. Their understanding of the land was the interconnectedness of life. Property, in and of itself, feeds no one.

This understanding of land is shared by the Maori in New Zealand, the Guaraní people in Brazil, the Luo people in Kenya, the Tswana people in South Africa, and many communities across the United States, especially the Wampanoag in southern Massachusetts and Rhode Island. The Colombian anthropologist and decolonial theorist Julia Suárez-Krabbe makes plain an important implication of this observation in the context of Colombia's Indigenous peoples. The imposed logic of settler "negotiations" is death.[20] For Africans in Africa, theft of land eventually shifted to negotiated transitions. The inhabitants of the remaining land were dispossessed, and their worth shifted to their value as laborers. The transition from noncapitalist ways of life into capitalism resulted not in a "proletarian" class, however, but in a racialized laboring one: blacks.[21] In countries where the white settlers did not successfully transform the majority of the land into property, the Indigenous African majority faces ongoing negotiations. Where settler domination is a fait accompli, the result is the colonized people becoming black and indigenous. In Africa's north, the various historical waves of European and West Asian settlements, from antiquity through to the time of the Caliphates, gave rise to dynamics similar to those in Latin America and South Asia, where waves of settlers each faced being conquered and colonized by new colonizers. Ironically, colonized settlers at times develop an anti-colonial consciousness premised upon ignoring the fact that they are settlers.

Colonialism thus imposes all five kinds of invisibility onto black people in Africa and Australia. Where African peoples were kidnapped into slavery, the invisibility focuses more on exploited labor than on the land. At the global level, black consciousness faced the implication of global Euromodern colonialism. Its globality promised the threat of an aspiring antiblack world. This global challenge brought black consciousness as an awareness of hatred of black people into facing Black consciousness—the kind that reaches for possibilities by which to become agents of history.

Blacks of the first kind, or with black consciousness, often avoid addressing the injustice of societal efforts to make the world antiblack. They attempt, instead, to fix themselves through adaptation. They seek a home in a society whose happiness is delusional; to be at home under colonialism, enslavement, and racism is the equivalent of being a happy slave. To appear "civilized," they master the language of those who dominate them. The problem is that what it means to be "civilized" has also been colonized. Rather than implying "city dwelling," or the capability of living as a citizen, Euromoderns changed the meaning of "civilized" to being white. Embracing their languages as a source of recognition comes at the price of not being a standard of value; blacks suffer the folly of imitation: "Now, the history of man / Snores in my language."[22] Never being able to be recognized as the original, they face intrinsic inequality. The pitfalls of recognition then follow. Seeking recognition through affections of the heart fails where its purpose is a flight or escape from blackness. To be loved as not black is sought from someone who is not black and, even better, is *antiblack*. Instead of a celebrated existence, there is an affirmation of self-loathing. Retreating inward, deep beneath the skin and consciousness into the realm of subconsciousness, even dream life, offers no escape. Reaching outward in a valorized opposition to whiteness is a reaction instead of the agency of creation. Creativity should transcend reaction to white conditions.[23]

A world in which there is no hope for normality is pathological.[24] If being depraved is the only authentic life awaiting blacks, we are lost. If being well adjusted is abnormal, we are also lost. What are we to do? Given the futility of seeking white recognition, the right question is whether that recognition is worthwhile. How could it be, when its history is marked by degradation? Looking to himself, Fanon, facing this situation, asked for his body—black and beaten—to reassert itself as a question.[25] Consciousness is a manifestation of existence. To be conscious is to stand out, to differentiate oneself as not identical to that of which one is conscious. To become a question is to become a possibility. That possibility requires looking to the future. If the beaten-down person belongs to the future, he or she has broken through melancholia into a different consciousness. Having a future possibility transforms the present. The black, with this realization, renders white recognition irrelevant and becomes Black.[26]

Realization of possibility also brings us back to the errors of language. The black looks to it as either a vessel into which he or she may be sealed or as an element, like fire, to steal. This is a distorted view of language as something one can possess, when it is not properly a thing—it's a disclosure of reality through participation. As a key, language opens other openings: learning one language facilitates learning another, and new dimensions are disclosed. It can be self-reflective and critical, or generate a metalanguage—a language about language;

it can offer a way to meet the new and unfamiliar. In time, it can even generate new language. The Black who looks to the future relates to language in this way. The future isn't preordained; it's possible to live, learn, and grow.

Fanon later recognized that this Black is an aberration from the perspective of a colonial society—an ill-fitting element, the exemplification of violence.[27] In the United States, there is a long-standing debate about how African Americans should fight for social justice. Many whites approach this debate in bad faith, since in truth their concern is not really about how African Americans protest but whether they should do so. The outrage many whites expressed over Black football players kneeling during the national anthem—a gesture of protest against police violence, and the failure of U.S. governing institutions to uphold the avowed ideals of equal protection for which the flag is supposedly a symbol—was an attempt to avoid the real issue. As the journalist Steve Chapman puts it:

> Are there better ways for them to make their point? Maybe so. But it wouldn't make much difference. To many whites, the only good black protest is no black protest.[28]

There is an additional interpretation. For whites who take the position that access is a zero-sum game, any expectation of black equality amounts to one thing: that they, whites, will be replaced. The desire to take the place of colonizers, to decolonize the colonial relationship, is violence as far as colonizers are concerned. But replacing them changes the players, not the game. If locked in the logic of imitation and replacement, the result would be continued colonization in black or colored face. The answer is something different. The logic of colonization and racism is Manichaean. This means it imagines the universal separation of two worlds—white and black. Interaction transforms this logic. It poses contradictions, and in doing so initiates new relationships, which we could call "open dialectical" ones.

Familiar, clichéd characterization of dialectics is "thesis versus antithesis with both resolved into a synthesis." This is boring and linear.

Another way of looking at dialectics is through "potentiated double consciousness."[29] Double consciousness is not dialectical; it simply connotes the consciousness of the colonizer and the negative black. Realizing that he or she is not a problem but a human being facing problems, the black comes to question the society, which is human-made and therefore changeable. Then, with that realization, the black becomes the Black, an agent of social change. That realization is born from the contradiction. Realizing an avowed universal was false raises many possibilities to consider. It's not only the Black who could emerge but also many other kinds of people.

Revisiting the black's condition of antiblack racism, blacks realize that in a world of limited options, choices can be made only about *how* to live with those limitations. Locked in this inward attention, the focus moves away from the world and onto the self. The body becomes the focus. Eventually, the inner world of madness is the last retreat.[30] The worst-case scenario? The black implodes.

Orienting outward, the task becomes the expansion of options. The more options one has, the sooner the futility of setting goals declines.

Institutions—governments; states; other mechanisms of power, such as economies, education, and cultural institutions—can change. But colonization, enslavement, and racism do not die easily. Their on-going life depends on blocking every path just outlined. Therein lies the tragic, violent struggle.

Building on potentiated double consciousness, James Davis III offers his experience of incarceration. He reflects on incarceration chipping away at his humanity behind a "concrete veil" in an ongoing dynamic of denied recognition. To survive, he must develop a "new consciousness," which he describes as a "double-double consciousness":

> Prisoners with this inflection of double-double consciousness are not content with being inmates. They develop an identity that allows them to thrive under the most hostile of conditions. They come to recognize that the denial of their humanity is predicated on social structures, and so critique those social structures that impose upon their self-consciousness

an unnatural unreality. They recognize that they are not the problem, the structure of society is the problem with its adherence to inhumane practices such as mass incarceration. These prisoners rebuke the prisoner identity.

. . . Double-double consciousness is a refusal to live a life completely within the lines drawn by institutional racism and enforced by law.[31]

A young South African medical student, political activist, and philosopher, Steve Bantu Biko, elucidated this problem in Apartheid South Africa.[32] Any state and society built on the degradation of a people must block the resources through which those people might threaten to appear as human beings. Waging war against their inclusion, it will also do so against anyone who assists them. Its goals become total; its focus becomes rule, and as that dominates, there is something that must be suppressed. That dangerous activity is politics.

In Apartheid South Africa, which regarded itself as making rigorous the racist values of Canada and the United States, the project of white supremacy required a strictly maintained Manichaean separation manifesting all five kinds of invisibility. The mere mention of "Black" and "consciousness" was a threat to the state's power and demanded its often violent reaction. This response makes it clear that Black consciousness is political.

9

BLACK CONSCIOUSNESS IS POLITICAL

We now largely think of the Euromodern city as the setting for politics. But politics was also practiced in ancient cities, which are often wrongly envisioned as having been devoid of dark peoples. Africans were for a long time considered rural in the Euromodern imagination, even though cities have existed in Africa for many millennia before their emergence in Europe. Such misconceptions might give the impression that politics is a novel thing to black people.

Today, however, blacks are inextricably linked with cities. So much so that despite the fact that the transformation of Africans into blacks under Euromodern colonialism initially took place in the rural contexts of the plantation and resources from mines, nearly a century of black migration into urban areas has made the phrase "rural blacks" seem outdated and perhaps oxymoronic.

The historical circumstances leading to urbanization arose in ancient times through a series of factors linked to citizenship. City-states sprouted up across Eastern Africa, Southwest Asia, Southern Europe, South America, and North America at least several thousand years ago.[1] Some were what Greek-speaking peoples called the *pólis*, in which the cultivation of citizenship eventually became known as *politeia*, or politics. Inside the polis, life was supposedly devoted to human flourishing. The polis was a structure wherein growing numbers of people led to population density. Keeping others outside put a premium on the limited space, and thus ceasing to spread outward, compression led to architectural innovations in which people increasingly lived in multistory housing that is a mark of many urban environments today.

We should bear in mind that a city can be open to others and spread outward. As long as practices of citizenship are at work, cities can take many physical forms, especially if the citizens face environmental challenges such as insufficient water and others caused by climate change.[2]

With urbanization, a new set of norms developed, leading to the notion of "civilization," which referred to the ability to live civilly—to live in cities—where "the civilized" became another way of saying "city dwellers." As the concept of the city became associated with urban centers, the urbane came to represent the civilized and the citizen. Yet an urban dweller needn't participate in the practices of citizenship. In fact, urban centers have been plagued by the simultaneous presence of those who practiced citizenship and those who either don't or were barred from doing so—in short, there can be cities within which the majority of the people are not citizens.

In some cases, the lack of citizenship is voluntary, where dwellers are simply passing through or freely choose to step outside public life. The ancient Greeks had a disparaging word for people who remained in a polis with access to citizenship but who eschewed politics: *idiōtēs*. The word, the English cognate of which is clear, stems from the Middle Kingdom (approximately 2030 B.C.E.–1640 B.C.E.) of Kmt's Mdw Ntr word *idi*, which means "deaf." This was not necessarily a ground for deaf exclusion in those parts of the world, as by 1000 B.C.E. there were Hebrew laws providing the deaf with limited rights to property and marriage. The presumption later espoused by the ancient Mediterranean Greek-speaking peoples was that a lack of hearing entailed isolation and a limited capacity to learn, though they were aware, as discussed in Plato's *Cratylus* (422e), of deaf people's capacity to communicate. The implication when applied to the polis is that without politics, many people would be packed together without ever listening to one another—a society, from the perspective of the ancients, of idiots.

Bear in mind that this portrait is from a tradition that served as the foundation of political life in what was Europe at least until the rise of Christendom. Curiously, the story of the normative significance of deafness had many twists and turns. For instance, the Spanish word for deaf is *sordo*. Its Latin roots are in *sordidus*, which means "dirty, filthy, foul, vile, mean, base," from *sordere*, "to be dirty, shabby," which in turn is related to *sordes* (dirt, filth). In addition to Spanish, it took form in Germanic languages through their pronunciation of *sordo* as *swordo* (black, dirty), which was the source also of Old English *sweart*, meaning "black." Think also of the English word "sordid." There is, as well, the contemporary German *schwarz* (black). Other languages—and by extension, cultures—had different associations with deafness and as a consequence held possibilities, for the most part, as in Hawai'ian sign language, that were almost lost. There is clearly a link between hostility to deafness and antiblackness in the European traditions, which raises questions of, as the political theorist Derefe Kimarley Chevannes argues, Deaf black and black Deaf consciousness.[3]

Where people are committed and willing to participate in practices of citizenship—speech and listening—but are barred, ignored, or deliberately thwarted from doing so by social elites in their society, an appeal to equal protection under the law is one recourse. Republicanism—the position that citizens should not live under arbitrary rules of a monarch and should stand as equals before the law under the governance of representatives—supports this view. This indirect egalitarianism of republicanism raises the inevitable question of the scope of the law.

The history of race in republics, including Australia, the Federative Republic of Brazil, the Republic of South Africa (founded in 1961), and the United States, is the story of a supposedly legitimate exclusion of certain people from the system on the grounds of protecting the system's integrity, meaning that their inclusion was forbidden. This rationalization takes the form of rejecting any critique of the system to the point of treating it like an idol or a god. Deified, the city or state can do no wrong; accounting for injustice and maledictions requires either ignoring them or blaming others, including the victims. Recall the earlier discussion of theodicy. The reasoning is the same: if the god is powerful and good, human suffering is for a greater purpose, or individual human beings must be blamed instead of the practices of adhering to the god's edicts. Treating a country, state, or city like a god in this way is what I call *cividicy*.

The logic of cividicy depends on contraries, which separate elements in a consistent system of who belongs inside and who doesn't. This logic is perfect for racist states with imposed systems of apartheid or segregation, in which the police as well as the military serve as physical borders between the inside groups and those paradoxically outside, despite them all being under the jurisdiction of the same government. Opposing contraries are contradictions, which are dialectical: they require interaction, negotiation, and the crossing of zones. Where, for example, do police officers and soldiers "belong" when they go home? Some, such as black police officers and soldiers, are also members of the outsider group. Such agents of the state "belong" instrumentally to its enforcers of exclusion but not to the very parts of society they are protecting. Think of the irony of off-duty black police officers and soldiers pulled over by white police officers who racially profile them. The initial logic of citizenship, in the context of the polis, was based on negotiating conflict—presumed to arise through intellectual and ideological differences—through communication. The police and the military represent where communication breaks down.

In the story of citizenship, race provides a peculiar twist. The urban spaces in Euromodern countries afforded only white men access to the benefits of full citizenship, a structure reminiscent of ancient Athens, with a similarly complicated relationship between the citizens and those noncitizens, historically women and the enslaved, who served them. In Euromodern societies, citizenship was racialized, which meant that its appearance, whether urban or rural, became white. Given the population density of urban centers, the possibility of violating boundaries was high; policing, as a way of restricting the mobility of subordinated racial groups, came to the fore. The often hysterical discussion of law enforcement became peculiarly urban, and urban centers became increasingly characterized as places of "crime." The expectation was that black and brown people should be present only where their labor was needed without them otherwise being "seen." Simply by existing, they committed violations of appearance.

Euromodern cities are divided into places of citizenship (white) and of criminality (black, brown, and colonized Indigenous), setting the stage for the former's use of citizenship *against citizenship*. Ironically, noncitizens such as documented permanent residents and undocumented immigrants often perform exemplary acts of citizenship, while legally designated citizens actively block immigrants' political appearance by leaning on law enforcement and supposed order.

Consider New York City, a historically vibrant center of political activity, burgeoning with institutions focused on civil society as an expression of possibility and the checking of governing institutions. It suffered a decline in citizenship in at least two moments. The first was white flight from the 1950s onward. The second was Mayor Rudolph Giuliani's draconian campaign, from 1994 to 2001, for what is called "law and order." Because expectations of citizenship and whiteness were in practice one and the same, this meant that citizenship (those people with racial and economic capital) migrated to the suburbs, exurbs, and rural areas. The remaining populations, largely of people of color fighting for democracy, suffered crackdowns from state violence, which continue into the third decade of the twenty-first century. Although urban centers such as Atlanta, Baltimore, Boston, Chicago, Los Angeles, Minneapolis, New York, San Francisco, and St. Louis are still called "cities," they have been marked by a decline and at times near lack of citizenship from the subordination of citizenship to the demands of so-called law—where *rule* subordinates political appearance in a continuous erosion of civil liberties, such as found in stop-and-frisk policies that mostly target black people. Urban centers across the globe face similar trends.

Dominated by rule instead of citizenship, the sociological and political functions of these urban centers have shifted. In the years since the 1990s, the aforementioned urban centers—Atlanta, Baltimore, Chicago, New York, San Francisco, and others mislabeled as "cities"— became urban places of entertainment for suburban whites. Younger whites, armed with capital, play in such places until they decide to raise families, at which point many take their white capital elsewhere. Like Disneyland or Disney World, many urban centers are managed places of consumption instead of production.

One can enjoy Disney World as a consumer because it is, at close inspection, a totalitarian state. Organized entirely on the management of consumption and pleasure, it monitors in detail the movements of its customers and staff; it is a harbinger of what the fetish of privatization offers: control in the hands of corporate management. Just as there is so much state violence hidden in plain sight in today's urban centers, there is much that remains invisible at such theme parks, such as the actual treatment of their workers.[4]

What this means is that criminality pertains almost exclusively to disruptions of state-sanctioned consumption or reverie. In effect, this means that many urban centers, increasingly drained of political efficacy and participation, are no longer cities.

Real cities are political. How can they continue to be so, however, when activities antipathetic to citizenship win the day? For one thing, the evacuation of citizenship, wherein the people take responsibility for how power functions in the society, marks their decline as places of politics.

Politics cannot exist without speech and power—or more specifically, power in speech. It is through communication of that kind that institutions are built. Yet an odd feature of contemporary political talk is a tendency to reflect on political issues in moralistic terms. The presumption is that if people were to become more moral, the organization of society would be "just." Order takes center stage at the expense of citizenship. A presumed well-ordered society could easily be thwarted through forms of cividicy, where "justice" depends on protecting a system's integrity from those who might sully it—not external enemies, unfortunately, but subordinated groups within its jurisdiction. The state violence waged in the United States against peaceful protestors during spring 2020—including those attacked by federal armed forces so that former president Trump could pose holding a Bible in front of St. John's Episcopal Church across from the

White House—reveals an environment of dissenters as the enemies within.[5] The antidemocratic efforts even included plans to use a "heat ray" against protestors.[6]

The moralistic appeal also fails to address crucial concerns about social change, the goal of those who have not appeared as citizens, as agents, as legitimate members of society, and would like to. They want societal transformation, which sets them at odds with a system that considers itself intrinsically just, marking them unjust. Their appearance is illicit; they are a violation.

Another problem with the moral applications model is that it makes sense if people really can, individually, put into effect what is right. But human beings are not divine and omnipotent; we are fallible and physically limited; we must find alternative ways of building society and living together. To do that requires community empowerment: we must foster community empowerment through which we can live and flourish.

"Power" is a word frequently used and rarely defined; it thus becomes a source of mystification and suspicion. It signifies the ability to make something happen, with access to the means for implementing it. Eurocentric accounts often point to the Latin word *potis*, from which came the word "potent," as in an omnipotent god, and the divine significance offers a clue. If we return to Middle Kingdom Kmt or ancient Egypt, we would find the word *pHty*, which referred to godlike strength, or the strength of pharaohs and other high officials. Going still further back to the Old Kingdom (2686 B.C.E.–2134 B.C.E.), we find the word *HqAw* or *heka*, which activates the *ka* (sometimes translated as "life force," "soul," "spirit," "womb," or "magic") that sparks reality.[7] The sun god Ra is illustrative here, since elements of that god flow through other gods and all reality, as in a ray of light or radiation. The *pHty* is achieved only through *HqAw*, which amounts to a straightforward affirmation of power as the ability with the means to make things happen. Today we also use the term "power" to refer to electricity. Lacking it, we say we are out of power. Associating electricity with power is why we sometimes refer to charismatic speakers as "electrifying." Such people are compelling. They move us. They make us do things. They make things happen.

We can now retell this story of speech and power and their relationship to politics this way. Our initial abilities and means are our bodies. Where our physical reach is our only means, our impact on the world is limited to material force. We directly touch or push things. We human beings have the gift of language, by which, through our understanding and production of meaning, we can expand our impact on the world not only through reaching one another but also by creating new kinds of meaning and things. It's alchemical. It's a key to bringing into being what did not precede it. Add our communication technologies, and we now create new kinds of life while sending probes through outer space in the hope of meeting others.

Our ability to affect one another builds the social world, enriching it with creativity and meaning. It also brings along responsibilities in need of constant negotiation. Culture, which Sigmund Freud aptly calls a "prosthetic god," signifies a major expansion of human options.[8] We may not be gods, but the social world of cultural meanings has enabled us to adopt the responsibilities once thought godly. We have ways of controlling our environment and preserving or cultivating our health, and we enact rules and regulations to mitigate our conflicts with one another. To aid the latter, we have built institutions, such as courts, governments, hospitals, markets, schools, temples, and unions, in which we divest some of our power for the expanded benefits of others. Expanding the capabilities of those in need is "empowerment." But where capabilities are hoarded by a few, the power of others is whittled away, to the point of locking them within their bodies. Pushed further inward, they suffocate or, worse, implode. That is oppression.

In racist societies, the state aims to disempower. Restricting the power of certain groups to the physical body requires neutering their capacities for expression, particularly speech. These people cease to affect the social world; they are unheard sounds. Antiblack racism, as an example, is antipathetic to the meeting of blacks and power. To prevent that meeting, the racist society must rally forces against speech, power, imagination, and politics. That is why all racist societies eventually become anti-political, anti-intellectual, and unimaginative. It's no accident that the struggle against racism is not simply moral (about how we should treat each other) but also political (about the expansion of freedom and capabilities). Since it involves communication and other kinds of interaction, political life reaches outward. Anti-political societies seek the breakdown of relations in an effort to force at least certain groups into the prison of non-relations or disconnectedness, which forces them inward.

Where political activity flourishes, so do citizenship and democratic institutions. There are activist groups in a variety of urban centers across the globe working at the rejuvenation of citizenship beyond the logic of racial exclusion. The effects of their hard work were witnessed in the multiracial populations who took to the streets in the fight against police violence and the struggle for democracy in what is now also known as "the American spring" of 2020.[9] From Brazil and Colombia to the Netherlands and the United Kingdom, similar protests against police violence occurred. Citizenship involves persistent democratic practice and struggle.

Rural areas, which are not only capable of but also increasingly exercising citizenship, become politically limited when they become ultra-rural—that is, places so remote with so few people that there is little sociality short of communication with the self. In the United States, there have been strategies to make people in those areas have more influence on election outcomes than people in densely populated areas. The result in the 2016 presidential election expressed an extension of the war against citizenship. People who rejected the need to live with others helped the ultra-affluent and the corrupt place in authority candidates with a set of directives against the majority of the country. By 2020, the outcomes were basically pillaging of the government coffers in the interest of the rich, the disruption and in some cases destruction of government services that could have saved many lives when the novel coronavirus reached the United States, invocation of police states and militarism, spiraling national debt for generations to come, and a frontal assault on democracy in the January 2021 insurrection at the U.S. Capitol followed by a systematic effort to disenfranchise particularly black voters across the country.

The waves of global protests since 2017 signaled a newly expanded struggle for citizenship.[10] The public protests from undocumented workers, refugees, and targeted black and brown peoples, in particular, also indicate a feature of true citizenship, one that arises in the face of adversity: courage. Today's defenders of citizenship could learn a great deal from the plight of those who have suffered from an imposed invisibility and have been denied the right to assert their humanity and potential as citizens. They are fighting for the options through which people could make meaningful choices and setting life-orienting goals.[11] Such efforts always face possibilities of becoming tragic, because although their success benefits all, we should remember their failures are also shared.[12] Examining this problem of political responsibility and risk in the United States, the famed autoworker-turned-Black-revolutionary intellectual James Boggs put it this way:

> What is man's greatest human need in the United States today? It is to stop shirking responsibility and start assuming responsibility. When Americans stop doing the one and start doing the other, they will begin to travel the revolutionary road. But to do this they must use as much creative imagination in politics as up to now they have used in production. The fact is that the more imaginative Americans have been in creating new techniques of production, the less imaginative they have been in creating new relations between people.[13]

Political responsibility is unfortunately often confused with moral responsibility. In his 1947 book *Die Schuldfrage*, the German philosopher and psychiatrist Karl Jaspers offered much insight on political responsibility in circumstances of profound assaults on the human spirit.[14] The word *Schuld* is related to the word *Schule* (school), the idea being that a person should learn something in a situation of guilt, blame, or responsibility. Guilt without learning is pointless and even pathological. The title of Jaspers's book has been translated into English, however, as *The Question of German Guilt*.[15] No doubt Germany's position as a vanquished country and a worldwide aberration at the end of World War II was the reason for translating the general "Guilt" into a specifically German one, since those who fought against Germany wanted to particularize it instead of addressing their shared responsibility for the imperialism and racism that had fostered the war. The United States, especially, continues to avoid the fact that its ill-treatment of its Indigenous and black peoples, bolstered by rationalizations from many of its eminent scientists, inspired the Nazis.[16] Jaspers, although at first addressing his fellow Germans, was speaking to every country and every person in the world.

Jaspers outlined four kinds of guilt, each with its own associated responsibilities. The first, metaphysical, addresses an individual's relationship with G-d or existence throughout the universe or pluriverse. Here one stands alone before the judgment of the all-knowing. This form of guilt and responsibility might not resonate with atheists, or people who reject the idea of a spiritual reality; they may weigh the existential question of whether they have lived a meaningful life. The crucial thing is that lack of spiritual belief does not absolve anyone of responsibility. Even the atheist faces the question of whether to have faith in or take responsibility for the very idea of responsibility; after all, if there is no G-d from which responsibility flows, the onus is left on all of us.

The second, moral responsibility, is about our character and relationship with the rules and mores of society. The main concern is summarized by the question "Have I done the right thing?" Morality pertains to the rules; ethics, to character, which also raises the question "Am I a good person?"

The third, legal responsibility, is the matter of whether one has followed or broken rules as legislated by relevant authorities. In what are known as *mala prohibita* (wrongs because prohibited) offenses, one's intentions need not matter. They are contrasted with *mala en se* (evil in themselves), which are prohibited even if no government or legal system has declared them so.

The last form of guilt and responsibility, political, is of primary interest here. It is responsibility, borne by every member of a society, for the actions of their government. This one raises the question of whether a government has acted that, should it fall, its people will deserve mercy. Jaspers counsels governments to remember that if they fail, it is the people, their citizens, who will be forced to pay their debts, and in some instances even merit a death sentence of their own doing.

In response to Jaspers, the feminist philosopher Iris Marion Young argues that political responsibility requires more than acting so that one will deserve merciful treatment.[17] It's not enough for those in power to avoid committing wrongs; it's also important that they do good or make the world better. This requires moving beyond what she calls a "liability model of responsibility." She proposes the following criteria for political responsibility:

> (1) Unlike responsibility as liability, political responsibility does not isolate some responsible parties in order to absolve others. (2) Whereas blame or liability seeks remedy for a deviation from an acceptable norm, usually by an event that has reached a terminus, with political responsibility we are concerned with structural causes of injustice that are normal and ongoing. (3) Political responsibility is more forward-looking than backward-looking. (4) What it means to take up or assign political responsibility is more open and discretionary than what it means to hold an agent blameworthy or liable. (5) An agent shares political responsibility with others whose actions contribute to the structural processes that produce injustice.[18]

While Young agrees with Jaspers that political responsibility is borne by everyone in a society, her reference to "the structural processes that produce injustice" is another way of referring to institutions of power. Implicit in being able to produce injustice is also the ability to produce a more just society; this is also why she says that political responsibility is forward-looking, which involves "participation in processes that produce structural injustice, [which] can be discharged only if those who share this responsibility organize collective action to transform the processes."[19] It's shared potentially by all members of a society.

Racism, as a system of institutional degradation, pertains to political responsibility. Too many whites' sense of political guilt creates a crisis, since their narcissism produces an imagined individual (moral) responsibility, which turns the question of fighting against racism into a topic that is all about them.

In his second and in his final accounts of his life, Frederick Douglass observed metaphysical guilt at play in white enslavers' pathological fear of graveyards.[20] Given Christianity's promise of the afterlife to the righteous, enslaved people were often more willing to meet their maker. This promise unfortunately also was the basis for the cruelty of slave owners and overseers. Perversely, many attempted to beat righteousness out of the enslaved in the hope of affirming their own right to salvation. Others needed G-d not to exist, which meant, for them, being able to be obscenely cruel without metaphysical punishment. In addition to the sadism Douglass chronicled, many scholars have offered accounts of acts ranging from chopping up enslaved peoples on slave ships and force-feeding the victims' remains to the "cargo," to the development of bizarre instruments of torture such as being hung by a hook through the ribs and having orifices stuffed with gunpowder and then ignited, to dismemberment and technologies of sexual violence on enslaved females and males of all ages.[21]

Moral guilt often leads to an obsession with being an individually good or moral person, which elides addressing the circumstances created by racism. Moral focus at times quickly retreats into moralism, where guilt is the prime objective. Catharsis is achieved from regarding the self as moral, while oppression—the systematic structures of dehumanization—remains. Then, legal guilt is about whether laws have been violated. Where racism is illegal, discrimination needs to be accounted for; guilt may be attributed without being experienced. A person could be found legally guilty for an action he or she does not consider immoral.

Political guilt is different. It's not that one's relationship to the gods, morality, personal virtue, and the law are irrelevant, but that everyone, even those who have not directly committed harm, is responsible. Even those who are harmed are responsible. Whites who attempt to disavow personal responsibility for their racist society fail to realize that blacks and other dominated nonwhites also, ironically, carry political responsibility. This question of political responsibility challenges two centuries-old fallacies about political action toward social transformation.

The first is that, somewhere out there, there is a group of people who have *got things right*. Find them, emulate them, and all that is right will come to fruition. The folly of this idea is that such people wouldn't be human if the rightness of their actions is a function of who or what they are instead of what they have done. If their actions and values are sources of learning, the rest of us should ask about their efficacy for the rest of us. If the idea is that there is something special about such people by virtue of who they are without examination of their practices, we would be facing problems of exoticization and fetish in which such people are intrinsically good or perfect. Investment in them would be an example of the spirit of seriousness. Focusing on the actions to be done would be a better stratagem.

The second fallacy seeks legitimacy in crowds, wherein a large-enough crowd can supposedly fix anything. The Spanish philosopher and statesman José Ortega y Gasset offered a response to this notion when he warned against what he called "mass man" and the near-metaphysical, hyper-democratic "massism" of the times.[22] Mass man is the enemy of wisdom, skill, expertise, propriety—indeed, he or she is the enemy of anything that would distinguish an individual in a way that makes him or her a "minority" or different. A healthy society appreciates these distinguishing skills and contributions. A large mass embodies force but rarely intelligence. The working class is not a mass, because as a class, it's distinguished by the labor it offers, which requires a broad range of experience and skills. An unhealthy society regards skilled or distinguished individuals with resentment, envy, and disdain. Arrogance follows, where those with a mass mentality presume they can do anything without the skill and time necessary for its fruition, or without at least the development of competence. In their view, they *have a right to everything* without accountability. They conflate mass identification into license and cruelty with strength. The right to everything, which involves also doing whatever one pleases, requires extremes. As having it all is impossible, this mentality cultivates resentment at not having all.

Much of the rhetoric of the "alt-right" and of many of the acolytes of Brazil's president Jair Bolsonaro, Turkey's president Recep Erdoğan, India's prime minister Narendra Modi, and former U.S. president Donald Trump is marked by resentment. To those who embody this mentality, the greatest affront is to be more capable than they. The brash, intellectual laziness of those leaders is what makes them attractive to their followers. The second affront is to be different from them. What is lost in the ascent of mass man—witnessed in the twentieth century in the rise to power of the fascists Franco (Spain), Hitler (Germany), and Mussolini (Italy)—is the task of what governing demands: the ability to set sensible rules and standards for living, which often means raising the standards of human potential instead of lowering them.

The bane of mass people's existence is a lack of legitimacy. Failure to achieve it leads them to wage war on clarity, evidence, facts, fairness, intelligence, persuasiveness, and truth in favor of sheer will. This antipathy fuels their decline into fascism. Incapable of building new and creative ideas and rules for the future, mass people appeal to a fictional, selectively glorified past, which they all promise marks them as the culmination of history. Fascism offers the lie of permanence and the false promise of eternal life.

The Italian philosopher and politician Antonio Gramsci understood the importance of cultivating legitimacy through actions connected to the interests and growth of a relevant community. He calls leaders who do this "organic intellectuals." These are intellectuals who are not necessarily born with the identity of a group or community but instead those who, by their commitments and actions, identify as its members. Organic intellectuals can thus come from other communities because their alternative program may be aligned with and organically linked to the goals of the one to which they have come. There can be black people with organic links to white communities and the reverse. Organic intellectuals can also, in today's language, be called "trans-intellectuals" in the sense of being born into one world but organically linked as a member of another. Think of an individual who is born rich but whose actions and commitments make her or him a working-class, left-wing intellectual.

Fanon made a similar argument in his critique of black leaders whose skill sets, organically linked to the struggle for decolonization or national independence, might not be best suited to the task of building their country. They could be organically linked only to the struggle against colonialism, which means their legitimacy derives from warding off continued colonial aggression. The problem is that the system of governance and the bases of legitimacy they build may not be organically linked to where their country needs to go. Colonialism might come to an end in legal terms, but continue, ironically, through the social and political avenues used to eradicate it. There are forms of antiracist struggles that result in more efficient racism, since their perpetrators belong to the group they are supposed to be liberating— for example, black perpetrators and perpetuators of antiblack racism.

Whereas black consciousness may be linked to the role consigned to the black person in an antiblack society, Black consciousness is organically linked to what black and all people ultimately need: the transformation of the society that produces antiblack racism and other kinds of dehumanization into something better. Black consciousness is linked to building a better world to come. This is the quest for liberation.[23] As liberation would require a radical change of society, we could also call it revolution.

Black consciousness is political because of its organic relationship to fighting against societal forces of disempowerment. Black consciousness therefore requires that concept, so terrifying to many whites and other antiblack peoples in antiblack societies: *Black power*.

What is Black power but the rejection of authoritarianism in favor of legitimacy born from the demand for liberation, to live with dignity and freedom? There is a distinction between being authoritarian and authoritative. Both are premised on legitimacy. An authority without legitimacy is often left with force and thus becomes authoritarian; an authority with legitimacy doesn't need force because authoritative. Black power demands not only the ability to make things happen—in this case, liberation from the degrading force of oppression—but also the development of legitimacy, justification, freedom, dignity, authoritativeness, worthiness.

Racism is the channeling of institutional mechanisms of power toward the disempowerment of targeted groups of people; its effectiveness depends on the meeting of state and cultural resources. People bring legitimacy to their society's formal aspirations. When a sufficient number of people oppose problematic formal social mechanisms and create alternative ones, others with stubborn individual attachments to the past become irrelevant. That is the ultimate fear of racists—their own irrelevance. As their relevance depends on a society wedded to racism, the empowerment of those they would exclude sounds the death knell of the racist system. And since systems can be built and sustained only by people, Black empowerment should be the goal of anyone committed to eradicating antiblack racism and other kinds of degradation of what it means to be human.

Fear of their irrelevance is among the reasons there are white people who need black people to "need" them.[24] In similar kind, there is no shortage of black people who appeal to that narcissistic fantasy. They tend to be blacks whom racist whites, from liberal to conservative, condescendingly call "smart." Reflecting on the old debate on whether black people should seek allies among white liberals or Marxists, James Boggs offered this reflection in his criticisms of Louis Lomax's undoubtedly "smart" text *The Negro Revolt* in 1963:

> Lomax ends his book by giving reasons why Negroes should stick with the liberals. Behind his reasoning is the assumption that Negroes want exactly what whites have. Lomax never faces the truth behind the common saying among Negroes that all the white man has is his "white." This "white" is exactly what the Negro despises . . . because it is nothing but

racial superiority. . . . When a Negro says that the whites have better opportunities . . . what he means is that he wants *a system of equality*. . . . Under these conditions, what the whites now have will no longer exist.[25]

Boggs's review is entitled "Liberalism, Marxism, and Black Political Power." As the title reveals, it's not only the white liberal who suffers from the need to be needed. He identifies this danger with regard to many Marxists who romanticize the working class, which invariably means the *white* working class despite the disproportionate number of black, brown, and Indigenous peoples belonging either to that class or among the unemployed and severely poor.[26] His critique is brutal:

Theoretically, the Marxists are worse than the liberals. The Marxists recognize that a revolution is involved in the Negro struggle but still they want the Negroes to depend upon the white worker being with them. The Negro worker who works in the shop knows that if he is going to depend on the white worker he will never get anywhere. The average white worker isn't joining any liberal organizations or radical organizations. If he is joining anything, he is joining racist organizations like the home improvement (i.e., keep the Negroes out) associations, the Ku Klux Klan, and the White Citizens Council.[27]

Boggs criticizes the failure to see how race and class can take separated forms in white worker versus black worker:

When the Negro fights, he fights not "in the last analysis"—i.e., not according to the thought patterns of Marxists—but *in reality*. His enemy is not just a class. His enemy is people, and the people are American whites of all classes, including workers.

Antiblack racism doesn't exist in a vacuum. It's a link in a chain of varieties of racism. Racism is antipathetic not only to equality but also to the form of belonging that is a connection to the future. What could the struggle against racism be but a quest for an egalitarian society premised on the openness of human possibility?

Getting rid of white supremacy doesn't entail the eradication of racism. While white supremacy is the thesis that whites must be superior and have *everything*—even the legitimate embodiment of oppression and victimization in a world where political subjects are constituted through having been harmed—antiblack racism is the conviction that blacks must have nothing. Rejecting both involves understanding that all people deserve something, and that an all-or-nothing mentality presents a false dilemma.

Fear of Black consciousness makes sense, then, in a society where white supremacists and antiblack racists desire to see without seeing the displeasing truth of what they have produced and the system of injustice on which they depend—namely, human degradation and the foreclosure of the breadth of human potential. Dignity, freedom, and respect with access to the conditions of meaningfully living are vital for a healthy society. If everyone should have something, equal access to the conditions on which to live meaningful lives of dignity, freedom, and respect is a significant thing to have.

10

BLACK CONSCIOUSNESS IN WAKANDA

Jack Kirby and Stan Lee, the legendary creative duo behind Marvel Comics, created the superhero Black Panther in 1966. The character appeared in *The Fantastic Four* no. 52. The Black Panther—T'Challa—is king of Wakanda, a fictional African country.

Kirby, born Jacob Kurtzberg, was the writer-artist; Lee, born Stanley Lieber, was the writer-promoter. I mention the birth names of these two giants in the history of comic books to indicate what many readers may already know: these two guys from New York City were Jews of European descent. What must this aspect of the Black Panther's origins mean to white supremacists, most of whom hate Jews? Their claims of Jewish conspiracies with blacks for overthrowing the white race must be on their minds.[1] Marvel's challenge to white supremacy, although never perfect, continues to the present. Like 2018's *Spider-Man: Into the Spider-Verse*, which features an Afro-Latino Spider-Man, and 2019's *Avengers: Endgame*, in which the white super soldier Steve Rogers hands over Captain America's shield to the African American Sam Wilson, aka Falcon, the 2018 film *Black Panther*, based on the original comic, poses an active threat to white supremacy in the arena of popular culture.

That the Black Panther was created by Jewish writers suggests that a Jewish reading of the character would not be out of place. The fictional country of Wakanda is located in East Africa, along eastern Uganda into western Kenya; it lies near the "Jewish territory" proposed by

Theodor Herzl at the sixth Zionist Congress in Basel, Switzerland, in 1903. The proposal was struck down by the British as impractical at the seventh Zionist Congress, two years later. The Balfour Declaration of 1917 announced the British government's support of Palestine as the location for the Jewish homeland and state.

The Black Panther could be interpreted as a messianic figure coming from a holy line. There are Jewish symbols throughout the character's fictional country; near the end of the 2018 film, many Jews may have noticed a boy blowing a shofar—an instrument made from the horn of a ram—as a new age begins. Jews blow the shofar on Rosh Hashanah, the beginning of the Jewish New Year.

It would be an error to interpret these Jewish elements as projections onto an imagined Africa. Though Lee and Kirby may be understood as white today, they were born at a time when nearly everywhere that would not have been the case (hence the Anglicizing of their last names). Moreover, anyone who knows African cultures and history could easily see the Africanness of Judaism (which not all Jews embrace or practice). African Jews, such as the Abayudaya of Uganda and the Lemba of Zimbabwe and South Africa, see no contradiction between *halakhic* living (living by Jewish law) and the historical practices they know as African. Many African American and Afro-Caribbean Jews, like me, also see in our Jewishness an affirmation of our Africanness.[2]

Although there are white-identified Jews who are also antiblack and anti-African, they are hardly representative. There are blacks who are also antiblack and anti-African, and there are blacks who are anti-Jewish. Considering those blacks representative of black people would be a misrepresentation, making some members represent all.

Ancient East Africans had no reason to stop at where the future geopolitical boundaries through which Africa and West Asia are now separated. For ancient migrants to have stopped at the location of what would later become the Suez Canal made no sense. The various people across what is today known as the Middle East were for the most part northeastern-dwelling people of Kmt/Egypt, and those along what is now the Arabian Peninsula were no doubt people from Nubia and other African countries nearby. Understanding ancient Jewish history is revelatory: the people who, living in those areas of East Africa and West Asia, eventually became Judeans and who, after the fall of the Second Temple of Jerusalem, their most sacred site, proselytized across the Roman Empire, converting many peoples and their descendants into what are now known the world over as Jews.[3]

In the Marvel mythology, Wakanda's wealth and technological power are fueled by a near magical substance, vibranium, which crashed into the country from the sky. A Jewish reading draws a connection to the Ark of the Covenant, which held the tablets Moses brought down from Mount Sinai. The holy cargo imbued the Ark with magical powers. The word "covenant" means "coming together." The enduring power of the tablets is the set of commandments under which the Hebrew people came together. The founding myth of the Black Panther tells of a great warrior, Bashenga, who ingested the vibranium-affected heart-shaped herb, attained extraordinary abilities, and united warring clans. It's no accident that Lee and Kirby chose T'Challa as the given name of his descendant, their superhero. Remove the "T" and add an "h" at the end, and one has "challah," the braided bread symbolizing the bringing together of the Jewish people at various ceremonial meals, especially the Friday-evening Shabbat dinner. T'Challa's name alerts at least Jewish readers to the kind of leader this protagonist is destined to become.

According to the myth, the heart-shaped herb—which radiates like a miniature burning bush—is poisonous. The great warrior survived because he was genetically immune. The warring clans thought he had died and buried him, but he was reborn with superpowers. Only his descendants, heirs of his genetic immunity, can become Black Panthers; in genetic terms, at least, they are chosen.

Identifying these mythic dimensions calls for some reflection on myth and the stories and one of the ways in which they are told—namely, allegorically. Taken literally, "allegory" means to speak openly about something else. The word comes from putting together the Greek words *allos* ("another," "something else," and, at times, "beyond") and *agoreuein* (to speak openly). Think of the agora, the open meeting place, in ancient Athens.

In his *Republic*, Plato argued for the importance of philosophy through his famous allegory of an ascent from a world of shadows to seeing the light, from the cave of deception and ignorance to illuminated truth and wisdom. That we could refer to the allegory as illuminative makes it a double movement of allegory, an allegory about allegory, so to speak. Illumination raises questions of what is being illuminated and what is achieved in making it apparent. Plato's answer was resolute: Truth.

Seeking truth is, however, not a simple affair. What's truth but that in which we could place our faith or trust? That could be many things and of many kinds. The English word "truth" comes from the old West Saxon word *triewð*, which refers to faith, faithfulness, fidelity, loyalty, and trustworthiness. It's from the old Germanic abstract noun *treuwitho*, from the earlier Proto-Germanic *treuwaz* (having or characterized by good faith). Truth is that or those in whom one can place one's faith. This expectation is not, of course, limited to Germanic languages. The story from words in other languages offers different insights. The ancient Greek word often translated as "truth," for instance, is *aletheia*, which is from the word *alethes*, which means "not concealing." The word *lēthē* means "forgetfulness, concealment." The prefix "a" means "not." Thus, even the word to which Plato manifested his allegory, since it also involves revealing or at least not concealing, is a metaphor of allegories. *Aletheia* was connected to an idea from the people of ancient Kmt, who in their more ancient language of Mdw Ntr spoke of *bw mAa*. The word *bw* (pronounced "bou") means "place," and the word *mAa* means "real." Together, they signify real place or location of the real. Bear in mind that *mAa* (pronounced "mei-a" or "may-a") also means "loyal." That more ancient Egyptian word is thus broader in scope and offers some connection between the ancient Greek and Germanic understandings. We could also explore related words in many ancient languages, of course, and there are living languages in which there is no single word for truth.[4]

The search for truth through allegory raises the question of its relation to myth. Many philosophers and scientists, for instance, argue that truth grows where myth dies. The result over the ages is often philosophers and scientists in league with each other against artists, especially poets, most of whom are at home in the world of myth. Some philosophers, especially Plato, protested that the poets—who in antiquity included storytellers, playwrights, orators, and writers of poems—beguiled the people with fiction. Sometimes, however, a poet or a philosopher would come along who raised the question of truth in fiction. To make matters worse, despite the tendency to question myth, its vitality was sometimes evident in such disavowals. To understand why, it is important to understand the distinction between theory and myth.

Theorizing involves experiencing moments of estrangement through which illumination occurs. Myth demands familiarity to the point of radical intimacy. Theory demands explanation and understanding. Myth seeks meaning. Theory ultimately adheres to evidence and facts. Myth addresses a peculiar *must* that haunts unreflective action. The stuff of myth comes from its retelling. Indeed the word is derived from the ancient Greek *muthos*, which means "told or recounted from the mouth" or "word of mouth." The narrative form is also a ritual. One repeats myth, which diverges a little in each retelling. Eventually, there are myths beneath myths, the inner or subterranean life of myth. The telling of myth is, thus, also mythical.

The act of theorizing, however, doesn't always offer a theory. The English word "theory" comes from the Greek *theoria* (contemplation, speculation, viewing, seeing), from *theoros* (spectator), from *thea* (a view—interestingly from which we also get "theater") and *horan* (to see), which in the Greek infinitive is *theorein* (to see, consider, look at). The interesting double moment of viewing what one sees offers reflection: not only to see but also to see that one sees. It's a meta-reflective—a reflection on reflection—move of double comprehension. To view what is seen and to see also that one sees offers the impression of seeing *all*. The primordial model of such is already embedded in the root *theo*, which means "god." As gods, especially when fully invested with power, bridge gaps between potency and thought, the conclusion should be clear. Embedded in theory is the effort to see what a god would see.

Theory, then, begins with a rather lofty goal for which theorizing faces, at least for human beings, an endless task. Human beings are, after all, not gods. This means we never begin with perfection. Our humanness is not ideal in the sense of perfect, but that doesn't and shouldn't prevent us from seeking what is reasonably ideal, given our limitations.[5]

All human seeing requires meaning. Seeing dissolves into mere sensing where meaning is lacking. Even reflection collapses into a sea of indistinctness. Meaning, then, is an unavoidable element of all efforts to get out of the cave of deception and ignorance. Seeing the source of all seeing, the source of all meaning, the light from which rays infuse reality, requires meaning; it's no accident that theory is grounded in myth, such as the sun god Ra.

Returning to the Black Panther, it should be evident that Kirby and Lee were informed by myth not only in the creation of their characters but also in the theories their stories—often allegories—illuminated. So, too, were the writers Ryan Coogler and Joe Robert Cole, who brought Lee and Kirby's famed comic book character to film. But the transition from comic book to film is not a seamless enterprise; what works in one medium doesn't necessarily translate well into others, and those who seek the original are often disappointed in the translated version, while those who begin with the adaptation sometimes find the original unappealing. In some cases, the muses of retellings intervene and multiple versions coexist, as with covers of a song to which each artist brings something different to its ongoing interpretation across generations. This is how I see the 2018 *Black Panther* movie. It came to the screen after the character had already appeared in several television cartoons, including a special 2010 BET miniseries with its own mythology created by Reginald Hudlin.

The film was met with various criticisms, among them the claim that the movie is racist. Some critics regard the film as racist against African Americans because the villain N'Jadaka/Erik Stevens/Killmonger, who was born in the United States of an African American mother (a descendant of enslaved Africans) and a Wakandan father, dies at the conclusion of a battle in which he claimed to have attempted to send Wakandan technology to mercenaries across the globe to inaugurate a world revolution for the liberation of black people.[6] That criticism has credence when we compare *Black Panther* with *Aquaman* (2018), which is its foil in this regard. Consider that the hero of that film, Arthur Curry (Aquaman), is "mixed race," a child of a princess (Atlanna) from the undersea Kingdom of Atlantis, and a Maori man (Thomas Curry) who lives on the coast. She returns to Atlantis to protect her lover and her son. She subsequently marries an Atlantean king and produces a "pure" child, Orm. The villain, King Orm, who has aspirations similar to Killmonger's, is a "pure" white man. Unlike Killmonger, Orm survives.

For the same reason, critics also see the film as counterrevolutionary. Those critics regard Killmonger as a liberator. They read the villain's demise as the triumph of, in this case, African complicity with white supremacy. Evidence for this is the character Everett Ross, the white CIA agent and former fighter pilot emerging as a heroic character who shoots down the last flying craft carrying the cargo of Wakandan technology.

Then there is the character M'Baku, the leader of the Jabari clan, whose totem is a white gorilla. The Jabari's way of voicing objection and making threats is to imitate the grunts of their totem. The social critic Sudip Sen expressed the humiliation of hearing white adolescents mimicking the grunts with laughter in the theater while watching those characters on the screen.[7]

That Wakanda is an ethnically homogenous monarchy with much military technology is hardly progressive, and, finally, though not exhaustively, critics claim that the film's portrait of Africans is inauthentic. Some also claim that its portrayal of African Americans is the same.[8]

In addition to all these, I offer a few criticisms of my own. First, I lament the unfortunate use of the words "tribe" and "king" to refer to the Wakandan people and their executive branch of leadership. As "chiefs," "kings," and "tribes" are European colonial designations imposed on many African peoples, it makes no sense for a never-colonized African country to refer to its people in such terms. "Ancestors," "clans," "elders," and "people" are closer to the terms used in many African communities.[9]

Additionally, as the anthropologist Claudia Gastrow observed when she and I spoke about the film, the high-rise buildings in Wakanda buy into presumed Euromodern urbanization as indications of development. The search for Euro-style urbanization is one of the follies not only of contemporary Africa but also of tropical regions of continents across the globe.

Finally, the comic books and cartoon miniseries make it clear that each Black Panther was superior intellectually and physically to Captain America, the iconic leader of white superheroes in the Marvel worlds, though this fact is neglected in the film adaptation. For this narrative, originally by Kirby and Lee, to have played out on the big screen would have been an additional strike against white supremacy. It's a sign of the politics of the times that making this point clear on the big screen may have been too much for many white superhero fans to bear.

There are many arguments one could offer in response to these many criticisms. One should bear in mind that those critics may find the comic books and magazines even worse. Though the comic book character preceded the birth of the Black Panther Party, the writers did for a time change the name of the character to the Black Leopard in *Fantastic Four* no. 119 to dissociate him from the Black Panther Party's politics. This was short-lived. Realizing the error of their ways, they reinstated the original name.

Other considerations are the comic book versions of M'Baku and Killmonger. M'Baku in the comics is actually a man-ape. He acquires his powers through killing Wakanda's white gorilla, eating its flesh, bathing in its blood, and wearing its skin. Killmonger, as well, is from Harlem in those versions and repeatedly attempts to conquer Wakanda. In one episode, he eats the herb and is poisoned. When he recovers, he lacks Black Panther powers. He doesn't have the immunity gene in that version, which raises questions of his actual ancestry. Additionally,

T'Challa's mother dies in his childhood in the comics. The woman who raises him, Romanda, his father's second wife, is from South Africa. All this is to say a faithful film adaptation of the character would not sit well with many of the black audiences who showed up in record-breaking numbers to view the film—in some cases, several times.

With the various criticisms in mind, let's turn to the movie. My goal here is not to defend or rebuke the film. My aim is to explore its mythic and allegorical implications and how they illuminate Black consciousness as being political, as opposed to black consciousness. It should also be borne in mind that this is a Marvel movie, which means it takes place in a fictional universe of gods and superheroes. From the standpoint of myth, gods are superheroes and superheroes are gods, or at least demigods.

The film steps outside the usual framework of superhero movies by focusing on the complexities of leadership, fidelity, and political obligation instead of physical prowess. Most superhero films—or to be precise, *white* superhero films—boil down to the hero discovering his powers, a villain doing the same, and then a conflict involving the hero's love interest. This usually ends with the hero's triumph over the villain, winning the love of the girl or woman in the process. But *Black Panther* breaks many rules of the genre beyond making the protagonist Black. Its "thesis," if it is appropriate to use that term, is that the real superhero is the political community, not one individual endowed with super strength and agility.

In an early scene, King T'Challa (the Black Panther) is on a mission to secure his beloved Nakia (Swahili for "pure and faithful"), a Wakandan spy on her own mission to liberate enslaved girls and boys from a Nigerian militia. Presumably the latter is a stand-in for Boko Haram, the group that infamously kidnapped 276 female secondary school students in Chibok, Nigeria, in 2014.[10] General Okoye (oddly, an Igbo—that is, Nigerian—name meaning "born on Orie market day"), Wakanda's highest military official, accompanies him. She warns him not to "freeze." In the following segment we see three women—his sister Shuri (unisex name from Japan meaning "village"), his beloved Nakia, and General Okoye—making fun of him for freezing after all when he saw Nakia in the midst of battle. T'Challa is the head of his country, and yet his fellow citizens are comfortable enough to tease and criticize him. This is an element of many accounts of African systems of leadership prior to colonialism and the propping up of "chiefs" in its service.[11] Colonial accounts indicate colonizers' shock not only at the difficulty of immediately identifying a given "king" in African societies but also at the seeming irreverence the people had for their highest officials.

The Amharic word *ras*, for example, means "high official." Up until the late twentieth century, there were many people in Ethiopia designated *Ras*, and the person elected among them as their leader was the head *Ras*. Tafari Makonnen Woldemikael, for instance, was known as Ras Tafari. He was not born as a preordained emperor but instead had to earn the title of head of state, through first having become a regent from 1916 to 1930, at which point he renamed himself, primarily to appease the European powers who would have diplomatic relations only with a leader who was a member of the Abyssinian Church. The name he chose was Haile Selassie, which translates into English as "hail the Trinity."[12]

Despite T'Challa's physical powers as the latest instantiation of the Black Panther, the general and his sister teasing him demonstrates that real power is ultimately being political. A tyrant lacks the love and commitment of the people; a true leader embodies their aspirations, goals, and values. The humor waged at T'Challa's expense is a reminder not to take himself too seriously, but instead to devote his energy to the people of Wakanda and, eventually, the world.

The film also offers two hours and fourteen minutes of African and African diasporic characters who do not once refer to each other as "niggers," "niggas," or "niggus." Additionally, women of Africa and the diaspora were from start to finish not called "bitches" or "hos." This aspect is worth special emphasis, since the rationalization for doing otherwise is often an appeal to "authenticity" and marketability to anti-black or predominantly white audiences. Black audiences have come to expect that we will hear black characters referred to with such invectives, but we should bear in mind that there are many black people, including among the working classes across the globe, who do not use such language. Richard Pryor once said that there are places where one could find Africans, even blacks, who are not "niggers." The film raises the idea that the United States in particular is a place that manufactures "niggers."

And so, *Black Panther* raises the question of what kind of consciousness is manifested in Wakanda. The Wakandans, after all, are not ignorant of the outside world. Their ancestors witnessed the rise of Euromodern colonialism, enslavement, and racism, and their response was a policy of nonintervention. It is important to examine the myths beneath the myths that encouraged this policy.

The first, and most obvious, is the importance of elders and ancestors. T'Challa kneels when he sees his father, T'Chaka, in his first visit with the ancestors, for which his father rebukes him, reminding him it is he who is now the "king." But the kneeling reveals fidelity to the tradition of respecting elders and ancestors. In most African societies, the earliest ancestors are the most potent exemplars of goodness. It's a world in which one relates to the descendants with the expectation that one will become their revered ancestor. In respecting T'Chaka, then, the normative chain is connected through to Bashenga, the very first Black Panther and "king" of Wakanda, who acquired his powers and used them to bring the warring clans together.

In many parts of Africa, ancestors are crucial for the continued life of the community, and power is most potent in the ultimate ancestor— namely, a god or the gods. Because of this, a "king" is no individual but instead a collection of sacred relationships across time. Pharaohs, for example, were considered reincarnations of the ancient Egyptian, or Kmt, god Horus. Bashenga set a high standard. He did not end war by scaring the various clans into submission, like the sovereign of Thomas Hobbes's *Leviathan*, who forces submission of all beneath him for the sake of order and security; instead, he organized a country and confederation of city-states. His "power" was not only his physical prowess but also his abilities as a leader. The subsequent Black Panthers, except for T'Challa and his first cousin N'Jadaka/Erik/Killmonger, focused on maintaining the peace he created among the clans. The movie concludes with T'Challa's decision that Wakanda will share its wealth and knowledge with the world; it is a statement that T'Challa has exemplified the true spirit of the first Black Panther, since he understands power as *political* and thus relational, not physical or even metaphysical.

A primary myth among the people of ancient Egypt, or Kmt, is the story of Isis and the "warring twins" Osiris/Horus and Set. The warring twins is a mythic motif in which there is a "sacred king/ancestor" who belongs to the mother and his antagonist through whom a second king/ancestor becomes the progenitor of profane life. Isis, the mother/ wife, symbolizes feminine power. We should bear in mind that the ancient African mother is different from the one who dominates mythic life in what became Europe. Isis is the offspring of Geb (Earth) and Nut (Sky). Geb is male; Nut, female. Their sex is reversed in the European myths such as the Greek and Roman ones, where Gaia (Earth) is female, and Ouranos (Sky) is male. In both versions, Sky is above Earth in the sexual act that produces divine offspring. The African version had the female above the male; the European placed her below him. The mythic theme of the African repetition of above and below is that the offspring of Geb and Nut would in some way be above the males. Thus Isis' role in the story of her relationship with her brothers Osiris and Set is active and powerful.

Isis and Osiris marry. Enraged, Set dismembers his brother Osiris multiple times, but Isis manages to find the pieces and reassemble them. Eventually Set devours most of Osiris (in some versions he feeds him to wild dogs), but Isis manages to secure the heart (in some versions, the penis), which she places into the Nile, where it becomes Horus. In another version, she bandages together the dismembered parts, thereby creating the first mummy, and becomes pregnant from coitus with the half-living body. In all versions of the myth, Osiris, during his periods of dismemberment, becomes a guide to the underworld. His various rebirths make him also a god of reincarnation. Horus exemplifies his final reincarnation, although this time as his son, who, by the way, also becomes the husband of his mother, Isis. Horus avenges Osiris through vanquishing Set.

Consider this myth now as we continue to unpack *Black Panther*. In order to become the Black Panther, T'Challa ritually drinks the brew of the heart-shaped herb and is buried in red soil; he visits with his father and the ancestors before awakening with his powers restored. This resurrection ritual eventually involves moving from soil to snow/water. Notice here the parallel to the familiar myth of Moses, the abandoned hero found by the riverbank. T'Challa is reborn as the Black Panther after being submerged in snow/water, which also, notably, makes him resemble a mummy. This is a crucial mythic element. T'Challa is in fact three manifestations of the Black Panther. The first is when he attempts to apprehend the killer of his father, who turns out to be Helmut Zeno in *Captain America: Civil War* (2016), the film in which the Black Panther makes his Marvel Cinematic Universe debut. The second is when he is reborn after his coronation through ritual battle. Both instances of resurrection occur after a burial in red soil, which connects to the founding ritual and both the Osiris resurrection myth and the myth of Geb, since all previous Black Panthers and he were placed into Father Earth below. The third, however, is different; he is reborn from water. He is really a *new* Black Panther—in effect, he is Horus grown from the shards in the river and the mountain snow.

It is significant that the soil is red. The Hebrew term for red soil is *adamah*, which means "blood-stained ground" or "red clay" and is the origin of the name Adam, meaning "human." T'Challa's mother, Romanda, is, in ancient mythic form, Isis. Romanda is the feminine version of "Rome," an adaptation of the Umbrian word *Rūma*, or "town of flowing rivers."

T'Challa's father, T'Chaka, in a line back to the first Black Panther, reiterated Osiris, but T'Challa is the manifestation of both Osiris and Horus, since Osiris is also the Black Panther; the process through which he is "born" as a leader is actually one of resurrection. The mother has her husband and her son in one, since the sacred consort was planted in the soil and the one aboveground who belongs to her is reborn from water. The result is the elimination of Set's temporary rule of Kmt/ancient Egypt/Wakanda.

Vibranium is also a symbol of *HqAw*, which, as we saw in our discussion of "power" in chapter 9, is the Kmt term for the life force through which even gods are animated. It also provides a form of legitimacy for the person who knows how to use it wisely, which requires *mAat* (breath, balance, health, justice, truth) against hubris. This myth brings to the fore one way *Black Panther* transcends the superhero-film model of vigilantism and individualized force. T'Challa embodies the Black Panther only when pursuing someone who has violated the laws of his country. When Nakia, Okoye, and he pursue the white South African villain Klaue in Seoul, South Korea, they are in fact working within the realm of law in pursuit of justice for their country. This theme challenges conceptions of Africanness and Blackness as intrinsically outside of law. That T'Challa takes the form of the Black Panther to pursue white men who violated Wakanda's laws means that he is not subsumed by white imperial justice, which asymmetrically allows whites to subordinate blacks to their laws but not vice versa.

The film therefore makes a distinction between strength and power. Super strength, achieved through a scientific energy source, does not entail power, which is instead achieved through character of leadership, the support of public opinion, and the general will of the people. The narrative thus distinguishes legitimate force from violence. The Black Panthers, except for the one embodiment of a tyrant, use their powers for justice, reparations, or addressing strife. Villainy comes from using instrumental force at the expense of others.

We come, then, to the distinction between politics and tyranny. Wakanda is a city-state with a federation of clans and an urban center. The "king" must go through a process of legitimation, but even after that the citizens of the country have a voice. The Wakandan "king," at least as exemplified by T'Challa and his ancestors, is contrasted with the tyrant N'Jadaka/Killmonger, who imposes an asymmetrical structure of power over the people. The name N'Jadaka has no origin. My best guess here is that it is a contraction of "Jade" and "aka," which could work if one imagines also-known-as-jade to signify his being born of royalty, since jade is also known as the "imperial gem." His villainous name Killmonger speaks for itself—a dealer or trader of death.

Curiously, "Erik" is an Old Norse name meaning "honored ruler." It also means to set in a straight line, to set the record straight. In the face of his orders, N'Jadaka the tyrant demands obedience and silence from them. There is a scene in which he grabs an elder by her neck and threatens to snap it if she fails to obey his orders.

A *political* leader is accountable to and affects the dignity of the people. This, in fact, troubles the notion of the "king" as a sovereign, since legitimacy rests with the will of the people. T'Challa always fights and makes decisions as part of a community, especially with female advisors, and communicates with the society's elders. N'Jadaka/Kill-monger, however, consults no one. In the dream world of his ancestors, T'Challa kneels and is told by his father to stand; Killmonger stands in the presence of his father, who sits.

To understand N'Jadaka before he became Killmonger, we must ask about his father in mythic terms. In addition to being a god of chaos or dismemberment, Set is also a god of secrecy; N'Jadaka's father, N'Jobu (Estonian name for "fool," "jerk," "loser"), was a spy and thus a man of secrecy. That element of his spirit is crystalized in his son, who also becomes a spy. Spies live multiple lives. Erik's include Killmonger and N'Jadaka. T'Chaka's reflexive decision to kill his brother to save Zuri, the Wakandan man sent to spy on N'Jobu and protect Wakanda's secrets, sets the tragedy in motion. "Zuri," by the way, is a Swahili female name meaning "beautiful." T'Chaka's killing his brother was no doubt a traumatic experience; his decision to conceal his actions, and failure to address that trauma, dooms it to return in the next generation. Secrecy has political consequences. The culminating struggle is over the people of Wakanda's voice being public or private. Wakandans, under T'Challa's model of leadership, expect a public or open voice; N'Jadaka/Killmonger's rule demands his voice only.

An issue about N'Jobu and T'Chaka, N'Jadaka's father and uncle, that is more complicated is what to make of avowed claims. N'Jobu was selling Wakandan technology to Klaue, a white supremacist. For anyone who thinks otherwise, note that he repeatedly calls black people, including Wakandans, "savages." How is N'Jobu, then, fighting for black liberation by doing such a thing? His motives appear more like resentment; after all, his brother, T'Chaka, was the official Black Panther or leader of Wakanda.

Spying is crucial to this political drama. Spies can become whatever their superiors or targets prefer them to be; the slippery N'Jadaka/Killmonger, as a special operative of the United States, has to earn the people of Wakanda's trust—although he makes no further effort to do so after delivering the body of Klaue.

This observation about spies makes Nakia a complicated character, since she, too, is a spy. Her character is established at the outset—her first appearance in the midst of a mission to rescue enslaved women, girls, and boys in Nigeria.

Throughout the film, spies exhibit extraordinary linguistic abilities. They can speak *locally* almost everywhere, as Nakia demonstrates when she speaks fluent Korean in Seoul. Spies know how to present themselves as working on behalf of anyone who holds power. Thus, the speeches of N'Jadaka/Killmonger must be taken with circumspection. He does not necessarily want to liberate black people; he wants to rule over Wakandans and everyone else. Remember, his declared aim is global imperialism under his leadership. If liberation were his goal, wouldn't he want future Black Panthers to rise, if even as his descendants?

I very much doubt N'Jadaka's plans for the rest of Africa and the diaspora are any different from what he has unleashed on Wakanda. It's also not clear if the factions to whom he sends the weapons are freedom fighters or warlords.

With regard to black consciousness, the question is raised about what N'Jadaka sees when he looks at not only Wakandans but also all black people. Recall that in a crucial scene, he lifts one of the female elders by her neck and threatens to snap it if she fails to heed his command to burn the remaining heart-shaped herbs. What are black people in his eyes?

Killmonger brings the problem of "niggerization" into Wakanda, where the identity of Wakandan as "human" offers dignity. However Wakandans see themselves, they need to take heed of powerful white-dominated countries invested in the ongoing production of "niggers," even if they now call themselves "niggas."

T'Challa and N'Jadaka's conflict also serves as an allegory of conservatism or the right, progressivism or the constructive left, and anarchic destruction, chaos, or the destructive left. These distinctions arise from how people respond to moments of crisis.

The origin of the word "crisis" is the Greek verb *krinein*, which means "to decide" or "choose." Situations that call for decisive action are "critical." In the face of crises, some people seek certainty, order, and security, sometimes through tradition, sometimes by turning to an idealized past. This is the conservative response. In contrast, the left believes that the past was never perfect; progressives see a long chain of previous efforts to make things better. The past, then, serves as the foundation for an ongoing project of improvement, a process through which a future is cultivated and some elements are discarded. This involves change, risk, and uncertainty, which affect how people think of time. Fanon offers this poignant reflection on such attitudes:

> Memory is often the mother of tradition. Now, if it is good to have a tradition, it is also agreeable to be able to go beyond that tradition and invent a new mode of living. Someone who considers that the present is worthless and that our sole interest lies with the past is, in a sense, a person who is lacking two dimensions and on whom you cannot count. Someone who deems that you must live with all your might in the here and now and that you do not have to worry about tomorrow or yesterday can be dangerous, since he believes that each minute is severed from the minutes that follow or precede it, and that he is the only person on this planet. Someone who turns away from the past and the present, who dreams of a distant future, both desirable and desired, is also deprived of the opposite everyday terrain on which one must act to accomplish the future sought-for. You thus see that a person always has to take into account the present, past, and future.[13]

Uncertainty means that positive change could happen right away, tomorrow, or after years, centuries, or millennia—or never. Many on the right would prefer to reach now for what was rather than to face uncertainty. This places right-wing leadership, which appeals to authenticity and homogeneity, at an advantage in moments of crisis. Plurality and heterogeneity are difficult to manage; practices of exclusion and suffering, which invariably lead to harm, are always easier and faster to achieve.

Turning toward the future leads to the question of responsibility over the actions that bring about change. For the right, the question is what people will be willing to give up for immediate security; if the answer is nearly all their liberties, the result is fascism. For the left, the question is what one is willing to give up for freedom. If the answer is order and security, the extreme case would be anarchy.

Black Panther is an allegory of how strength or prowess could lead to tragic results, despite avowed good intentions. Bashenga, the first Black Panther, transformed strength into power by uniting the warring factions into one country, which maintained a relationship with the one faction that refused to participate (the Jabari). Subsequent Black Panthers adopted an isolationist policy and, ultimately, conservatism, despite Wakanda's technological innovations. The new Black Panther finally rises as the spiritual synthesis of the first, as he overcomes the hatred and resentment of the destructive foe. This new Black Panther faces uncertainty and questions of Afrofuturity and Afromodernity, yet he reaches out to the world despite the risks.

Disillusioned by his father's imperfection, T'Challa realizes that the greatest leader of Wakanda was not T'Chaka but the first Black Panther, Bashenga. The name is made up, but closest to the Arabic "Bashir," which means "the one who brings good news." If the name is conjoined with *shenga* or *śēṅga*—a Marathi word for a pod or legume—we also gain an allusion to the heart-shaped herb. I doubt the authors realized this, but myth always draws from submerged myths, and its meanings are fecund.

T'Challa learns a version of Fanon's insightful observation: "Each generation must, in relative opacity, discover its mission, fulfill it, or betray it."[14] Other Black Panthers lost their way, perhaps through a form of Wakandan nationalism. They failed to see that the role of leadership is not only protecting one's people but also nurturing their growth, which requires reaching beyond the self to the outside world. The youth, creativity, and technological savvy embodied by T'Challa's precocious, ingenious sister Shuri, who in the comics becomes a future incarnation of the Black Panther, support this conclusion. That T'Challa takes on Bashenga's example instead of that of the other Black Panthers, including T'Chaka, means he is thinking about a different future. Simply put, conservative Wakanda preserves the past and seeks order and security; left-wing or progressive Wakanda, which was there in its origins, addresses the uncertainty of possibility and a different future. An imperial Wakanda would be right-wing, since it would seek its security through ruling the world. All this is paradoxical, since looking to Bashenga is a form of nostalgia, but understanding his example means not fetishizing him, and thus transcending him. Bashenga, after all, did not have a precedent; he had to look forward while maintaining awareness of the conflicts he quelled.

The Wakandans do not trust white people, but they do not trust black or any other kind of people either. They trust *individuals*. We see this in what cultivates their trust. Zuri trusts T'Chaka because that Black Panther saved his life at the expense of his own brother's; he repays that debt by sacrificing himself to save T'Challa. Everett Ross, who is controversial because he is both white and a CIA agent, earns T'Challa's and Nakia's trust by taking a bullet for Nakia, and he was unaware of Wakandan medical technology. Still, the Wakandans' lack of trust in white people leads to the question of why the writers added Ross to the comic and included him in the movie. The psychologist Mikhail Lyubansky offers this explanation:

> If [Klaue] is the representation of white supremacy, then Ross is the comforting antithesis. He not only likes and respects T'Chaka's son, T'Challa (the Black Panther) but essentially earns his "pass" by stepping in front of a bullet to save one of T'Challa's guards.
>
> Though in many ways, Ross essentially functions as a reverse "magic negro"—a character whose sole purpose seems

to be to promote the well-being of the lead (in this case, black) characters—he is also an avatar, an audience surrogate who represents the way the Panther is perceived by well-meaning white men (and women).

In the words of Ross's creator, Christopher Priest, "Comics are traditionally created by white males for white males. I figured, and I believe rightly, that for *Black Panther* to succeed, it needed a white male at the center, and that white male had to give voice to the audience's misgivings or apprehensions or assumptions about this character."[15]

As this is a fictional universe governed by Marvel's drive for sequels and crossover stories of Marvel characters, subsequent developments could change the material on which this white-token interpretation of Ross is based. For our purposes, it should be clear that the Wakandans' trust, at least in the film, must be earned.

Yet, through the thrice-resurrected T'Challa's leadership, Wakandans introduce their technology directly to the black youths of the Oakland projects, and they even offer to share some with the dignitaries of the United Nations. By way of that final ironic scene, Wakanda stands as a challenge to the racist "not out of Africa" thesis (that is, nothing positive comes out of Africa), raising the question of what Africa could offer the world if it were seen with open eyes.[16] Innovation need not always take the European form. As Okoye remarks, guns are "so primitive."

Not only Africans but also members of the African diaspora are critically intelligent in this movie, and they exemplify that trait through political virtue, intelligence (especially technological), and ethical virtues (courage, fidelity, integrity). Even where they are not virtuous, they are still intelligent. It is Killmonger's anger that is his downfall, but his intelligence is never brought into question.

Black women in the film have high self-esteem, skills, brilliance, beauty, and creativity, and they are sexy without being sexualized. Romanda, T'Challa's mother and the Isis figure, is one example. But there are so many others. Nakia exemplifies the virtue of language and courage through her work in reconnaissance; Shuri is not just a prodigy but also a genius (the most intellectually gifted person in the Marvel universe);[17] and General Okoye is the epitome not only of courage and military leadership but also of intelligence, as she is always assessing a given situation strategically, tactically, and politically.

Black men in the film have dignity, skills, beauty, and creativity, without being structurally subservient or lascivious; they, too, are sexy without being sexualized. They are also complicated in their rivalry, as each manifests special skills and aspirations. The "good" characters in the film are all fighters of one kind or another, and the "bad" characters are not simplistic. Each can be measured against what Richard Wright wrote about Bigger Thomas, the anti-hero protagonist of his classic novel *Native Son*.[18]

Wright outlined five manifestations of Bigger Thomas: Bigger 1 is the bully who coerces other blacks to concede his superiority. Bigger 2 is the black who challenges white authority and lives as he pleases but who, Wright confesses, "was in prison the last time I heard from him." Bigger 3 is the proverbial "bad nigger"; he takes advantage of fellow blacks and defies the law. His fate is death, often at the hands of the police. Bigger 4 is more complicated; he plays with proverbial fire in his efforts to outwit whites and avoid being exploited. His fate, if he is not killed or incarcerated, is madness. Bigger 5 is another "bad nigger," but unlike Bigger 3, who persecutes other blacks, he challenges whites. Among blacks, Bigger 5 stimulates "an intense flash of pride," Wright observes. Bigger 5's fate, however, is often the same as Bigger 3's.

Although Bigger Thomas is a man, Bigger could also be a woman. The anti-lynching activist Ida B. Wells-Barnett, the revolutionary anarchist Lucy Parsons, the communist activist Claudia Jones, the civil and human rights activist Ella Baker, the former Black Liberation Army activist Assata Shakur, and the prison abolitionist Angela Y. Davis are exemplars of Bigger 5. Winnie Madikizela-Mandela, the second wife of Nelson Mandela, could be added to this list, although there would be much debate over which Bigger she represents, especially given her reputation for having also harmed the powerless. What these women have in common is not only their fearlessness but also their anti-imperial commitments.

N'Jadaka/Killmonger's false binary—that one must conquer or be conquered—makes it clear that he is no Bigger 5. Though angry, and *rightfully so*, he is not Bigger 4, since he was clearly exploited as a special agent. He is, at best, Bigger 3. Fanon, writing on decolonization and the postcolonial bourgeoisie, wrote that these inheritors of power often ignored the goal of building infrastructures for freedom. Their aims turned out to be simple: they wanted to take the place of those who dominated them. As with N'Jadaka/Killmonger, this meant that their only continued source of legitimacy was to hold their nation hostage to the violence amid which their style of leadership was most in demand.

Failing to see his body become dust and blown to the wind, N'Jadaka/Killmonger could always, as in the comic books or in the world of myth, return. Indeed, even if his corpse were turned to ash, that would not rule out his return in that fictional multiverse of human beings, superhuman beings, gods, and who knows what else to come. This raises a central question of governance for his admirers. Under whose *rule* would they prefer to live, should he return?

A question to consider is whether T'Challa is Bigger 5, since he does not fear whites. The same question pertains to the other Wakandans, especially the women who accompany him on his missions. But Bigger 5, per Wright, is the product of alienation imposed by Euromodernity. Wakanda has self-imposed isolation, facilitated by its cloaking technology; it stands outside Euromodernity, with its citizens observers of the horrors of colonialism and racism. Its relationship to the rest of the world is asymmetrical, setting Wakandans outside the framework of white and antiblack recognition.

Recall Fanon's theorem of antiblack racism: "A normal black child, having grown up with a normal family, will find himself [or herself] abnormal from the slightest contact with the white world."[19] It is clear that various Black Panthers and Wakandan spies have made contact with the white world over the centuries. Were they, then, abnormal? Can T'Challa, given his contact with whites, remain normal in Wakandan terms?

The nature of that contact is crucial. In every instance, Wakandans are *agents*. Bigger Thomases result from the frustration of agency. They suffer from the low glass ceiling imposed over their ambitions, one that doesn't equally limit whites and other nonblack populations. For Wakandans to become any of the Bigger Thomases, such limitations must be imposed upon them.

T'Challa suffers from ambivalence; his freezing in battle when he sees Nakia foreshadows the eventual hibernation he must endure. When he resurfaces, he is prepared for the long struggle his people and he will now take on through their contact with the wider world, much of which is saturated with condescension and disdain for black people.

The film is a critique of contemporary global turns to the right, to fascism and xenophobia. T'Challa's closing speech at the UN is a clear refutation of the likes of former U.S. president Donald Trump and his supporters. Barriers, T'Challa declares, need to be broken down, not built up.

N'Jadaka's death at sunset also marks the beginning of T'Challa's new era of leadership, which also brings different ways of meeting conflict. Instead of "conquer or be conquered," an alternative stratagem is to destroy that false dilemma—that is, to reject conquest and build a world in which dignity, freedom, and respect can be gained without it.

At the release of *Black Panther*—and the writing of this critique—many liberal democracies are struggling for their legitimacy, which is equally laughable as tragic, as imbeciles ascended to governance in their two most recent representatives of global imperial power: the United Kingdom and the United States. Having presumed themselves triumphant at the end of the Cold War, and having ruled the world with military might and economic force, the two Anglo powers failed to see that China and Russia continued to fight by other means. Information warfare proved far more damaging to the credibility and effectiveness of the United States and the U.K., and the European Union is jeopardized by rising fascism as France and Germany try to hold it together. In the meantime, China looks at Africa and Australia as investments for its future, and Russia regards the countries of Africa in particular as a possible site of military opposition to China. Where they will eventually face off depends on whether African countries can develop viable strategies to articulate their future beyond the dictates of such imperial forces.[20] In the meantime, the devastation wreaked by the COVID-19 pandemic brought forth crises of justification in the United States and the U.K. and countries whose harsh policies against social services make the police and military the bases of their claim to legitimacy.

T'Challa's decision to build Wakandan centers across the globe might not be the altruistic gesture that proponents of black liberation would at first interpret it to be. Building Confucius Institutes was, after all, part of China's strategy of global ascent. Legitimacy achieved through understanding, rather than force, may be more effective. This model of world citizenship was also advanced by the U.S. national security experts who authored *A Strategic Narrative* (2011). The authors' advice to the United States, ignored for the most part, is to become a better citizen of the world. Their reasoning was that being a bad neighbor investing primarily in its military is not sustainable.

In a similar vein, T'Challa recognizes the importance of taking on a global political consciousness. Fanon, little more than half a century earlier, recommended going beyond Europe and building new institutions and ideas for a new humanity.

We already know that "black" meant something entirely different in Wakanda than the negative connotations forged by the age of Euromodernity that left the fictional country unscathed. In Wakanda, "black," associated with its totemic panther, is positive. It is not a construction of white supremacy and thus need not necessarily be the overcoming of a negation.

Killmonger, however, brought the question of negation to the center of Wakandan society—he actually is, as my son Elijah quipped, "the African American Panther." Elijah was making fun of race evasion marked by efforts of ethnicization, as when an American refers to an African politician like the late South African president Nelson Mandela as "African American." But the use of "African American" as a metonym for all African peoples and their diaspora, or all black peoples, also demonstrates the imperial reach of U.S. norms. The importation of U.S. black consciousness to African countries is full of contradictions. Africans in Africa are racialized in countries where they are not only Indigenous people but also the vast majority. This majority status enabled many African communities to maintain their ethnic diversity, including keeping their Indigenous languages alive. In the Caribbean, majority black countries face different political realities from U.S. blacks while sharing the experience of not being the Indigenous people. But in countries such as Australia, Canada, India, Pakistan, the United States, and all of those in Europe, black consciousness is a distinct minority perspective on those societies, and each country has a unique history because of elements such as slavery in the United States, indigeneity in Australia, and immigration from the colonies as a distinct feature of the majority of blacks in Europe. The hegemonic status of the United States centers its black experience over all these countries', including those in Africa, the Caribbean, South Asia, and South America. Killmonger's request to be buried at sea with his ancestors marks his origin, through his mother, in the Middle Passage and the horrors that continued through enslavement, Jim Crow, and ongoing racism. One could wonder if he is reborn from water, would he no longer be Killmonger?

The irony is that Black Panther, the character, is not an African creation, nor even an African American one, but the brainchild of European Jewish Americans, descendants of people intimately linked to both diaspora and the foundations of race. Kirby and Lee struggled with their tenuous whiteness, and their creation, mediated by the cinematic creativity of screenwriters Coogler and Cole, was brought to the screen in an African-Jewish creolized and dialectical offering with its own imperfect suggestions of what could be. This phenomenon is not unique to the world of fiction. Historically, a similar fusion was a step toward self-determination in transforming untouchability in South Asia, where "Dalit" is a term not imposed upon but instead formulated from the people themselves: "'Dalit' is the only name which the Black Untouchables of India have given themselves. Its root word is 'Dal,' which in Hebrew means broken, crushed."[21] Rejecting the Brahmanic

Hindi, the Dalits used the language of an ancient people whose under-standing of calling is *Tikkun olam*—repairing the world.

Wakanda begins with its own consciousness of blackness, encoun-ters a Euromodern-affected black consciousness, and asks for nothing less than an African-creolized relation that can live with a new kind of Black consciousness: one committed to no longer remaining the same.

PART IV

EVEN WHEN BLACK AND BLUE

How difficult it must be

To bring light to the world
Emanating love
Behind which
Stands loneliness

Do not despair
Physical distances
Can always be bridged
By longings of the heart

—Author's poem

11

BLUE

The battering of colonized people over the past five hundred years has left many black and blue. Abuse can choke the soul with the spirit of seriousness. The march of Black consciousness, accompanied by black consciousness, is a struggle for freedom, a struggle for breath. Even though for black consciousness life is posed as already foreclosed, invisible beyond the eyes of antiblack society—it yearns for possibility. Resentful, it sometimes cries; understanding, it knows the value of its tears. In the context of the United States, black consciousness inaugurated its path to Black consciousness through transforming reflection and sorrow into the blues. This is a form of awakened play, taking responsibility for the rules by which we live and releasing them from the bonds of seriousness. This, along with antiracist or decolonized education, is a pathway to political action and building institutions devoted to dignity, freedom, and social health.

Amiri Baraka wrote a work of love devoted to this sensibility under the title *Blues People*.[1] It's a testament to Black challenges to Euro-modern practices of dehumanization. Blues music and lyrics address dissonance and responsibility, and let forth a wail in which the blues poets and singers cry, despite it all, that their lives matter. The dehumanization of black people—not only by being forced into the status of property and stigmatized labor but also by subjection to the legacies of this presumption of subhuman status—leads many to interrogate what it means to be human. It makes sense that people who were enslaved, colonized, and disenfranchised would reflect on the meaning of free-dom and liberation. It also makes sense that self-justification would be a concern for people whose efforts to interrogate their condition are frequently met with insinuations about their supposed lack of intellec-tual capacity to do so.

Racist societies have devised mechanisms of not-mattering for many groups of people. Their tenuous foundations even delude many whom they claim matter more than others. This is because many of the rationalizations of racist societies are misanthropic; they degrade hu-manity. This degradation, among other existential challenges, makes blacks, as representatives of degradation, produce a powerful leitmotif: the blues.

The blues is a form of black music. It is also a mode and a mood beyond musical performance—the musical form itself, in other words, is an expression of the blues. The artistic creation of Africans who were degraded by European colonization and enslavement and who struggled to articulate their condition, the blues is at times presumed "particular" to black people, but a better understanding of black lives in antiblack societies offers a different conclusion. The realization that negative views of black people are *imposed* demands that they be jus-tified, a demand that itself refutes negative black self-consciousness as the culmination of black consciousness. The logical response to a false consciousness, posed as universal, is to seek what transcends it, and regardless of what alternative one is able to find, there is already achievement in liberation from that false reality. Where a supposed universal is unattainable, that very inaccessibility is shared by all. This, of course, is a paradox: a universal lack of access to a universal.

The message should now be obvious. The blues, as black music, may actually be more universal than other kinds of music proposed as universal. This comparison, however, is like contrasting apples and oranges without remembering the nutritional value of both. For those to whom a kind of music, mode of thought, or mood connects, do they ultimately care whether their source of joy is universal? Many do, but others—perhaps most—don't.

Blues music helps us think about the blues that fueled it. What is behind Louis Armstrong's lamentation when he sings Fats Waller's "(What Did I Do to Be So) Black and Blue" (1929) and Ralph Ellison's ruminations on it in *Invisible Man*?[2] There is so much battered blackness in blue.

The blackness that contextualizes the blues is a peculiar misery borne of a struggle for existence gone mad. Euromodern racism, based on the expansion of an old theological order into a global secular one, led to whole groups of people having to ask, "In reality, who am I?" Generalized, this becomes "What are we?"[3] Unpacked, the question returns us to the problem of justification: "What is the meaning of who and what we are?" Or, "Are we, given who and what we are, supposed to be here?" And, made plain, "What is the meaning of black suffering?"

We have seen that black consciousness faces a problem of legitimacy and the melancholia born from that problem. To be black in this sense is to be rejected from normative life in antiblack societies, even while being indigenous to them. As there was no reason for people to consider themselves black in racist terms before that understanding of blackness was brought into being, all Euromodern blacks face the condition of not belonging to the only world in which we could possibly be indigenous. The resulting condition of black consciousness in the Euromodern world is nothing less than the blues.

But why invoke the color blue and not any other? Addressing that question, the rock musician and author Debra Devi speculates that the phrase originated with the seventeenth-century English expression "the blue devils," eventually shortened to "the blues," which referred to the intense effects, even hallucinations, associated with severe alcohol withdrawal.[4] This account does not explain, however, why "the blue devils" were indeed blue. Blue, after all, might refer to something positive, such as the expression "blue skies ahead."

The African American Jewish curator and historian Catherine E. McKinley points to the use of blue among West African ethnic groups, where bright blue signifies royalty, and indigo is used for mourning.[5]

The blues was born when Africans and Europeans converged in the new world under conditions of misery that reverberate through the present. This adds a dimension, perhaps psychoanalytical, to the "blue devils" theory: the high of Euromodern global exploitation and profit wreaked the low of the hangover humanity is now enduring. To these interpretations, we could add the initial color of bludgeoned skin, which is sometimes literally and always idiomatically black and blue.

An antiblack society, in attempting to overcome its contradictions and to make itself complete and one with itself, nurtures an obsession with completeness. This produces in nonblack people childlike expectations that the world will be consistent and neat; meanwhile, for black people who cannot avoid reality, these circumstances produce an adult awareness of the paradoxes, contradictions, and life's unfair burdens. In other words, the blues.

The blues tells us that what is rational is not always reasonable. Racism, as those who suffer it understand, is never reasonable but always offers itself as coldly logical and rational. As Fanon puts it:

> The racist in a culture with racism is . . . normal. He has achieved a perfect harmony of economic relations and ideology in his environment. . . . In fact, race prejudice obeys a flawless logic. A country that lives, draws its substance from the exploitation of other peoples, makes those peoples inferior. Race prejudice applied to those peoples is normal.[6]

Others, those who do not belong, are always supposedly in the wrong. Realizing this pleasing falsehood for most whites is a lie would give everyone in antiblack societies cause to sing the blues. The self-deception of living with ongoing injustice, if one claims to uphold justice, requires enormous energy. Fanon, ironically, faced such a situation in his early reflections on the blues. As he concludes:

> Thus the blues, "the slave lament," is presented for the admiration of oppressors. It is some stylized oppression returned to the exploiter and the racist. There is no blues without oppres-

sion and racism. The end of racism is the death knell of great black music.[7]

Born from racial suffering, the blues, according to Fanon, could be maintained only by that continued suffering. Whites listening to the blues are entertained by the suffering caused by the world created for their benefit. This argument suggests that identification with an aesthetic production such as blues music requires awareness of and connection to the source of the pleasure it brings. Many people, however, not only enjoy music that is not intimately linked to their personal experience; they also freely attach their own experiences to music influenced by others' vastly different experiences. Another person's misery could be artistically personalized and enjoyed without incorporating one's own personal suffering. As Kierkegaard writes of the poet:

> An unhappy man who in his heart harbors a deep anguish, but whose lips are so fashioned that the moans and cries which pass over them are transformed into ravishing music. His fate is like that of the unfortunate victims whom the tyrant Phalaris imprisoned in a brazen bull, and slowly tortured over a steady fire; their cries could not reach the tyrant's ears so as to strike terror into his heart; when they reached his ears they sounded like sweet music. And men crowd about the poet and say to him, "Sing for us soon again"—which is as much as to say, "May new sufferings torment your soul, but may your lips be fashioned as before; for the cries would only distress us, but the music, the music is delightful."[8]

Kierkegaard's description points to the beauty of poetry and music born of suffering. He does not say why the reader or listener is able to experience the joy or identify the beauty. There must be something that *connects* the audience to the performance. After all, it's not only black people who sing the blues and listen to it. There are nonblack people listening to the blues in Australia, Brazil, China, India, Italy, South Korea, Portugal, Russia, Serbia, Spain, Sweden—everywhere—

and I very much doubt that all of them are relishing the suffering of black people. They are probably not imagining themselves as enslaved blacks on cotton, sugarcane, or tobacco plantations or those occupying prison cells in unfair criminal justice systems, any more than the Brahman would imagine being among the lowest caste of Southwest Asian society, the Dalits.

Understanding the lived reality of the damned of the earth requires transitioning to potentiated double consciousness of the societal conditions that degrade them. While emerging from black suffering, the blues speaks to suffering through the challenges of Euromodern life and its concomitant antiblackness. It speaks to anyone confronting the entrails of living in such societies. Ellison puts it this way:

> The blues is an impulse to keep the painful details and episodes of a brutal experience alive in one's aching consciousness, to finger its jagged grain, and to transcend it, not by the consolation of philosophy but by squeezing from it a near-tragic, near-comic lyricism. As a form, the blues is an autobiographical chronicle of personal catastrophe expressed lyrically.[9]

The blues is about dealing with life's suffering in any form. Blackness speaks to contemporary life through the many musical descendants of the blues: swing, jazz, rhythm and blues, soul, rock 'n' roll, beguine, mambo, salsa, samba, rocksteady, reggae, calypso, the many styles of hip hop, and more.

Blues music is full of irony. Its sadness exemplifies an adult understanding of life that is sorrowful, sober, and sometimes happy. It is a non-delusional happiness often marked by self-deprecation and critical evaluation, the kind of happiness or good humor motivated by clear-eyed realization instead of diversion. It's the beauty of moonlight versus sunshine, although a sunny day can foster the blues—so much can hide in plain sight. If one seeks numbness in alcohol, the blues would tell you that numbness gets you nowhere.

The blues reminds us that life is not something to escape but some-

thing to face. And it does so in its very form. The classical blues structure is full of repetitions that reveal new layers of meaning about the
cyclicality of life. And in this structure, although a story is retold, it is
understood at different levels with each retelling, the effect of which
is cathartic, provoking a renewed understanding of the beginning.
Blues artists take responsibility for their existence, and in so doing can
also transcend their present in flights of shared imagination. This dimension of blues performance, especially in bebop music, did not always amuse white patrons of exoticized blackness, an observation that
Fanon did not fail to notice. He reflects with delight:

> A memorable example, and one that takes on a certain impor-
> tance because it is not entirely about a colonial reality, was the
> reaction of white jazz experts when after the Second World
> War new styles such as bebop established themselves. Jazz
> could only be for them the broken, desperate nostalgia of an
> old "nigger," taken with five whiskeys, cursing himself and the
> racism of the whites. As soon as he understands himself and
> the world differently, as soon as he raises hope and forces the
> racist world to recoil, it is clear that he will blow his trumpet
> to his heart's content and his husky voice will ring out loud
> and clear.[10]

Fanon is responding to the musical dexterity and complexity of bebop. Performances of bebop music—sometimes played so fast that white
Euro-classical musicians thought the records were being spun at the
wrong speed—often challenged what most non-jazz musicians thought
impossible to perform. There are also harmonic variations, with subtle
use of dissonance, that rose the music to levels of art instead of entertainment. Antiblack racism relaxes when black people are reduced to
entertainment instead of the challenge and complexity of art. Bebop
transcends the misery of stereotypical blackness, which is exoticized
and fetishized by white critics and consumers of black performance,
by raising the standards in virtuoso flights of imagination. It offers a

triple threat to white supremacy. It's not imitation; it demonstrates an overwhelming history of black artistic achievement, beyond the potential of most whites participating in the genre; and it's independent of white recognition. Whites who perform bebop enter a world in which the highest standards are Black. The scale of achievement not only in bebop but also in many other forms of jazz is still being deciphered, as the theoretical physicist and saxophonist Stephon Alexander explains in his analysis of John Coltrane's "Giant Steps" (1960) and the double helix.[11] No matter how much those early critics hated it, bebop musicians continued working on the artistic potential of the music without regard to its commercial value. If it produced "hits," such as Dizzy Gillespie's "A Night in Tunisia" (1942) and "Groovin' High" (1945) or Charlie Parker's "Confirmation" (1946) and "Yardbird Suite" (1946), great. If it didn't, to channel a Miles Davis title: So what?

Yet, with respect to Fanon, we should not dismiss the blues' wails and moans. Evading suffering is neither mature nor wise. The blues' reflective expression of suffering brings understanding. The blues transitions, in other words, from pre-reflective experience to self-reference, self-assessment, and self-transcendence.

This means that the blues reveals an aspiration manifested beautifully in bebop and its other musical descendants—an aesthetic and ethical maturity in which the question of political life is never ignored. This music comes from societies in which the dominant sentiment is that black people have no point of view, and even if one is expressed, it's at best childlike. This is one of the goals of racism—disempowerment from political institutions through to levels of aesthetic expression. To produce music in which the lives and aspirations of black people matter—and to do so at a level of musical virtuosity that few white performers can match—is already an affront to antiblack racist society. This political element is present in the international offshoots of the blues. In Brazil, it's in samba and other consciously Black Afro-Brazilian forms, such as the fusions found in Milton Nascimento's music. The blues' political critique is there in reggae, that outgrowth of ska and rocksteady. From the Abyssinians to the Heptones, the Melodians, the Wailers, and many other artists, reggae began with dance rhythms and later articulated protest and critique in its own fusions; nearly every country has its own style of reggae. On the African continent, other forms of the blues offer distinct kinds of political critique; in Nigeria, the Yorùbá multi-artist and freedom fighter Fela Anikulapo Kuti's is a great example.

In his philosophical memoir, the South African philosopher Mabogo P. More reflects that jazz, especially bebop, and music intimately connected to its ethos, was a source of inspiration and affirmation for many of his fellow black South Africans and him while growing up under the brutal apartheid system.[12] Despite the messages they received of white supremacy and black inferiority, in jazz, a creation of black people taking the stage as Black, was one in which whiteness was ultimately *not* the standard. Additionally, how jazz musicians dressed and stood on the stage was striking: no jazz artist of African descent exemplified being a "boy" or "girl." One was always listening to a man or a woman, even when the artist was a teenager.

But More's observation raises one thorny issue in contemporary discussions of Black music. There is always a market for those willing to pull Black back into black; back into "negro" and "nigger." This is unfortunately a pervasive feature of recent popular music, where black instead of Black music is preferred, in which the end goal is entertainment and not political or even philosophical or artistic. The problem with Black music, from the perspective of a music industry dominated by white-market tastes, is that it is supposedly not "authentic." This is a coded way of saying that it doesn't match the stereotypes sought by predominantly white consumers. There is, as well, the view that authentic blackness could be marked only by suffering. Consider, however, this: suffering stinks. Put another way, it's *funky*. That term now of course refers to dance music that moves the body so as to release the funk, a form of cathartic purging of the soul or, more crudely, a fart. "Let it out!" is its credo, and dancers move their lower abdomen, hips, and buttocks, in multiple meanings of released excrement and orgasm. And while catharsis can be healthy, attachment to it can ironically lead to rigidity. Play, which can be a critical activity, then becomes pure entertainment, which is amusement without reflection. Where blackness is solely entertainment, minstrelsy is soon to follow.

Entertainment is also, as we have seen, a model of black consciousness easily accessible to white reverie, imitation, and theft. Into the first decade of hip hop, the group Run-DMC anticipated this problem in the music video for "It's Tricky" (1987). The song is about how rapping is not as easy to do as people think, and the video depicts the group's mistake of teaching their craft to two white hustlers after outwitting them at three-card monte in the streets. The video begins with an African American woman being hoodwinked out of her gold jewelry, a clear allusion to gold stolen from Africa. At the end of the video, Run-DMC show up to their gig in Japan to discover that not only are the two white hustlers on the stage posing as them, but the Japanese audience believes the white hustlers are the *real* Run-DMC.

Back in the mid-2000s I wrote an essay on problems of maturity in hip hop that garnered some critical reaction from my students, many of whom later came to confess agreement with my argument.[13] I had asked what would come out of hip hop as bebop came out of swing music. My point was not to measure hip hop by the standards of bebop, but to raise a critical question faced by both—namely, artistic growth or maturation. Hip hop artists often perform a valorization of authentic blackness as perpetual adolescence, and so does the market commodification of the genre: black people, to be authentic, must supposedly never grow up. Ensnaring black people in perpetual adolescence as a mark of authenticity is the return of the patronization against which many Black revolutionaries protested and continue to work at eliminating.

Although the center of hip hop music is the United States, we should bear in mind that it is global, which means that how a problematic music industry packages what it deems authentic blackness affects black people everywhere. This packaging includes its history. What many proponents of the genre often elide is the multinational history of how hip hop was formed. It was organized by Anglophone and Hispanophone Caribbean peoples along with varieties of other Black youths converging in the Bronx in New York City. Many were Jamaicans; others, Puerto Ricans; and the range spanned from Barbadians and Trinidadians in the Caribbean to African Americans who spent their childhoods between New York and summertime with family members in the U.S. South and the Caribbean. Hip hop, in other words, varied widely from its inception. The stereotypical presentations of black authenticity through which it is marketed are indicative of decay. In this regard, hip hop followed a classic movement from lively ascent to hallmarks of—albeit not entirely so—decadence.

Nietzsche outlined the dialectics of aesthetic production that map out with uncanny accuracy developments in much contemporary music.[14] He argued that in the stage of creative development, music comes out of the chorus (the community) and is linked to the embodied affirmation of life in dance. It then transitions to self-absorption (the individual) in portraits of the ego and recession of the chorus. It descends eventually into a search for agency through the body (corporeality), often with a focus on gender, sex, and sexual pleasure.

The ancient Athenian expression of this movement was exemplified by the poets Aeschylus, Sophocles, and Euripides—think of the *Oresteia*, *Antigone*, and *The Bacchae*. Aeschylus is the eldest of the three, and Euripides the youngest. The *Oresteia* is a trilogy in which the first part tells the tragic story of the hero Agamemnon, who is murdered by his wife, Clytemnestra, and her lover, Aegisthus; the second, the *Choephoroi*, relates Agamemnon's daughter Electra and son, Orestes, slaying their mother and her lover; the third, the *Eumenides*, features Orestes' trial. The chorus and music are central features of all three. The ancient Athenian philosopher Socrates and the nineteenth-century German philosopher G.W.F. Hegel loved the Sophoclean tragedies, especially *Antigone*, which focuses on the conflict between Antigone (the daughter of former king Oedipus) and her maternal uncle, King Creon. The death of Oedipus led to civil war in which her brothers, Eteocles and Polynices, died in battle on opposing sides. Eteocles received ritual burial; Polynices, who opposed Creon, was left to be devoured by vultures. Antigone repeatedly buries Polynices, which leads to her trial and eventual condemnation to death. The chorus has a smaller role in that play than in the Aeschylean plays, and the main characters are wrapped in a conflict of obligations to the gods versus those to the state. Nietzsche saw *Antigone* as the beginning of the decline of classical Greek society. Succeeding it were the Euripidean plays, in which the plight of women was central. In *The Bacchae*, for example, the androgynous god Dionysus—god of drama, wine, and women—visits and tricks the young king Pentheus to dress as a woman to infiltrate the gods' female followers lost in ritual reverie. Pentheus' deception is revealed, and he is torn to pieces by the women, which include his mother, Agave. Critics in Nietzsche's time praised the Sophoclean plays as the highest artistic expression of what is known as Attic Greece, which was also marked by the flourishing of philosophy. Nietzsche read the transition from dance and the chorus to monologues and philosophical reflection and then to female-centered themes as a decline.

Turning to the present, the evolution of certain popular music forms such as rock 'n' roll, reggae, and hip hop reveals movements from dance music to a stage of critical and often self-referential protest to a release of libidinal forces in highly sexualized and often misogynous lyrics. The last is paradoxical because, as female-focused, there are critics who interpret it as also emancipatory and liberatory.

The parallels in the history of popular music are striking. Early rap came from the voice of the chorus over music devoted to dance. That early period, when the Sugarhill Gang's "Rapper's Delight" (1979) introduced rap to a wider audience, brought people to the dance floor. The next stage focused more on the experience of the individual rapper whose favorite words were "I," "me," and "my." Think here of KRS-One's "My Philosophy" (1988). I don't think KRS-One would object to this being the Socratic/Sophoclean stage since he identifies as a philosopher. This period also produced prescient social critique. The next stage featured the rise of female rappers such as Salt-N-Pepa, known for their highly sexual lyrics, alongside male performers obsessed with referring to women as "bitches" and "hos." Perhaps the best exemplar of the misogynist turn is the group 2 Live Crew. New styles reasserted themselves, but the cycle from dance to protest to sexual degradation and reverie returned. Artists such as Missy Elliott, TLC, and Outkast, for example, brought listeners back to their feet with wit and pizzazz. As the music is about much more than getting people to the dance floor or into bed, *Plantation Lullabies* (1993) and *Bitter* (1999), by Meshell Ndegeocello; *Black on Both Sides* (1999), by Mos Def (Yasiin Bey); and, in France, *Paradisiaque* (1997) and *Cinquième As* (2001), by the Senegalese rapper MC Solaar (Claude M'Barali) followed. More recently, there is Kendrick Lamar's oeuvre, which includes the lauded *To Pimp a Butterfly* (2015) and the Pulitzer Prize–winning *Damn* (2017). Yet the tradition continues, as Lamar's achievements are succeeded by Cardi B's "WAP" (2020), featuring Megan Thee Stallion, which, despite being from a female point of view, follows the formula of women and sex as a dialectical response to male political reflection.

Nietzsche also argued that art never sprouts from unfertile soil. That means it is never free of material economic and political forces. Contemporary music—of which rock 'n' roll, reggae, and hip hop are not the only varieties—evolved in a world necessarily characterized by capitalism, colonialism, and racism, all of which rally against any effort for art to stand beyond their reach. Nietzsche's conservatism may make him unsympathetic to these considerations, but his argument that music reflects the growth and decay of society make this material observation appropriate.

The descent into "niggerization" as a mark of authenticity is but one current that is, unfortunately, highly marketable to largely white audiences. The more decadent, the better. One could point out that jazz performances also often draw majority white audiences, but those audiences do not observe the self-deprecation of those on the stage. "Nigger," "nigga," and "nigguh" are not part of the jazz lexicon and are incompatible with jazz identity, whose performers also call it "African American classical music." Oddly enough, early rap recordings rarely used such invectives.

Where even politics can be commodified, the supposedly revolutionary potential of this kind of self-negating expression is able to find its audience and its market. Those who have fought the good fight

against racial self-deprecation have taken notice. Out of both frustration and love, some, such as the philosopher and poet Richard Jones,
issue a wake-up call:

> In 1959 it was niggrah please
> Git yo' lazy black ass offa de bus
> And then soon enuf it waz
> Neegrow please for da
> Econonomic gains and boogie-woogie bougie shit
> And den kneegrow pleas
> For *merci beaucoup* and
> Hippity hoppity down
> The bunny trail to
> Niggaz pleezee and wheezee
> Negro-ese easy peasee
> And shit for the Nigaratti
> Makes a nigger wanna go
> Crazy/home/back to Afrika/
> To da crib/fuck hisself/
> Loop-de-loop/eat chitlins/
> Go-go!!! Chuck Brown
> Go fist-bump and drag-a-leg
> *Niggah pa-leeze*!!![15]

An objection could be made about whether this critical comparison is an assertion of what is called "the politics of respectability."[16]
This is an attitude advanced by bourgeois black communities in which
their class sensibilities and values occlude poor black populations
whom they judge as uncouth. There is, however, a difference between
respectability and respect. Respectability at times leads to quiescence
when political conditions may require confronting antiblack society
for the sake of respect. Fighting an unjust society takes many forms, as
we saw in chapter 10 in our discussion of Richard Wright's portrait of
five kinds of challengers of the antiblack racist system, which he char-

acterized as Bigger Thomases. The various Bigger Thomases end up terrorizing their fellow blacks or getting killed by the police. The fifth, however, focuses on rejecting any system in which the only roles are conquering others or becoming conquered. That is the one with revolutionary import. Bigger 5's struggle is not built on self-degradation. That is why Sojourner Truth, Ida B. Wells-Barnett, Ella Josephine Baker, Claudia Jones, Amílcar Cabral, Frantz Fanon, El-Hajj Malik El-Shabazz (Malcolm X), and Steve Bantu Biko—all courageous freedom fighters who regarded themselves as fighting against cruel and unjust systems—are historic examples of Bigger 5.

To state the obvious, not all aesthetic productions are politically insightful and revolutionary—in other words, marked by maturation in their understanding of radical social change. Some are reactionary. Some valorize returning to a supposed authentic past. Others may call for burning everything down, which leaves no future for anybody. Some can be so self-absorbed that there is no room for others to make creative contributions to the growth of the art form. The political question for hip hop, then, is, whether maturity is offered where liberation is posed. To live perpetually as a counter-aesthetic—that is, simply being against white society—is a life of dependency, since whites would set the terms against which to react, which offers little short of pessimism and, worse, despair.

This is not to say that maturity and politically nuanced performances are impossible in hip hop—see the already mentioned list of Meshell Ndegeocello, Mos Def, and MC Solaar, and we could add the group the Roots, especially their album *Things Fall Apart* (1999), whose title is an homage to the great Nigerian Igbo writer Chinua Achebe, whose novel *Things Fall Apart* (1958) is the most read book in African literature. We could also consider the activist, musician, and filmmaker Boots Riley, who initially rose to fame with the politically critical group the Coup. In his 2018 film *Sorry to Bother You*, Riley brings into focus many of the themes and objections posed for hip hop as an ideal meeting of politics and art.

The challenge of maturation is that it requires transformation with the hope of growth. *Sorry to Bother You* addresses struggles for maturation in the claustrophobic context of contemporary capitalism. Recall that myth, from the Greek word *muthos* (which means "told" or "narrated from the mouth"), raises what must be told, which are not only stories but also their attendant rituals of repetition. Retelling brings forth the meaning beneath meaning; this is why we are often able to recognize a familiar story in what at first appears to be a new story, revealing the truth at work in its narrative. There is thus truth in fiction, where fictional stories reveal the lore we tell again and again.

One myth *Sorry to Bother You* retells is Carlo Collodi's novel *The Adventures of Pinocchio* (1883), no doubt more familiar to most moviegoers through the Disney retelling, simply entitled *Pinocchio* (1940).[17] One of the wooden puppet Pinocchio's adventures in his quest to become "a real boy" is most relevant here. In Collodi's novel, Pinocchio and friends put themselves in danger by venturing to the Land of Toys, called Pleasure Island in the Disney film. In both versions, children are lured there with the promise of pure license or liberty without responsibility. The unsuspecting children—in the novel they are boys and girls, but in the Disney version, only boys—devolve into donkeys and are then sold into slavery.

The second-century North African Roman Lucius Apuleius's *Metamorphoses*, most popularly known by Saint Augustine's preferred title *The Golden Ass*, explores similar themes of transformation: the protagonist Lucius is transformed into a donkey, is enslaved, and then suffers through a series of misadventures.[18] (The name Lucius, by the way, means "light," "clarity," as in "lucid," and also "man of light," which, incidentally, also means "white man.") Apuleius's novel is based on an earlier, now lost Greek work *Loúkios è ónos* ("Loukios or the Ass"). *Ónos* not only means "ass," as in a "donkey," but also "burden," as in "onus." The Greek version is itself likely based on a more ancient story probably originating in Kmt/ancient Egypt, where donkeys were first domesticated.[19]

Whether or not Boots Riley realized he was retelling an episode from the Pinocchio story or from *The Golden Ass*, the parallels in his film are undeniable: *Sorry to Bother You* is also about transformation, the exploitation of labor, and enslavement.

Riley uses all-too-obvious metaphors, metonyms, and plays on words to plant his clues. There is the nefarious corporation, Worry-Free, which offers a devil's bargain for a worry-free life. There's our protagonist Cassius Green ("cash green") and the villainous Steve Lift (likely Steve Jobs), with the name Lift here standing for employment without wages—"lift" as in theft. There's Squeeze, the union organizer, and Cassius's artist girlfriend, Detroit—in other words, the city where Riley grew up, a place devastated by neoliberal economic policies but making its comeback through activism, art, and urban agriculture. "Mr. ___" is a top telemarketer with one eye, a Cyclops. His one eye turns out to be his right one, a foil to the radical group called the Left Eye, which vandalizes WorryFree advertisements. There's Diana De-Bauchery, Langston (Langston Hughes, the great blues poet);[20] and Coke (both the cola and cocaine). The phrase "stick to the script" is also often repeated, which is the telemarketing motto for communicating social consumption and submission. And, of course, consider the title: "sorry to bother you" is not only an annoying telemarketing catchphrase but also a reference to the political reality of those who prefer to live, to borrow from Stanley Kubrick, with eyes wide shut.

The title is also a meta-cinematic self-reference to what the film is actually doing to its viewers. It breaks the fourth wall, speaking directly to the audience.

The movie begins as a garage door, behind which Cassius lives, opens unexpectedly to interrupt his morning intimacy with Detroit; it concludes with the door smacking him in the face as he attempts to shut out the world. What happens between the open and closed door is a process that begins with Cassius's search for employment, at first through deception. Cassius brings a large fake trophy to a telemarketing job interview, and he is offered the job despite—like Pinocchio's elongated nose—the exposure of his lies. This seems at first a stroke of good fortune, but one should always be careful about what one wishes for. The next stage of transformation occurs when Cassius opens the

door to success by using his "white voice." Next come questions of
class struggle, the racial and gendered elements of which become increasingly clear as the telemarketers organize. Cassius's transformation continues, as his white voice in black skin leads to his promotion
to "power caller" and his eventual discovery that workers are being
transformed into workhorses—half-man, half-horse monstrosities—
dubbed "equisapiens."

This movement is also reminiscent of a crucial understanding in
Marxism, which is all about social transformation. Marxism is critical
of valorized transformation for its own sake. Some kinds of transformations could involve the radicalization of enslavement. Revolution
requires responding to contradictions by changing the conditions that
maintain them.

Steve Lift offers Cassius the opportunity to become the "Martin Luther King, Jr.," of the equisapiens. He does not mean the historic political fighter Martin Luther King, Jr., who was assassinated in Memphis a
little more than a half century earlier while fighting for workers' rights
as part of his Poor People's Campaign. He means the King caricatured
and memorialized as a moralistic pacifist dreamer.

Despite Lift's efforts, the leader Cassius becomes is more like the
Dr. King whose affinities were with the revolutionary fighters Frantz
Fanon, El-Hajj Malik El-Shabazz (Malcolm X), and the boxer Muhammad Ali (formerly Cassius Clay)—that is, Bigger 5. Muhammad Ali is
especially pertinent here, since his "slave name" honored a white abolitionist. His life was also one of transformation, and as a fighter, he
also changed or rediscovered his religion through converting to Islam
and being anointed with names in Arabic that mean being praise-
worthy and most high, or, appropriately, worthy of praise from the
most high.[21]

Although Cassius Green at first thinks of himself as "woke" when
he joins the telemarketers' union, he naively expects that he will be able
to return to his community with modest reforms. When he attempts
to close the garage door on the world near the film's end, it smacks him
in the face and reveals the revolutionary community to which he actually belongs—the equisapiens—whether he likes it or not. His swollen,

equisapien nose reveals the bad faith, the lie, with which he was living, which was the expectation that deception would not change him.

Capitalism's quest to gobble up *everything* makes human beings an unfortunate inconvenience. The desire is for the maximization of profit, which requires taking away whatever might limit that goal—and that includes humanity. The fantasy is to replace workers with robots. The word "robot," by the way, is from the Czech *robota*, which means "forced labor" or "slave," which is striking since Czechs are a Slavic people. The word "slave" comes from "Slav."

The convergence of class, gender, and race imposes a cruel joke on the enslaved equisapiens. They are all males with large, *limp* penises. Theirs are penises but not phalluses; in psychoanalytical terms, the equisapiens lack power. Their penises are thus not erect or, alluding to their perverse creator, neither uplifted nor upright.

The characters Langston, Squeeze, and Detroit also provide provocative nuance. Recall Langston signifying Langton Hughes, the African American blues poet of the Harlem Renaissance. Hughes was part of the radical left. He was publicly supportive of the Communist Party USA, even though his biographers say he was not a formal member of the party. Hughes's literary achievements gave him access to white commodification, which he rejected through his political commitments. He was part of a group of left-oriented poets such as the Jamaican Claude McKay, the Cuban Nicolás Cristóbal Guillén Batista, and the Haitian Jacques Roumain, to name three. In the film, Langston functions as the Virgil to Cassius's Dante, leading the protagonist through limbo and the many levels of hell to see what he needs in order to be released from his fears and hatred, and thereby find his way out.[22] Langston always sees beyond appearances. A crucial indication of who he is becomes apparent when he joins his comrades for a drink at a bar; he demands that the bartender serve him "the good stuff"—from a bottle hidden within another bottle.

Squeeze is a Korean American union activist. According to the cultural theorist and literary critic Brian Locke, U.S. films tend to position Asian Americans, particularly Asian American males, as a threat to security, through which a bonding of blacks and whites would save the American nation.[23] Squeeze breaks this and other stereotypes of Asian American males in Hollywood cinema. He is a courageous leader whose speech is not marked by presuppositions of foreignness, and he is not only a sexual being but also a desirable one. He works across class and racial lines. And the proposed deal of a capitalist bond between Steve Lift and Cassius Green, wherein unionization and an equisapien revolution are considered the threats, is derailed through alternatives already set in play because of Squeeze's unionizing efforts across class, gender, and race. In short, in the film, working-class people of color and white people who believe capitalists are on their side are deluded.

Squeeze not only puts pressure on the bosses but also is a squeeze in the sense of a lover. Squeeze's relationship with Detroit is a complicated one. The impact of Korea and Japan in relation to the U.S. automobile industry was felt in Detroit since the 1970s perhaps more than in any other American city. Detroit and Squeeze's affair signifies the South Korean and Japanese automobile factories and dealerships in the United States.

Detroit is a performance artist. Her projects include working as a "human directional," a person who carries signs promoting businesses. A member of the Left Eye militants, she defaces WorryFree ads, and her artistic performances include reciting, while wearing a black-leather-glove bikini, lines from the Berry Gordy–produced *Last Dragon* (1985)—another Afro-Asian fusion—while her audience throws old cell phones, bullet casings, and balloons filled with lamb's blood on her. Since Gordy was the mogul who founded and ran the Detroit-based Motown Records, the question becomes what people like him would sacrifice for material wealth. The answer of today's plutocrats, oligarchs, and kleptocrats comes down, by the nihilistic implications of their practice, to reality, truth, and, ultimately, the future.

Although a class- and race-inspired hip hop film that crosses genres from comedy to science fiction to horror, *Sorry to Bother You* is also very much a blues movie. This is to be expected since the genealogy of hip hop points back to blues music mixed with critical speech from a tradition that points back to African griots. Its undercurrent is a struggle for humanity in the face of degradation or, specific to Riley's film, animalization. It brings that element of racism to the fore.

Racism is a form of degradation that attempts to bar certain people from the rights and privileges of adult life, such as the dignity of images of self-worth, while also blaming them for their lack of access to those goods. That is why people who become objects of racism are treated as perpetual children, people under the guardianship of a supposedly adult race. In the 1968 sanitation workers' strike in Memphis, the picketers' signs declared, I AM A MAN. Black nationalist women in earlier global struggles for freedom used the same slogan, altered for their gender.[24] Their signs echoed the famous speech the nineteenth-century abolitionist and preacher Sojourner Truth delivered at the 1851 Women's Rights Convention in Akron, Ohio: "Ain't I a Woman?"

Let us reflect on the blues through the conditions of enslaved peoples who made daily ethical decisions, and were conscious of doing so, but suffered under the designation of being property. Nearly every blues performance and lyric illustrates this contradiction. How can one be responsible when the fact of one's responsibility is dismissed or obstructed? Thinking about political responsibility, where one carries the burden of those who govern even when one rejects that governance, such a circumstance makes *all* actions of enslaved peoples into political responsibility while contradictorily denying them political life. This dimension of enslavement and its accompanying racism mark the struggle for full citizenship after slavery met its official, though not actual, end.[25]

We see here the primordial distinction between how things appear and what they are. But the difference is not always so clear. The blues point to this lack of clarity in both form and content. There is repetition in the blues, but each re-instantiation of a theme is uniquely significant. There is repetition without being the same.[26] In blues music, it is usually at a point just before resolution (often at the dominant fifth chord) where revelation occurs. This moment is often ironic in that it points back to the performer's role in some element of the condition at hand; it is an assertion of adult sensibility. Here the blues artist or pro-testor, after outlining the conditions of and living the suffering, raises the question of agency and responsibility. I call this "adult sensibility" because it points to a central moment in development that all parents, at some point, reveal to the child who must now grow up: life is rarely fair, and one must nonetheless improvise and make do.

Improvisation is one of the central features of Black music. An over-looked element of improvisation is that it's not random; the improviser faces responsibility for each creative riff. It's thus play as a challenge to the spirit of seriousness. It's also paradoxical, since mature play is open-ness to continued growth. In jazz, the melody, harmony, and rhythm set the stage for what can no longer be expressed with spoken words. It calls, always, to bring meaning to the seemingly ineffable.

With regard to the unfairness, which amounts to injustice through-out the course of black life in antiblack societies, there is much with which to contend. To cry out loud about this injustice is not simply a revelation of wrong but also an acknowledgment of having been wronged. To do so as a wail or moan is to assert the value of self, for if you aren't valuable, why should anyone care what has happened to you?

The blues thus extracts from the inner life of the afflicted the value of defiance, and along with that, dignity and self-love.

The Black Jewish queer activist Alicia Garza, who, in collaboration with Patrisse Cullors and Opal Tometi, formulated and tweeted the hashtag #BlackLivesMatter on July 13, 2013, in response to George Zimmerman's acquittal for what was clearly at least the manslaughter if not the second-degree murder of Trayvon Martin, said it was "a love note to our folks."[27] Her tweet five minutes later was: "Black People. I love you. I love us. Our lives matter."[28] Love notes from black becom-ing Black, in moments of the blues, are like messages in bottles from a people marooned on islands over an uncaring, temporal sea. They are music, poetry, and other modes of expression ranging from speeches to varieties of arts, bubbling out of the blues mixed with other re-sources. The Afro-Cuban percussionist Ramón "Mongo" Santamaría

Rodríguez's classic "Afro Blue" (1959), with the lyrics of Oscar Brown, Jr., added in Abbey Lincoln's *Abbey Is Blue* (1959), anticipated Garza, Cullors, and Tometi's offering through singing to the world about the "shades of delight" in "cocoa hue," that beauty in night that is, in continued struggle and affirmations of life, afro blue.

12

VALUED

Frederick Douglass grappled throughout his life with the meaning of his experiences, documented in three of his books.[1] When the first was published, Douglass was a fugitive. His crime? He had "stolen" his enslaver's "property"—himself.

That this "property" was capable of stealing itself suggests having legal responsibility without political life. Douglass's first book was protected under U.S. copyright law, yet he himself was not; his book bizarrely had more rights than he. The details he revealed in the book put him in danger of extradition to Maryland and re-enslavement by the Auld family. Douglass found refuge in England and Ireland, where his supporters brokered a deal with Hugh Auld for his manumission in 1846. Legally "free," he returned to the United States, where he devoted his life first to the ongoing struggle against legalized slavery, which led to his involvement in the U.S. Civil War, and then to the fight against its structural reassertion in the United States and abroad, including in the Caribbean during his years as ambassador to Haiti (1889–1891). Fighting against slavery meant, for Douglass, fighting *for* freedom, including women's rights, with which he was involved as early as the Seneca Falls women's rights convention of 1848. This commitment never wavered.

Douglass was born Frederick Augustus Washington Bailey in Talbot County, Maryland, where he was separated from his mother,

Harriet Bailey, and placed, along with other enslaved children, under the care of Betsy Bailey, his enslaved elderly grandmother. In the first book, he claims that he saw his mother, Harriet, only a few times and developed no emotional attachment to her, perhaps to emphasize the cruelty of slavery. This avowed lack of emotional attachment between children and their mothers has unfortunately persisted even in contemporary narratives of paternal abandonment in black families. I often have to remind those who accept this misinformed portrait that it was devised by proponents of black pathology in bourgeois societies that treat families as normal if, and only if, they are run by men.[2] But more, the narrative of black families traumatized by abandonment from times of slavery through to the present fails to account for the fact that mothers were sold away, too, and not just fathers—hence the birth of spirituals such as "Sometimes I Feel Like a Motherless Child," which dates back to the 1870s. Consider also that distant or unacknowledged fathers, such as Douglass's, were often white enslavers.[3]

In his final account, Douglass discards the story of emotional detachment from his mother. Taken from his grandmother to labor at the house of the former Maryland governor Lieutenant Edward Lloyd, he was introduced to the full brutality of enslavement around the age of seven. His mother, Harriet, worked on the fields of a plantation twelve miles away. In the evenings, she walked those miles to spend time with him, leaving an hour or two before dawn to return to the fields. She brought what little food she had to share with him, as the child Frederick was reduced to fighting with the enslaver's dog for table scraps. The last time she saw him, she rescued him from the abuse of the cruel, enslaved cook. Soon thereafter, Harriet passed away.

As any psychologist would attest, children cannot understand parental absence. Even when the parent is enslaved, the child's response to the loss, experienced as abandonment, is to blame the parent; similarly, the extenuating circumstances of poverty, war, and other sources of separation do not always lead children to forgive the absent parent. That Douglass's mother endured hardship to see him—walking each night through rural Maryland was a perilous venture—compelled this reflection in her son's later years:

My mother had walked twelve miles to see me, and had the same distance to travel over again before the morning sunrise. I do not remember ever seeing her again. Her death soon ended the little communication that had existed between us, and with it, I believe, a life full of weariness and heartfelt sorrow. To me it has ever been a grief that I knew my mother so little, and have so few of her words treasured in my remembrance. I have since learned that she was the only one of all the colored people of Tuckahoe who could read. How she acquired this knowledge I know not, for Tuckahoe was the last place in the world where she would have been likely to find facilities for learning. I can therefore fondly and proudly ascribe to her, an earnest love of knowledge. That a field-hand should learn to read in any slave State is remarkable, but the achievements of my mother, considering the place and circumstances, was very extraordinary. In view of this fact, I am happy to attribute any love of letters I may have, not to my presumed Anglo-Saxon paternity, but to the native genius of my sable, unprotected, and uncultivated mother—a woman who belonged to a race whose mental endowments are still disparaged and despised.[4]

The world in which the child Frederick lived was one in which he was valued only as property. To be valued was to be of use to the master, or to the person to whom the master leased him. He was a thing of market value; his point of view did not matter. His wants, his desires, his dreams were not valuable. For enslaved women and men, this included their flesh; as many chronicles attest, the bodies of the enslaved were sources of sexual gratification and other forms of physical amusement for those who owned or rented them. Harriet Bailey, in her efforts, introduced something empowering into the young Frederick's consciousness—*love*. As far as he knew, even when he was a child, he had worth only as a commodity. Love, however, offers a different kind of value. It is a judgment on existence beyond being. It says that existence is worth immeasurably less without the beloved.

In her extraordinary efforts to spend time with Frederick, Harriet showed that she loved him. She was saying, "Frederick, you're valuable. Your life matters." Love offered Douglass a glimpse of a possibility beyond black and enslaved melancholia; it is an emotion that affirms where and with whom one *belongs*.

But if that sense of worth were all that Douglass learned from Harriet's efforts, that would be a loss. Knowing he was valuable could have made him cocky toward his fellow enslaved; it could also have made him an obnoxious freedman. He could have had pride and a sense of superiority to the still enslaved and many unloved freedmen and freedwomen. But would he have had dignity?

The rules of young Frederick's world were clear; only enslavers bestowed value, so what was the value of an enslaved woman's love? If Frederick had rejected Harriet's love, he would have also undermined the value of any love of his own. It was not sufficient, then, to be loved by Harriet. Frederick had to value that love. The spark of love, and the flame that grew from valuing it, nurtured a revolutionary spirit. Frederick went on to learn to read and write, to fight against the slave breaker Reverend Covey, to eventually escape from Maryland, and, despite the liberties afforded him under the shadow of his new name, to throw himself into the struggle for abolition and the subsequent, lifelong political fight for the living practice of freedom.

Douglass's story is of a journey from enslaved to black to Black consciousness. Its message is clear: the movement to Black consciousness requires that one value being valued by the damned of the earth.

Recall that political responsibility looks to the future while learning from past challenges. The decision to launch oneself into a struggle on behalf of the damned of the earth can be regarded only as absurd. History rarely appears to decide for the oppressed. Lacking any assurance of a positive outcome, commitment is the only basis of action against oppression. Struggles for liberation therefore become more than political responsibility; they embody political commitment.

Political commitment defies ordinary models of action. Consider acting out of love. A popular model of love claims that the beloved is seen as an extension of the self. One's beloved is similar to oneself, and thus all love is an expression of self-love. Yet anyone who knows love can see the error here—most people with the ability to love are capable of loving those who are not like them, just as we also have the capacity to hate most intensely those who are most like us. The French philosopher Simone Weil reflects on love as follows:

> Lovers and friends have two desires. One is to love so much that one enters the other to make a single being. The other is to love so much that with half the earthly globe between them, their union would not suffer any diminishment. . . . Those impossible desires are within us as a mark of our destination, and it is good for us when we don't hope to accomplish them.[5]

Weil first raises the implications of assimilation, a core element not only of one dominant model of love but also of ethics and morality. Her second consideration is premised on distance and separation, which produce "impossible desire." Impossibility here is rhetorical, since, as the example shows so well, what is supposedly impossible does happen, and with sufficient regularity to be familiar. Love is not just based on similarity but also possible through difference. Some people claim to love the divine, including the Absolute or G-d, and what could be more different from us and more beyond our reach? Similarly, political love is an expression of our capacity to love that which is beyond the self.

This observation is a revolutionary insight from freedom fighters over the ages: to act from commitment defies imitation and requires expecting that subsequent generations will receive the gift of not having to be like those who precede them.

Many who turn politically to the right do so to oblige a need for immediate order and security. They look not to the future but to the now and the past. The future that is not a repetition of the past is, for them, a source of fear and dread; for some, a future that brings in the new points to a world without them. As no one lives forever, a future without them is inevitable, and that prospect, in addition to reality, is the enemy of all narcissists. Although those who turn to the left look forward to the future, some also do so with narcissistic expectations; they expect it to be *their* future. Others, however, understand that contributing to the future requires transcending the self, or at least attachment to the self. Letting go is a gift of freedom to subsequent generations not to be repetitions of us.

"Reforms and revolutions," James Boggs writes, "are created by the illogical actions of people. Very few logical people ever make reforms and none make revolution. Rights are what you make and what you take."[6] Harriet Bailey did not think about what she could receive from Frederick. She thought about what to do. She had no way of knowing what would become of her son's generation, and Frederick realized that he had no way of knowing what would become of the generations after his own. We, too, as we reckon with establishing the conditions of possibility for those who will succeed us, must act without knowing the outcome. We must embrace or reject our commitments. If we do not repeat what we are trying to overcome from the past, what could the future to which we contribute be but revolutionary?

We return to *Get Out*, Jordan Peele's allegory of the failure to listen to one's ancestors and learn about the traps that ensnared them. The film is as much about listening as it is about what is seen, as the images' leitmotif is the haunting "Sikiliza Kwa Wahenga" ("Listen to your ancestors"). The ancestors suffered; heed their warning. They eventually whisper, "*Run!*"

Yes, get out.

Chris, the photographer protagonist, works with his eyes, but his vulnerability is that he fails to listen. A blind member of the sinister cult makes his own intentions clear: "I want your eyes, man," he says. "I want those things you see through."

There is a form of hearing that is not listening. Part of what Chris has to learn is what not to hear, or how to attune his ears away from that which stifles reality. He needs to listen. "The sunken place," into which he is thrown and immobilized, is the stratification of trauma. Chris fails to realize that he is living in another stage of a struggle suffered by ancestors such as Paul Bogle, Ottobah Cugoano, Frederick Douglass,

Harriet Jacobs, Solomon Northup, Toussaint Louverture, Tula Rigaud, Sojourner Truth, Harriet Tubman, and countless others whose names are no longer preserved in the reservoir of historical memory. The key to his sunken place is his reassociation with his mother's death from a car accident, triggered when his girlfriend, Rose, hits a deer with her car. At Rose's childhood house, which is obviously "the Big House" of slave narratives, Chris sees his counterpart in the buck on the mantel.

Andre, a young black man abducted at the beginning of the film, delivers the title's imperative. Momentarily released from the grip of white consciousness through the flash of light from Chris's smartphone, he quickly warns him: "Get out!"

Ancestors and predecessors come before us. They offer knowledge. They offer history. The choice of Kiswahili as their initial voice points to Africa, though Kiswahili is a creolized language of East African Kingozi with Arabic, Persian, and various other African additions. That there was an Arab and Persian trade in the enslavement of Africans brings to the fore the African American story of creolization from enslavement. Yet the basilect, the often-suppressed African voice, speaks. That voice, in a way, gets out. Where does one go if one gets out?

Freedom is a perpetual, never-completed journey. Permanently "getting out" is a paradox. Does one get out "as black" or get out of the ensnarement of a world dependent on a particular construction of blackness? The first would require a different kind of black, as we have seen, than those premised on white agency and black passivity. That black, however, would be something radically different and possibly unrecognizable to anyone locked in the idea of blackness as a negative term—a redemptive historical development.

Can anyone get out alone? Not when living in a human world. In *Get Out*, the character Rod Williams, despite his surface role as comic relief, is much more than he appears. Rod is a TSA agent. His job is to monitor migration. He is the mythic gatekeeper: he manages transgressions, pathways. When he goes to the police in an attempt to rescue Chris and other blacks from whites illegally migrating into their bodies, he is, in effect, doing his job. But what is invisible to the law is the transmigration of one consciousness into another's.

Rod's significance is complicated by the two endings of *Get Out*. In the official, released version, Rod shows up and rescues Chris from the carnage that has resulted from his fight for his life. "Rod," as in a lightning rod, is a conduit; he negotiates passages. When he drives Chris away from the Armitage house, he is similar to mythic guides such as the god Aker in Kmt/ancient Egypt, Virgil in Dante's *Inferno*, and even Glinda, the Good Witch of the North in *The Wizard of Oz* (1939). *Get Out*'s similarities with *The Wizard of Oz* are from its black-and-white opening to its shift into technicolor and the journey ahead, and Rod does take Chris home, but they drive away in color on a dark night, not in black and white. In the original ending, it's white police officers, not Rod, who show up at the aftermath of Chris's bloody struggle with the Armitage family. The scene shifts to black for five seconds. We then see Rod enter a glass booth. He looks down, almost as if in preparation for prayer. There is a black woman in an adjacent booth having what seems to be a cheerful conversation with the prisoner she is visiting. Chris appears behind the glass divide in front of Rod. He is wearing an orange prison jumpsuit with a white T-shirt underneath. Rod offers to use his detective skills to exonerate Chris, but Chris discourages him. He says, with little emotion, "Rod. I'm good. I stopped them. I stopped them." As Chris walks away in handcuffs, accompanied by a white guard down a white hall, "Sikiliza Kwa Wahenga" returns, and white bars slide shut behind him.

"Chris," we should remember, means savior. Whom does Chris save? In the released version, Chris saves himself and, indirectly, those to come, the other black people who might have been abducted by the cult. It was not only the question of the audience's response to the bleak original ending that led to this change. Peele set out to subvert the tropes of the horror genre, where the death of black characters is pre-ordained. The 1968 horror masterpiece *Night of the Living Dead* had Ben, the heroic Black protagonist, shot dead and thrown onto a pile of burning corpses after fending off zombies throughout the night. In the released ending of *Get Out*, Chris has perhaps also saved the black "hosts" whose white parasites will no longer have the help of hypnotist Missy Armitage in suppressing their consciousness.

"I stopped them." Chris's closing words in the original ending make him a messiah. It also makes Rod someone who knows the truth but is no longer a guide. In the alternative ending, as the one who knows the truth and seeks balance, breath, justice, life, and order, Chris is the ancient African goddess MAat. At the level of myth, male and female distinctions may hide undercurrents of meaning. Among MAat's many functions is to weigh the souls of the deceased to determine their suitability for paradise in the afterlife. Her positive judgment allows the deceased to breathe and thus live. In the confessional structure of Chris and Rod's last meeting, Chris is already in a form of living death, and he tells Rod, as he has done throughout the film, the truth. Yet his final journey doesn't lead to paradise.

Chris's words "I'm good" signify that he has accomplished what he was supposed to do. He can breathe. This is another feature of myth: the one who gets others out does not himself get out. Think of the biblical story of Moshe or Moses. In Numbers 20:10, Moses shouts, "Listen, you rebels, shall we get water for you out of this rock?" His referring to his brother Aaron and himself was an affront to G-d. Both paid by being barred from entering the Promised Land.

Many groups and individuals have positioned themselves as gods. Their efforts to become eternal inevitably led to tragedy, folly, and, over time, their insignificance. Those who want to have everything eventually lose, despite the power they hoard, to those who want little, and even to those who may seek nothing.

Fernando Meirelles and Kátia Lund's 2002 Brazilian film *Cidade de Deus* (City of God) reminds us of this truth. In a mythic retelling of historical gangsters in Rio de Janeiro in the last quarter of the twentieth century, the film begins with a chicken that seems to witness the slaughter of its fellows in preparation for a feast. As the dead chickens are plucked and chopped up, the witnessing chicken kicks free of the tether on its leg, then takes off, pursued down perilous steps and into the streets by a gang of young men. With them in pursuit from one direction, other slaughterers, the police, show up from another, and the protagonist Rocket—a dark-skinned native of the eponymous favela—and the chicken wind up facing each other in the middle.

A rocket is a projectile that can achieve great heights. By the end of the film, Rocket is a newspaper photographer. Yet, in truth, Rocket and the chicken are one and the same—both have taken flight and landed in the middle of danger.

The film tells the story that leads up to the moment when the boy and chicken face each other between gangs of would-be butchers. Ascending favela hierarchy on a long ladder of murders is the ruthless gang leader Li'l Zé. As a child he is known as "Li'l Dice," a name fitting a boy whose life is a murderous game of chance. To prove his manhood, he slaughters the staff and guests of a motel during a robbery in which the older gangsters insisted on taking no lives. In his twenties, Li'l Dice is renamed "Li'l Zé" by a Candomblé priest. The name, a Portuguese version of José (graced or favored by G-d or the gods), is also reminiscent of "Zeus." If the favela is the City of God, it is *his* city, and this god wants to control everything. He despises what is beyond his reach. His only sexual experience is a violation—he rapes the girlfriend of Knockout Ned, a man whom women desire. As Li'l Zé—laughably, "little favored" or "little Zeus"; only little men imagine themselves as gods or the gods' favored—his domain is actually a small and marginalized part of Rio. But his actions make him the symbolic father of a new generation of killers, "the runts"—children who terrorize the streets without mercy. Returning to the first scene of the film, Li'l Zé and his gang of runts stand on one side of Rocket and the chicken, and the police—another gang: they are the source of the weaponry and drugs in the favela and throughout the city—stand on the other.

In the mayhem that ensues, Li'l Zé encounters the runts—his true progeny, made, as he realizes too late, in his own image. They murder him and Rocket photographs his corpse in the gutter. Rocket had also photographed the police in the midst of one of their illicit transactions. Still in flight, Rocket gives the papers the photograph of Li'l Zé's corpse instead of the one that would have exposed the cops and the system, and no doubt endangered his life.

City of God is a remarkably beautiful movie even where it reveals spectacular cruelty. Like Chris in *Get Out*, Rocket is a photographer—and he is also trying to get out. The subjects of both characters' photography are also similar; they address the underside of racialized urban life in antiblack societies, that which the affluent and white learn to avoid seeing. The original ending of *Get Out* is what Rocket would have faced if he had decided to expose the police. But he decides to be neither a god nor a sacrifice. Like the chicken, he flees but is not free.

Transformation, as a feature and goal of the movement from black to Black consciousness, hits a wall in *City of God*. Li'l Dice changes his name, yet he remains the same. Beginning with his initial acts of murder, he is already killing himself, a sentence his protégés, the runts, carry out. And Rocket, as we see, continues to flee.

Chris and Rocket could have perhaps looked for inspiration from Harriet Bailey, Frederick Douglass, Harriet Jacobs, Harriet Tubman, Sojourner Truth, and many others. The ancestors are a community; the act of listening to them affirms their value and commits the listener to valuing what they learned. This valued knowledge, in turn, makes sense only in a world where, in valuing the ancestors one will someday join, one values beyond the self. No one can be free alone.

Bringing forth Black consciousness requires offering the social world, the community across time, the power of possibility through commitment. The only way to combat the enemies of this movement is to build productive and life-affirming institutions of empowerment. What are these but the conditions of belonging—that is, home? What is there being summoned if not cultivating the fruits of freedom and respect for those to come?

In 1952, Fanon asked his body to make of him a man who always questions. By 1961, he had learned it was more important for communities to fight and build new concepts and institutions through which to better the lives of those not yet named. That is also the challenge we—not only those who have taken to the streets in times of converging pandemics, but also all of us across times in which it is increasingly impossible to breathe—have inherited. Consider, along our way:

> O, how different our journey could be
> Whose life is also its undertaking,
> Whose commitments are without idols?
>
> —Author's tercet

NOTES

INTRODUCTION: STRUGGLING TO BREATHE

1. See, for example, Julian Borger, "Maga v BLM: How Police Handled the Capitol Mob and George Floyd Activists—in Pictures," *The Guardian*, January 7, 2021, https://www.theguardian.com/us-news/2021/jan/06/capitol-mob-police-trump -george-floyd-protests-photos (accessed February 21, 2021).
2. See Jane Anna Gordon, *Statelessness and Contemporary Enslavement* (New York: Routledge, 2020).
3. W.E.B. Du Bois, *The Souls of Black Folk: Essays and Sketches* (Chicago: A. C. McClurg, 1903).
4. Frantz Fanon, *Peau noire, masques blancs* (Paris: Éditions du Seuil, 1952), 183 (my translation). The book is available in two translations as *Black Skin, White Masks*. I will refer to the text in English, but all references will be to the French edition, with my translations.
5. Alfredo Saad Filho and Fernanda Feil, "COVID-19 in Brazil: How Jair Bolsonaro Created a Calamity," *The Conversation*, April 23, 2021, https://theconversation .com/covid-19-in-brazil-how-jair-bolsonaro-created-a-calamity-159066 (accessed May 1, 2021).
6. Chacour Koop, "'THANK YOU GOD': Darnella Frazier, Who Filmed George Floyd's Death, Reacts to Verdict," *Miami Herald*, April 20, 2021, https://www .miamiherald.com/news/nation-world/national/article250821594.html (accessed May 1, 2021).
7. This is not to say that there weren't ancient organizations of maintaining order, whether by the use of military troops or clan councils and "kin policing," in which members of a community police themselves. In some societies, such as ancient Athens, the enslaved were used to protect goods at markets. See Bruce L. Berg, *Policing in Modern Society* (Oxford: Butterworth-Heinemann, 1999). For a critical discussion of what contemporary police actually do and their growing obsolescence, see Alex S. Vitale, *The End of Policing* (London: Verso, 2017),

and Geo Maher, *A World Without Police: How Strong Communities Make Cops Obsolete* (London: Verso, 2021).

8. Frantz Fanon, *L'an V de la révolution algérienne* (Paris: Maspero, 1959), 174 (my translation). This text is available in English as *A Dying Colonialism*. My references will be to the original French.

PART I: BOUND

1. From Sojourner Truth, "Ain't I a Woman?," delivered at the 1851 Women's Convention in Akron, Ohio. It's reprinted in many places. See, for instance, Feminist.com, https://www.feminist.com/resources/artspeech/genwom/sojour .htm (accessed February 21, 2021).

1. FEARED

1. The Mayo Clinic is the top hospital in the United States. Its nonprofit medical research center produces findings and criteria used for diagnoses of illness across the globe. The description of malignant narcissism offered here is from its website: "Disease Conditions: Narcissistic Personality Disorder," Mayoclinic .org, https://www.mayoclinic.org/diseases-conditions/narcissistic-personality -disorder/symptoms-causes/syc-20366662 (accessed February 21, 2021).

2. The literature on this false belief is vast. For a recent study, see New York University, "Children Associate White, but Not Black, Men with 'Brilliant' Stereotype, New Study Finds," *ScienceDaily*, October 10, 2019, https://www.sciencedaily .com/releases/2019/10/191010075418.htm (accessed February 21, 2021).

3. Frantz Fanon, *Peau noire, masques blancs* (Paris: Éditions du Seuil, 1952), 96.

4. Fanon, *Peau noire, masques blancs*, 117. One may wonder about racially mixed families, whose children cannot avoid the white world by virtue of one of their parents being white. Fanon was not talking about racially mixed families. After all, from the perspective of racist societies, there is no such thing as a normal racially mixed family. Beyond such prejudice, there is another consideration. As intimate contact and ongoing conversation are already present in racially mixed families, a study of ripe neurosis or the triumph of overcoming social adversity may be their story. And, of course, there is still another consideration. Not all racially mixed families are the same. Although this should be obvious, readers may wish to consult Lori L. Tharps, *Same Family, Different Colors: Confronting Colorism in America's Diverse Families* (Boston: Beacon Press, 2016).

5. The list would probably take up the rest of this book. The *New York Times* web page "Race and Ethnicity" is an excellent source: https://www.nytimes.com /topic/subject/race-and-ethnicity (accessed February 21, 2021).

6. Ta-Nehisi Coates, *Between the World and Me* (New York: Random House, 2015); and Ibram X. Kendi, *How to Be an Antiracist* (New York: One World, 2019).

7. Classic discussions of this understanding of consciousness as embodied include Jean-Paul Sartre's *Being and Nothingness*, trans. Hazel E. Barnes (New York: Washington Square Press, 1956); and Maurice Merleau-Ponty's *Phenomenology of Perception*, trans. Colin Smith (London: Routledge and Kegan Paul, 2002).

For an analysis in the context of antiblack racism, see Lewis R. Gordon, *Bad Faith and Antiblack Racism* (Atlantic Highlands, NJ: Humanities International Press, 1995). See also Susan Schneider, *Artificial You: AI and the Future of Your Mind* (Princeton, NJ: Princeton University Press, 2019), for similar conclusions and their implications for contemporary studies of artificial intelligence (AI).

8. "Lewis Black on Broadway Talking About How America Isn't #1," DailyMotion, https://www.dailymotion.com/video/x2not0t (accessed May 1, 2021).

9. I recommend reading Christopher Columbus's diary, *The Four Voyages of Christopher Columbus*, trans. J. M. Cohen (London: Penguin Classics, 1992); Bartolomé de las Casas's *A Short Account of the Destruction of the Indies*, introduced by Anthony Pagden and trans. by Nigel Griffin (New York: Penguin Classics, 1999); C.L.R. James's *The Black Jacobins: Toussaint L'Ouverture and the San Domingo Revolution* (New York: Vintage, 1989); Hilary McD. Beckles, *Britain's Black Debt: Reparations for Caribbean Slavery and Native Genocide* (Kingston, Jamaica: University of the West Indies Press, 2013); Robert Hughes, *The Fatal Shore: The Epic History of Australia's Founding* (New York: Vintage, 1986); Adam Hochschild's *King Leopold's Ghost: A Story of Greed, Terror, and Heroism in Colonial Africa* (Boston: Houghton Mifflin, 1999); Julius S. Scott, *The Common Wind: Afro-American Currents in the Age of the Haitian Revolution* (London: Verso, 2018); and Lamonte Aidoo's *Slavery Unseen: Sex, Power, and Violence in Brazilian History* (Durham, NC: Duke University Press, 2019), among a long and easily accessed list of sources.

10. This observation of a mind taking hold of a consciousness raises a philosophical problem. We move from consciousness to mind, since the two are not identical. One could be conscious of things without having a mind. The latter is a particular type of consciousness. It's a consciousness capable of being aware of itself as conscious with a reservoir of resources through which to make experience meaningful. It doesn't just see. It also sees that it sees. The "sunken place" is one in which there is a conscious mind under control of another conscious mind, but as controlled, the former's mind is imprisoned. The formulation of seeing that one sees is from Søren Kierkegaard, *Works of Love: Some Christian Reflections in the Form of Discourses*, trans. Howard V. and Edna H. Hong (New York: Harper and Row, 1962), 5.

11. Fanon, *Peau noire, masques blancs*, the beginning of chapter 6.

2. BLACKENED

1. See Sartre's *Being and Nothingness*, trans. Hazel E. Barnes (New York: Washington Square Press, 1956), 566. Where I refer to the absolute deity of monotheism, I use the Jewish convention of eliminating the vowel so it will not be confused with a proper name.

2. It's no accident that animal studies is a peculiarly white phenomenon in which blacks are more recently entering by responding to discussion in which animal discourse is being paired with black studies. For a meeting of animal studies

and black studies, see Bénédicte Boisseron, *Afro-Dog: Blackness and the Animal Question* (New York: Columbia University Press, 2018).

3. Alex Hannaford, "The Tiger Next Door: America's Backyard Big Cats," *The Observer* (London), November 10, 2019, https://www.theguardian.com/global/2019/nov/10/the-tiger-next-door-americas-backyard-big-cats (accessed February 21, 2021). See also Sharon Guynup, "Captive Tigers in the U.S. Outnumber Those in the Wild," *National Geographic*, November 14, 2019, https://www.nationalgeographic.com/animals/2019/11/tigers-in-the-united-states-outnumber-those-in-the-wild-feature/ (accessed February 21, 2021); and Worldwildlife.org, "More Tigers in American Backyards Than in the Wild," July 19, 2014, https://www.worldwildlife.org/stories/more-tigers-in-american-backyards-than-in-the-wild (accessed February 21, 2021).

4. See Stacey Venzel, "Whatever Happened to Michael Jackson's Animals at Neverland Ranch?," Wide Open Pets (May 2020), https://www.wideopenpets.com/whatever-happened-michael-jacksons-animals-neverland (accessed August 12, 2020); and for a discussion of race and pets, including attitudes toward black people owning pit bull terriers, see Boisseron, *Afro-Dog*.

5. Akilah Johnson, "That Was No Typo: The Median Net Worth of Black Bostonians Really Is $8," *The Boston Globe*, December 11, 2017, https://www.bostonglobe.com/metro/2017/12/11/that-was-typo-the-median-net-worth-black-bostonians-really/ze5kxC1jJelx24M3pugFFN/story.html (accessed February 21, 2021).

6. Shawn D. Rochester, *The Black Tax: The Cost of Being Black in America* (Southbury, CT: Good Steward Publishing, 2017). Relatedly, see Mehrsa Baradaran, *The Color of Money: Black Banks and the Racial Wealth Gap* (Cambridge, MA: Harvard University Press, 2017); and William A. Darity, Jr., and A. Kirsten Mullen, *From Here to Equality: Reparations for Black Americans in the Twenty-First Century* (Chapel Hill: University of North Carolina Press, 2020). Beyond the United States, see Hilary McD. Beckles, *Britain's Black Debt: Reparations for Caribbean Slavery and Native Genocide* (Kingston, Jamaica: University of the West Indies Press, 2013).

7. *Blanqueamiento* policies are well known and continue across much of Latin America. For history and critical discussion, see Tanya Katerí Hernández, *Racial Subordination in Latin America: The Role of the State, Customary Law, and the New Civil Rights Response* (Cambridge, UK: Cambridge University Press, 2014); and Johanna Ferreira, "How Latin America's Obsession with Whitening Is Hurting Us," *Hiplatina*, June 5, 2020, https://hiplatina.com/latin-americas-obsession-with-whiteness/ (accessed June 1, 2021).

8. Bear in mind that Mani's ideas were a fusion of Christian and earlier Persian or Aryan myths. Those peoples seem to have established mythologies of hierarchies wherever they settled, including in the Indus Valley. For a succinct discussion of their historical and linguistic impact, see John Fiske, "Who Are the Aryans?," *The Atlantic*, February 1881, https://www.theatlantic.com/magazine/archive/1881/02/who-are-the-aryans/521367/ (accessed February 21, 2021).

9. James P. Comer and Alvin F. Poussaint, *Black Child Care* (New York: Simon & Schuster, 1975).

10. James P. Comer and Alvin F. Poussaint, *Raising Black Children: Two Leading Psychiatrists Confront the Educational, Social and Emotional Problems Facing Black Children* (New York: Plume, 1992).

11. Alison Gopnik, *The Gardener and the Carpenter: What the New Science of Child Development Tells Us About the Relationship Between Parents and Children* (New York: Farrar, Straus and Giroux, 2016).

12. See, for example, Noel A. Cazenave's *Killing African Americans: Police and Vigilante Violence as a Racial Control Mechanism* (New York: Routledge, 2018); Alex S. Vitale, *The End of Policing* (London: Verso, 2017); and Geo Maher, *A World Without Police: How Strong Communities Make Cops Obsolete* (London: Verso, 2021).

13. See his reflections on why he made his turn to developing sociological work on American blacks in W.E.B. Du Bois, *The Autobiography of W.E.B. Du Bois: A Soliloquy on Viewing My Life from the Last Decade of Its First Century* (New York: International Publishers, 1961).

14. For an excellent history of this process from antiquity through to the twentieth century, see Joseph E. Harris, *Africans and Their History* (Nairobi, Kenya: Mentor, 1972).

15. For historical demonstration, see, for example, Walter Rodney, *How Europe Underdeveloped Africa* (Washington, DC: Howard University Press, 1982).

3. ERASED; OR, "I DON'T SEE RACE"

1. See Fanon's famous paper "Racism and Culture," which he presented in Paris at the First Congress of Black Writers and Artists in 1956, available in Frantz Fanon, *Pour la révolution africaine: Écrits politiques* (Paris: François Maspero, 1964), and available in English as *Toward the African Revolution*.

2. See, for example, Ruth Bogin, "'Liberty Further Extended': A 1776 Antislavery Manuscript by Lemuel Haynes," *William and Mary Quarterly* 40, no. 1 (January 1983): 85–105; and from Benjamin Banneker, see, for example, "To Thomas Jefferson from Benjamin Banneker, August 19, 1791," National Archives, Founders Online, https://founders.archives.gov/documents/Jefferson/01-22-02-0049 (accessed February 21, 2021).

3. Catherine E. Walsh, "The Decolonial *For*: Resurgences, Shifts, and Movements," in Walter D. Mignolo and Catherine E. Walsh, *On Decoloniality: Concepts, Analytics, Praxis* (Durham, NC: Duke University Press, 2018), 21. For reflective discussions of these themes from across the globe, see Sayan Dey, ed., *Different Spaces, Different Voices: A Rendezvous with Decoloniality* (Mumbai, India: BecomeShakespeare.com, 2018).

4. See, for example, Viola Cordova, *How It Is: The Native American Philosophy of V. F. Cordova*, ed. Kathleen Dean Moore, Kurt Peters, Ted Jojola, and Amber Lacy (Tucson: University of Arizona Press, 2007); and Vine Deloria, Jr., *Custer Died for Your Sins: An Indian Manifesto* (Norman: University of Oklahoma Press, 1988 [1969]).

5. For an eyewitness account, see Bartolomé de las Casas, *A Short Account of the Destruction of the Indies*, introduced by Anthony Pagden and trans. by Nigel Griffin (New York: Penguin Classics, 1999). And for critical discussions of this "I" as formulated here, see C.L.R. James, *The Black Jacobins: Toussaint L'Ouverture and the San Domingo Revolution* (New York: Vintage, 1989); Hilary McD. Beckles, *Britain's Black Debt: Reparations for Caribbean Slavery and Native Genocide* (Kingston, Jamaica: University of the West Indies Press, 2013); and Enrique Dussel, "Anti-Cartesian Meditations: On the Origins of the Philosophical Anti-Discourse of Modernity," *Human Architecture* 11, no. 1 (Fall 2013): 25–29.

6. Tanya Katerí Hernández, *Racial Subordination in Latin America: The Role of the State, Customary Law, and the New Civil Rights Response* (Cambridge, UK: Cambridge University Press, 2014), 47–72.

7. For an outline and even advocacy of this position—with regard to woman as "subject"—see Judith Butler, *Gender Trouble: Feminism and the Subversion of Identity* (New York: Routledge, 1990). The argument is premised primarily on Michel Foucault's discussion of subjects and subjugation in *Discipline and Punish: The Birth of the Prison*, trans. Alan Sheridan (New York: Vintage Books, 1995), original French *Surveiller et punir: Naissance de la prison* (Paris: Gallimard, 1975). The translation of the original French title, by the way, is "to watch [as in keeping an eye on] and punish."

8. I offer detailed discussions of bad faith in Lewis R. Gordon, *Bad Faith and Antiblack Racism* (Atlantic Highlands, NJ: Humanities International Press, 1995), and *Existentia Africana: Understanding Africana Existential Thought* (New York: Routledge, 2000).

9. Henry Cornelius Agrippa, *Three Books of Occult Philosophy: The Foundation Book of Western Occultism, Completely Annotated, with Modern Commentary*, trans. James Freake (Woodbury, MN: Llewellyn Publications, 2014 [1531]).

10. See, for example, the French philosophers Simone de Beauvoir, *The Ethics of Ambiguity*, trans. Bernard Frechtman (New York: Citadel, 2000 [1947]); and Jean-Paul Sartre, *Being and Nothingness*, trans. Hazel E. Barnes (New York: Washington Square Press, 1956).

11. Jean-Paul Sartre, *L'imaginaire: Psychologie phénoménologique de l'imagination* (Paris: Gallimard, 1940).

12. For recent studies, see Lamonte Aidoo's *Slavery Unseen: Sex, Power, and Violence in Brazilian History* (Durham, NC: Duke University Press, 2019); and Jane Dailey, *White Fright: The Sexual Panic at the Heart of America's Racist History* (New York: Basic Books, 2020).

13. See Beauvoir, *The Ethics of Ambiguity*.

14. Dena Neusner, *Simply Seder: A Passover Haggadah and Family Seder Planner* (Millburn, NJ: Behrman House, 2011).

15. Simone de Beauvoir, *The Second Sex*, trans. Constance Borde and Sheila Malovany-Chevallier (New York: Citadel, 2000 [French, 1947]).

16. Butler, *Gender Trouble*.

17. Friedrich Nietzsche, *The Gay Science: With a Prelude in Rhymes and an Appendix of Songs*, trans. Walter Kaufmann (New York: Vintage, 1974), and *On the Genealogy of Morals*, trans. Walter Kaufmann and R. J. Hollingdale (New York: Vintage, 1989).

18. Simone Weil, *Gravity and Grace*, trans. Emma Crawford and Mario von der Ruhr (New York: Routledge, 2002 [1947]), 78, 80.

19. Keiji Nishitani, *Religion and Nothingness*, trans. Jan Van Bragt (Berkeley: University of California Press, 1982 [1961]).

20. Thomas Meagher, "Creolization and Maturity: A Philosophical Sketch," *Contemporary Political Theory* 17, no. 3 (August 2018): 382–86.

21. Henri Bergson, *Laughter: An Essay on the Meaning of the Comic*, trans. Cloudesley Brereton and Fred Rothwell (Mansfield Center, CT: Martino Publishing, 2014 [1912]), 4.

22. Bergson, *Laughter*, 23 (emphasis in the original).

23. Bergson, *Laughter*, 28.

24. Bergson, *Laughter*, 29 (emphasis in the original).

25. For discussion, see Lucy Collins, "Fashion and Personal Identity" (Philosophy Department dissertation, Temple University, 2011).

4. RACE-MAKING

1. Death Penalty Information Center, retrieved on April 8, 2018 (site updated daily), https://deathpenaltyinfo.org/race-and-death-penalty (accessed February 21, 2021).

2. This is now well known. For information in the United States, see the Centers for Disease Control and Prevention report "Health Equity Considerations and Racial and Ethnic Minority Groups," https://www.cdc.gov/coronavirus/2019-ncov /community/health-equity/race-ethnicity.html (accessed June 1, 2021); and APM Research Lab Staff, "The Color of Coronavirus: COVID-19 Deaths by Race and Ethnicity in the U.S.," June 10, 2020, https://www.apmresearchlab.org /covid/deaths-by-race (accessed February 21, 2021). In the U.K., see Mélissa Godin, "Black and Asian People Are 2 to 3 Times More Likely to Die of COVID-19," U.K. Study Finds," *Time*, May 6, 2020, https://time.com/5832807/coronavirus -race-analysis-uk/ (accessed February 21, 2021); and Robert Booth and Caelainn Barr, "Black People Four Times More Likely to Die from COVID-19, ONS Finds," *The Guardian*, May 7, 2020, https://www.theguardian.com/world/2020 /may/07/black-people-four-times-more-likely-to-die-from-covid-19-ons-finds (accessed February 21, 2021). And in Brazil, see Kia Lilly Caldwell and Edna Maria de Araújo, "COVID-19 Is Deadlier for Black Brazilians, a Legacy of Structural Racism That Dates Back to Slavery," *The Conversation*, June 10, 2020, https://theconversation.com/covid-19-is-deadlier-for-black-brazilians-a-legacy -of-structural-racism-that-dates-back-to-slavery-139430 (accessed February 21, 2021).

   Data from countries with a long history of racism are so many that they would, as one might guess, make this note eclipse the chapter.

3. See V. F. Cordova, *How It Is: The Native American Philosophy of V. F. Cordova*, ed. Kathleen Dean Moore, Kurt Peters, Ted Jojola, and Amber Lacy (Tucson: University of Arizona Press, 2007); Vine Deloria, Jr., *Custer Died for Your Sins: An Indian Manifesto* (Norman: University of Oklahoma Press, 1988 [1969]), and *The Metaphysics of Modern Existence* (Golden, CO: Fulcrum, 2012 [1979]); and Glen Sean Coulthard, *Red Skin, White Masks: Rejecting the Colonial Politics of Recognition* (Minneapolis: University of Minnesota Press, 2014). For a history and portrait of weaponized diplomacy as a means of invasion, see Suzan Shown Harjo, ed., *Nation to Nation: Treaties Between the United States and American Indian Nations* (Washington, DC: Museum of the American Indian in association with Smithsonian Books, 2014).

4. See Sebastián de Covarrubias's *Tesoro de la lengua castellana o española* [Treasury of Castilian or Spanish language], published in Madrid in 1611. For an excellent discussion, see David Nirenberg, "Race and the Middle Ages: The Case of Spain and Its Jews," in *Rereading the Black Legend: The Discourses of Religious and Racial Difference in the Renaissance Empires*, ed. Margaret R. Greer, Walter D. Mignolo, and Maureen Quilligan (Chicago: University of Chicago Press, 2007), 71–87.

5. For research on the Moors, see, for example, Ivan Van Sertima, ed., *Golden Age of the Moor* (New Brunswick, NJ: Transaction Publishers, 1992).

6. Stanford Joines, *The Eighth Flag: Cannibals. Conquistadors. Buccaneers. Pirates. The Untold Story of the Caribbean and the Mystery of St. Croix's Pirate Legacy, 1493–1750* (independently published, Amazon.com, 2018), 11.

7. Joines, *The Eighth Flag*, 11–12.

8. For a concise history of Semitism and antisemitism, see Mustafa Selim Yılmaz, "Bir Terimin Arkeolojisi: Antisemitizmin Teolojik ve Politik Tarihi / The Archaeology of a Concept: The Theological and Political History of Antisemitism," *Cumhuriyet İlahiyat Dergisi / Cumhuriyet Theology Journal* 21, no. 2 (December 2017): 1181–216. See also Lewis R. Gordon, Ramón Grosfoguel, and Eric Mielants, eds., "Historicizing Anti-Semitism," special issue, *Human Architecture: Journal of the Sociology of Self-Knowledge* 7, no. 2 (Spring 2009).

9. See, for example, Falguni A. Sheth, *Toward a Political Philosophy of Race* (Albany: State University of New York Press, 2009).

10. Enrique Dussel, "Anti-Cartesian Meditations: On the Origins of the Philosophical Anti-Discourse of Modernity," *Human Architecture* 11, no. 1 (Fall 2013): 21–24.

11. Jane Anna Gordon, *Creolizing Political Theory: Reading Rousseau Through Fanon* (New York: Fordham University Press, 2014).

12. Lucius Annaeus Seneca, "De Superstitione." The original survives only in fragments and quotations in writings such as Saint Augustine, *The City of God*, trans. Marcus Dods (New York: Modern Library, 1950), 204.

13. Catherine Nixey, *The Darkening Age: The Christian Destruction of the Classical World* (London: Pan Books, 2017), xxiv.

14. Nixey, *The Darkening Age*, xxix.

15. I elaborate on this aspect of Fanon's thought in Lewis R. Gordon, *What Fanon*

Said: A Philosophical Introduction to His Life and Thought (New York: Fordham University Press; London: Hurst; Johannesburg: Wits University Press, 2015).

16. W.E.B. Du Bois, *The Souls of Black Folk: Essays and Sketches* (Chicago: A. C. McClurg, 1903), *Black Reconstruction in America, 1860–1880* (New York: Harcourt, Brace, 1938 [1935]), and *The World and Africa* (New York: International Publishers, 1979 [1947]). For discussion, see Lewis R. Gordon, "An Africana Philosophical Reading of Du Bois's Political Thought," in *A Political Companion to W.E.B. Du Bois*, ed. Nick Bromell (Lexington: University of Kentucky Press, 2018), 57–81. See also Terrence Johnson's thoughtful study, *Tragic Soul-Life: W.E.B. Du Bois and the Moral Crisis Facing American Democracy* (New York: Oxford University Press, 2011).

17. Sterling Stuckey, "Twilight of Our Past: Reflections on the Origins of Black History," in *Amistad 2: Writings on Black History and Culture*, ed. J. A. Williams and C. F. Harris (New York: Vintage, 1971), 291.

18. Deloria, *Custer Died for Your Sins*, 81.

19. Lewis R. Gordon, *Disciplinary Decadence: Living Thought in Trying Times* (New York: Routledge, 2006).

20. See Du Bois, "The Study of the Negro Problems" and *The Souls of Black Folk*; and my chapter "What Does It Mean to Be a Problem?," in *Existentia Africana: Understanding Africana Existential Thought* (New York: Routledge, 2000), in addition to *Disciplinary Decadence*.

5. RACISM INTERSECTED

1. A genealogy of this line of thought points to Anna Julia Cooper, *A Voice from the South* (Xenia, OH: Aldine Printing House, 1892); Angela Y. Davis, *Women, Race, and Class* (New York: Vintage, 1983); Hortense J. Spillers, *Black, White, and in Color: Essays on American Literature and Culture* (Chicago: University of Chicago Press, 2003); and Kimberlé Crenshaw, "Mapping the Margins: Intersectionality, Identity Politics, and Violence Against Women of Color," *Stanford Law Review* 43 (July 1991): 1241–99. There are, of course, many others who could be named. See also Evelyn M. Simien and Ange-Marie Hancock, "Intersectionality Research," *Political Research Quarterly* 64, no. 1 (March 2011): 185–243.

2. In addition to Crenshaw, "Mapping the Margins," see Bim Adewunmi's interview with Crenshaw, "Kimberlé Crenshaw on Intersectionality: 'I Wanted to Come Up with an Everyday Metaphor That Anyone Could Use,'" *New Statesman*, April 2, 2014, http://www.newstatesman.com/lifestyle/2014/04/kimberl-crenshaw-intersectionality-i-wanted-come-everyday-metaphor-anyone-could (accessed February 21, 2021).

3. Again, see Noel A. Cazenave, *Killing African Americans: Police and Vigilante Violence as a Racial Control Mechanism* (New York: Routledge, 2018); Alex S. Vitale, *The End of Policing* (London: Verso, 2017); and Geo Maher, *A World Without Police: How Strong Communities Make Cops Obsolete* (London: Verso, 2021). See also Matthew Clair, *Privilege and Punishment: How Race and Class Matter in Criminal Court* (Princeton, NJ: Princeton University Press, 2020); and for a more

global perspective, Jean Comaroff and John L. Comaroff, *The Truth About Crime: Sovereignty, Knowledge, Social Order* (Chicago: University of Chicago Press, 2016).

4. I introduced this approach in Lewis R. Gordon, *Her Majesty's Other Children: Sketches of Racism from a Neocolonial Age* (Lanham, MD: Rowman and Littlefield, 1997), in the chapter "Sex, Race, and Matrices of Desire."

5. Sri Aurobindo, *The Future Evolution of Man: The Divine Life upon Earth* (Twin Lakes, WI: Lotus Press, 1963).

6. This literature is vast, but the lay reader could consult the following for summaries of the research: Greta Jochem, "Neanderthal Genes Help Shape How Many Modern Humans Look," NPR, October 5, 2017, https://www.npr.org /sections/health-shots/2017/10/05/555592707/neanderthal-genes-help-shape-how -many-modern-humans-look (accessed February 21, 2021); and Matthew Warren, "Biggest Denisovan Fossil Yet Spills Ancient Human's Secrets," *Nature*, May 1, 2019, https://www.nature.com/articles/d41586-019-01395-0 (accessed February 21, 2021). For those wishing to delve into the specialized literature, see, for example, Kwang Hyun Ko, "Hominin Interbreeding and the Evolution of Human Variation," *Journal of Biological Research-Thessaloniki* 23 (December 2016): 17, https://www.ncbi.nlm.nih.gov/pmc/articles/PMC4947341/ (accessed February 21, 2021); and Michael Dannemann and Janet Kelso, "The Contribution of Neanderthals to Phenotypic Variation in Modern Humans," *The American Journal of Human Genetics* 101, no. 4 (October 5, 2017): 578–89, https://www.cell.com /ajhg/fulltext/S0002-9297(17)30379-8 (accessed February 21, 2021).

7. See, for example, Megan Gannon, "How Smart Were Neanderthals?," *Live Science*, March 23, 2019, https://www.livescience.com/65003-how-smart-were -neanderthals.html (accessed February 21, 2021); Sarah Kaplan, "Humans Didn't Outsmart the Neanderthals. We Just Outlasted Them," *The Washington Post*, November 1, 2017, https://www.washingtonpost.com/news/speaking-of-science /wp/2017/11/01/humans-didnt-outsmart-the-neanderthals-we-just-outlasted -them (accessed February 21, 2021); "Neanderthals Were Too Smart for Their Own Good," *The Telegraph*, November 18, 2011, https://www.telegraph.co.uk /news/science/science-news/8898321/Neanderthals-were-too-smart-for-their-own -good.html (accessed August 12, 2020); and Joe Alper, "Rethinking Neanderthals," *Smithsonian Magazine*, June 2003, https://www.smithsonianmag.com /science-nature/rethinking-neanderthals-83341003/ (accessed February 21, 2021). And for those wishing to read something more substantial, see Clive Finlayson, *The Smart Neanderthal: Cave Art, Bird Catching, and the Cognitive Revolution* (Oxford: Oxford University Press, 2019).

8. For a succinct summary, see Karl Gruber, "Europeans Did Not Inherit Pale Skins from Neanderthals," *New Scientist*, September 26, 2012, https://www .newscientist.com/article/dn22308-europeans-did-not-inherit-pale-skins-from -neanderthals/ (accessed February 21, 2021). For a recent detailed, scientific account, see Dannemann and Kelso, "The Contribution of Neanderthals to Phenotypic Variation in Modern Humans."

9. Sharon R. Browning, Brian L. Browning, Ying Zhou, Serena Tucci, and Joshua

M. Akey, "Analysis of Human Sequence Data Reveals Two Pulses of Archaic Denisovan Admixture," *Cell* 173, no. 1 (2018): 53–61.

10. See Gruber, "Europeans Did Not Inherit Pale Skins from Neanderthals," and for elaboration of specific genes associated with mutations for color variation, see University of Pennyslvania, "Genes Responsible for Diversity of Human Skin Colors Identified," *ScienceDaily*, October 12, 2017, https://www.sciencedaily.com /releases/2017/10/171012143324.htm (accessed February 21, 2021). See also Olivia Godhill, "How Europeans Became Tall and Fair-Skinned 8,500 Years Ago," *Quartz*, November 28, 2015, https://qz.com/561034/how-europeans-became-tall -and-fair-skinned-8500-years-ago/ (accessed February 21, 2021).

11. Danny Vendramini, *Them and Us: How Neanderthal Predation Created Modern Humans* (Armidale, NSW, Australia: Kardoorair Press, 2009). For scientific criticism, see Adam Benton, "Them and Us: Predatory Neanderthals Hunted Humans?," *Filthy Monkey Men*, May 25, 2015, https://www.filthymonkeymen.com /2015/05/25/them-and-us-predatory-neanderthals-hunted-humans/ (accessed February 21, 2021).

12. Danny Vendramini, "Neanderthal: Profile of a Super Predator," YouTube, December 4, 2010, https://www.youtube.com/watch?v=mZbmywzGAVs (accessed February 21, 2021).

13. Catherine Shoard, "Liam Neeson: After a Friend Was Raped, I Wanted to Kill a Black Man," *The Guardian*, February 4, 2019, https://www.theguardian.com/film /2019/feb/04/liam-neeson-after-a-friend-was-raped-i-wanted-to-kill-a-black-man (accessed February 21, 2021); Elisha Fieldstadt, "Liam Neeson Says He Wanted to Kill a Black Man After a Friend Close to Him Was Raped," NBC News, February 4, 2019, https://www.nbcnews.com/pop-culture/celebrity/liam-neeson-says-he -sought-black-man-kill-after-friend-n966676 (accessed February 21, 2021).

14. This is old news across the African diaspora and many communities of racial mixture. It is usually referred to as "colorism" since most empirical examples are within the context of an overarching white power structure functioning as the racial one. See, for example, Lori L. Tharps, *Same Family, Different Colors: Confronting Colorism in America's Diverse Families* (Boston: Beacon Press, 2016). See also Suzanne Oboler and Anani Dzidzienyo, eds., *Neither Enemies nor Friends: Latinos, Blacks, Afro-Latinos* (New York: Palgrave Macmillan, 2005).

15. See Robert E. Washington, "Brown Racism and the Formation of a World System of Racial Stratification," *International Journal of Politics, Culture, and Society* 4, no. 2 (Winter 1990): 209–27. See also Joanne L. Rondilla and Paul Spickard, *Is Lighter Better? Skin-Tone Discrimination Among Asian Americans* (Lanham, MD: Rowman and Littlefield, 2007); and Nikki Khanna, ed., *Whiter: Asian American Women on Skin Color and Colorism* (New York: NYU Press, 2020).

16. V. T. Rajshekar, *Dalit: The Black Untouchables of India*, 3rd ed. (Atlanta, GA: Clarity Press, 2009), 37. See also Chandramohan S., *Love After Babel and Other Poems* (Ottawa, Canada: Daraja Press, 2020); and Manoj Kumar Panda, *One Thousand Days in a Refrigerator: Stories*, trans. Snehaprava Das (New Delhi: Speaking Tiger, 2016).

17. William Loren Katz, *Black Indians: A Hidden Heritage* (New York: Atheneum, 1986).

18. Osagie K. Obasogie, *Blinded by Sight: Seeing Race Through the Eyes of the Blind* (Palo Alto, CA: Stanford University Press, 2013).

19. Mark Hubbe, "Walter Neves and the Pursuit of the First South Americans," *PaleoAmerica* 1, no. 2 (2015): 131–33. For readers wishing to consult Neves's work directly, see Walter A. Neves and Hector Pucciarelli, "The Zhoukoudian Upper Cave Skull 101 as Seen from the Americas," *Journal of Human Evolution* 34, no. 2 (February 1998): 219–22; and Walter A. Neves, Joseph F. Powell, and Erik G. Ozolins, "Modern Human Origins as Seen from the Peripheries," *Journal of Human Evolution* 37, no. 1 (July 1999): 129–33.

20. See, for example, Saint Augustine, *The City of God*, trans. Marcus Dods, with an introduction by Thomas Merton (New York: Modern Library, 1950); Gottfried Wilhelm Leibniz, *Theodicy*, ed. Austin Farrer and trans. E. M. Huggard (New Haven, CT: Yale University Press, 1952); Kwame Gyekye, *An Essay on African Philosophical Thought: The Akan Conceptual Scheme*, rev. ed. (Philadelphia: Temple University Press, 1987); John Hick, *Evil and the God of Love*, rev. ed. (New York: Harper and Row, 1978); William R. Jones, *Is God a White Racist? A Preamble to Black Theology*, 2nd ed. (Boston: Beacon Press, 1997); Sherman A. Jackson, *Islam and the Problem of Black Suffering* (New York: Oxford University Press, 2009); and Anthony B. Pinn, *Why, Lord? Suffering and Evil in Black Theology* (New York: Continuum, 1999). See also Lewis R. Gordon, *An Introduction to Africana Philosophy* (Cambridge, UK: Cambridge University Press, 2008), and *Freedom, Justice, and Decolonization* (New York: Routledge, 2021).

21. Gyekye offers an excellent critique along these and other lines in *An Essay on African Philosophical Thought*. See also Hick's *Evil and the God of Love*. I offer critical discussion in many contexts, including in *Freedom, Justice, and Decolonization* and, with Jane Anna Gordon, *Of Divine Warning: Reading Disaster in the Modern Age* (New York: Routledge, 2009).

22. In South Africa and the United States, constitutionalism has become a form of idolatry through which the larger picture of their constitutions often stopping short where the lives of the damned of the earth are concerned is often ignored. I discuss this problem in *Freedom, Justice, and Decolonization*; see also Rozena Maart, "Philosophy Born of Massacres. Marikana, the Theatre of Cruelty: The Killing of the 'Kaffir,'" *Acta Academica* 46, no. 4 (2014): 1–28.

23. For a detailed discussion of Kant's misadventures in the study of race and how they affected even his conception of ethics, see J. Reid Miller, *Stain Removal: Ethics and Race* (New York: Oxford University Press, 2016).

24. This has been well known and kept relatively quiet for decades. For a recent summary, see Sarah Spain, "Africa Is Most Genetically Diverse Continent, DNA Study Shows," *BioNews*, May 10, 2019, https://www.bionews.org.uk/page _91054 (accessed February 21, 2021). She should have, of course, stated "genetically diverse continent of human beings." For those who would like to consult specialized literature on this diversity, see L. B. Jorde, W. S. Watkins, M. J.

Bamshad, M. E. Dixon, C. E. Ricker, M. T. Seielstad, and M. A. Batzer, "The Distribution of Human Genetic Diversity: A Comparison of Mitochondrial, Autosomal, and Y-Chromosome Data," *American Journal of Human Genetics* 66, no. 3 (March 2000): 979–88, https://www.sciencedirect.com/science/article/pii /S0002929707640245 (accessed February 21, 2021).

25. For a compilation of the literature in question, from Bernier through to Galton, see Robert Bernasconi and Tommy L. Lott, eds., *The Idea of Race* (Indianapolis, IN: Hackett Publishers, 2000).

6. PRIVILEGE, LUXURY, LICENSE

1. Peggy McIntosh, "White Privilege and Male Privilege: A Personal Account of Coming to See Correspondences Through Work in Women's Studies," Working Paper 189, Wellesley, MA: Wellesley College, Center for Research on Women, 1988.

2. Ben Montgomery, "FBI Closes Book on Claude Neal's Lynching Without Naming Killers," *Tampa Bay Times*, August 3, 2014, https://www.tampabay.com /features/humaninterest/fbi-closes-book-on-claude-neals-lynching-without -naming-killers/2191344 (accessed February 21, 2021). This was not, unfortunately, unusual. See Anne P. Rice, ed., *Witnessing Lynching: American Writers Respond* (New Brunswick, NJ: Rutgers University Press, 2003).

3. The literature is vast. For a recent summary, see Maurício Brum, "How Belgium Cut Off Hands and Arms, and Killed over 15 Million in Africa," *Gazeta do Povo/ Wise Up News*, July 2, 2019, https://www.gazetadopovo.com.br/wiseup-news/how -belgium-cut-off-hands-and-arms-and-killed-over-15-million-in-africa/. See also Adam Hochschild's *King Leopold's Ghost: A Story of Greed, Terror, and Heroism in Colonial Africa* (Boston: Houghton Mifflin, 1999); and Walter Rodney's classic, *How Europe Underdeveloped Africa* (Washington, DC: Howard University Press, 1982).

4. This literature is also vast. For a succinct discussion, see Norimitsu Onishi and Melissa Eddy, "A Forgotten Genocide: What Germany Did in Namibia, and What It's Saying Now," *The New York Times*, May 28, 2021, updated May 29, 2021, https:// www.nytimes.com/2021/05/28/world/europe/germany-namibia-genocide.html.

5. Adolf Hitler, *Mein Kampf* (Munich: Franz Eher Nachfolger, 1925). Critical discussions of Hitler's logic are many. For a more recent analysis, see Jason Stanley, *How Fascism Works: The Politics of Us and Them* (New York: Random House, 2018).

6. W.E.B. Du Bois discusses this phenomenon in "Of the Sons of Master and Man," chapter 9 in *The Souls of Black Folk: Essays and Sketches* (Chicago: A. C. McClurg, 1903). See also Ida B. Wells, *The Light of Truth: Writings of an Anti-Lynching Crusader*, ed. Mia Bay and Henry Louis Gates, Jr. (New York: Penguin Classics, 2014). Contemporary writers include Michelle Alexander, Noel A. Cazenave, William Darity, Jr., Angela Y. Davis, Roxanne Dunbar-Ortiz, A. Kirsten Mullen, and Alex S. Vitale.

7. See Cherryl Walker, ed., *Women and Gender in Southern Africa to 1945* (Claremont, South Africa: David Philip Publishers, 1990). See also Jonathan Hyslop,

"White Working-Class Women and the Invention of Apartheid: 'Purified' Afrikaner Nationalist Agitation for Legislation Against 'Mixed' Marriages, 1934–9," *The Journal of African History* 36, no. 1 (1995): 57–81.

8. Frantz Fanon, *Peau noire, masques blancs* (Paris: Éditions du Seuil, 1952), introduction and chapter 7.

7. TRANS BUT NOT TRANSCENDED

1. For elaboration, see Rogers Brubaker, *Trans: Gender and Race in an Age of Unsettled Identities* (Princeton, NJ: Princeton University Press, 2016).

2. Nkiru Uwechia Nzegwu, *Family Matters: Feminist Concepts in African Philosophy of Culture* (Albany: State University of New York Press, 2006); and Oyèrónké Oyěwùmí, *The Invention of Women* (Minneapolis: University of Minnesota Press, 1997), and *What Gender Is Motherhood? Changing Yorùbá Ideals of Power, Procreation, and Identity in the Age of Modernity* (New York: Palgrave, 2015).

3. Simone de Beauvoir's *The Second Sex* is the classic statement of this argument.

4. Rebecca Tuvel, "In Defense of Transracialism," *Hypatia* 32, no. 2 (2017): 263–78. See also Rebecca Tuvel, "Changing Identities: Are Race and Gender Analogous?," *Black Issues in Philosophy*, July 6, 2021, https://blog.apaonline.org/2021/07/06/changing-identities-are-race-and-gender-analogous.

5. The reactions are too many to list here. The reader can consult the special symposium on the controversy, with critical essays and a reply, in *Philosophy Today* 62, no. 1 (January 2018), where Rebecca Tuvel's re-articulation of her position is available in "Racial Transitions and Controversial Positions: Reply to Taylor, Gordon, Sealey, Hom, and Botts," 73–88, and in the aforementioned "Changing Identities: Are Race and Gender Analogous?"

6. For a summary of these arguments and their proponents, see Paul C. Taylor, *Race: A Philosophical Introduction*, 2nd ed. (Cambridge, UK: Polity, 2013).

7. For a classic study of this argument, see Peter L. Berger and Thomas Luckmann, *The Social Construction of Reality* (New York: Random House, 1966).

8. For elaboration and histories of Jews and Muslims who converted to Christianity—referred to as "Conversos" and "Moriscos"—in medieval Iberia, see Geraldine Heng, *The Invention of Race in the European Middle Ages* (Cambridge, UK: Cambridge University Press, 2018); and Lisa Vollendorf, *The Lives of Women: A New History of Inquisitional Spain* (Nashville, TN: Vanderbilt University Press, 2005).

9. See Angelina Chapin, "Of Course White Women Voted for Trump Again," *The Cut*, November 17, 2020, https://www.thecut.com/2020/11/many-white-women-still-voted-for-trump-in-2020.html (accessed February 21, 2021). Worse, their numbers for Trump increased while the number of white male votes decreased; see Ruth Igielnik, Scott Keeter, and Hannah Hartig, "Behind Biden's 2020 Victory: An Examination of the 2020 Electorate, Based on Validated Voters," Pew Research Center, June 30, 2021, https://www.pewresearch.org/politics/2021/06/30/behind-bidens-2020-victory.

10. Blacks in the United States who identified as "strong Republicans" in 2016 were only 2 percent of the black voting population. See "Black Party Affiliation," BlackDemographics.com, https://blackdemographics.com/culture/black -politics (accessed February 21, 2021).

11. For elaboration, in addition to Brubaker's *Trans*, also see Judith Halberstram, *Female Masculinity* (Durham, NC: Duke University Press, 1998). See also Judith Butler, *Gender Trouble: Feminism and the Subversion of Identity* (New York: Routledge, 1990); and Lewis R. Gordon, *Bad Faith and Antiblack Racism* (Atlantic Highlands, NJ: Humanities International Press, 1995), and *Her Majesty's Other Children: Sketches of Racism from a Neocolonial Age* (Lanham, MD: Rowman and Littlefield, 1997).

12. For a historical study, see C. Riley Snorton, *Black on Both Sides: A Racial History of Trans Identity*, 3rd ed. (Minneapolis: University of Minnesota Press, 2017).

13. There are, of course, white-looking black people who do identify as black. The examples are many, but for a most recent popular story, see Khushbu Shah, "They Look White but Say They're Black: A Tiny Town in Ohio Wrestles with Race," *The Guardian*, July 25, 2019, https://www.theguardian.com/us-news /2019/jul/25/race-east-jackson-ohio-appalachia-white-black (accessed February 21, 2021).

14. The Pew Research Center reveals that whites marry outside their group the least. See the data on its web page "Intermarriage," https://www.pewresearch .org/topics/intermarriage (accessed February 21, 2021). For discussion and data, see, for example, Gretchen Livingston and Anna Brown, "Intermarriage in the U.S. 50 Years After *Loving v. Virginia*," Pew Research Center: Social and Demographic Trends, May 18, 2017, http://www.pewsocialtrends.org/2017/05/18 /intermarriage-in-the-u-s-50-years-after-loving-v-virginia/ (accessed February 21, 2021). Marriage, of course, is not identical with dating, and, of course, there is the question of producing children outside marriage.

15. See, for example, Anténor Firmin, *The Equality of the Human Races: A Nineteenth Century Haitian Scholar's Response to European Racialism*, trans. Asselin Charles (New York: Garland Publishers, 2000 [1885]); Frantz Fanon, *Peau noire, masques blancs* (Paris: Éditions du Seuil, 1952); Angela Y. Davis, *Women, Race, and Class* (New York: Vintage, 1983); Hilary McD. Beckles, *Natural Rebels: A Social History of Enslaved Women in Barbados* (New Brunswick, NJ: Rutgers University Press, 1989); Lamonte Aidoo, *Slavery Unseen: Sex, Power, and Violence in Brazilian History* (Durham, NC: Duke University Press, 2019); Jane Dailey, *White Fright: The Sexual Panic at the Heart of America's Racist History* (New York: Basic Books, 2020); Jane Ward, "The White Supremacist Origins of Modern Marriage Advice," *The Conversation*, August 27, 2020, https://theconversation.com/the -white-supremacist-origins-of-modern-marriage-advice-144782; and Rebecca Stevens, "White Men and the Sexual Fetishization of Black Women," *Illumination*, September 9, 2020, https://medium.com/illumination-curated/white-men -and-the-sexual-fetishization-of-black-women-ca046b8d1da8.

16. Cara Rose DeFabio, "If You're Black, DNA Ancestry Results Can Reveal an Awkward Truth," *Splinter*, September 29, 2016, https://splinternews.com/if-you-re -black-dna-ancestry-results-can-reveal-an-awk-1793862284 (accessed February 21, 2021). For the relevant study, see Katarzyna Bryc, Eric Y. Durand, J. Michael Macpherson, David Reich, and Joanna L. Mountain, "The Genetic Ancestry of African Americans, Latinos, and European Americans Across the United States," *The American Journal of Human Genetics* 96, December 8, 2014, http://www.cell .com/ajhg/fulltext/S0002-9297(14)00476-5 (accessed February 21, 2021). For demographics and genomic information on the proportion of blacks who are of European ancestry versus whites who are of black ancestry, see Lizzie Wade, "Genetic Study Reveals Surprising Ancestry of Many Americans," *Science*, December 18, 2014, https://www.sciencemag.org/news/2014/12/genetic-study-reveals -surprising-ancestry-many-americans (accessed August 12, 2020); and "How African Is Black America," BlackDemographics.com, https://blackdemographics .com/geography/african-american-dna/ (accessed February 21, 2021).

17. Vine Deloria, Jr., *Custer Died for Your Sins: An Indian Manifesto* (Norman: University of Oklahoma Press, 1988 [1969]), 2–3.

18. For elaboration, see Jane Anna Gordon, *Creolizing Political Theory: Reading Rousseau Through Fanon* (New York: Fordham University Press, 2014); and Michael J. Monahan, *The Creolizing Subject: Race, Reason, and the Politics of Purity* (New York: Fordham University Press, 2011).

19. I am here referring to the guiding idea of the influential text by Alain Badiou, *Being and Event*, trans. Oliver Feltham (London: Bloomsbury, 2013).

20. See Sara Ahmed, *Queer Phenomenology: Orientations, Objects, Others* (Durham, NC: Duke University Press, 2006); and David Ross Fryer, *Thinking Queerly: Race, Sex, Gender, and the Ethics of Identity* (New York: Routledge, 2008).

21. See Meg-John Barker and Alex Iantaffi, *Life Isn't Binary: On Being Both, Beyond, and In-Between* (London: Jessica Kingsley Publishers, 2019).

8. FIVE KINDS OF INVISIBILITY

1. For those in doubt, see Ryan Sit, "Trump Thinks Only Black People Are on Welfare, but Really, White Americans Receive Most Benefits," *Newsweek*, January 12, 2018, http://www.newsweek.com/donald-trump-welfare-black-white -780252, accessed August 12, 2020; and Tracy Jan, "The Biggest Beneficiaries of the Government Safety Net: Working-Class Whites," *The Washington Post*, February 16, 2017, https://www.washingtonpost.com/news/wonk/wp/2017/02/16 /the-biggest-beneficiaries-of-the-government-safety-net-working-class-whites/ ?utm_term=.bc219d2e03a1 (accessed February 21, 2021). See also William A. Darity, Jr., and A. Kirsten Mullen, *From Here to Equality: Reparations for Black Americans in the Twenty-First Century* (Chapel Hill: University of North Carolina Press, 2020).

2. For discussion of the recurrence of these arguments, along with scientific demonstrations of their flaws, see Stephen Jay Gould, *The Mismeasure of Man*,

rev. and expand. ed. (New York: W. W. Norton, 1996); and Angela Saini, *Superior: The Return of Race Science* (Noida: HarperCollins Publishers India, 2019). See also Lewis R. Gordon, *Bad Faith and Antiblack Racism* (Atlantic Highlands, NJ: Humanities International Press, 1995).

3. See W.E.B. Du Bois, *The Souls of Black Folk: Essays and Sketches* (Chicago: A. C. McClurg, 1903); and Angela Y. Davis, *Angela Davis: An Autobiography* (New York: Random House, 1974), *Are Prisons Obsolete?* (New York: Seven Stories Press, 2003), and *Abolition Democracy: Beyond Empire, Prisons, and Torture* (New York: Seven Stories Press, 2005). See also Michelle Alexander, *The New Jim Crow: Mass Incarceration in the Age of Colorblindness* (New York: New Press, 2010); Angela J. Davis, *Arbitrary Justice: The Power of the American Prosecutor* (New York: Oxford University Press, 2009), and, as editor, *Policing the Black Man: Arrest, Prosecution, and Imprisonment* (New York: Pantheon Books, 2017); Marie Gottschalk, *Caught: The Prison State and the Lockdown of American Politics* (Princeton, NJ: Princeton University Press, 2015); Ibram X. Kendi, *Stamped from the Beginning* (New York: Bold Type Books, 2017); Khalil Gibran Muhammad, *The Condemnation of Blackness: Race, Crime, and the Making of Modern Urban America* (Cambridge, MA: Harvard University Press, 2011); and Michael Tillotson, *Invisible Jim Crow: Contemporary Ideological Threats to the Internal Security of African Americans* (Trenton, NJ: Africa World Press, 2011).

4. See Frank R. Baumgartner, Derek A. Epp, and Kelsey Shoub, *Suspect Citizen: What 20 Million Traffic Stops Tell Us About Policing and Race* (Cambridge, UK: Cambridge University Press, 2018).

5. Nathalie Etoke, *Melancholia Africana: The Indispensable Overcoming of the Black Condition*, trans. Bill Hamlett (London: Rowman and Littlefield International, 2019).

6. Vine Deloria, Jr., *Custer Died for Your Sins: An Indian Manifesto* (Norman: University of Oklahoma Press, 1988 [1969]), 215.

7. Russell Thornton, *American Indian Holocaust and Survival: A Population History Since 1492* (Normal: University of Oklahoma Press, 1990).

8. Duane Brayboy, "Two Spirits, One Heart, Five Genders," *Indian Country Today* September 7, 2017, https://indiancountrytoday.com/archive/two-spirits-one-heart -five-genders (accessed February 21, 2021).

9. See, for example, the Igbo philosopher and art historian Nkiru Uwechia Nzegwu's *Family Matters: Feminist Concepts in African Philosophy of Culture* (Albany: State University of New York Press, 2006); and the Yorùbá sociologist Oyèrónkẹ́ Oyěwùmí's *The Invention of Women* (Minneapolis: University of Minnesota Press, 1997), and *What Gender Is Motherhood? Changing Yorùbá Ideals of Power, Procreation, and Identity in the Age of Modernity* (New York: Palgrave, 2015).

10. Christine de Pizan, *The Book of the City of Ladies*, trans. Rosalind Brown-Grant (New York: Penguin Classics, 2000 [1405]), and *The Treasure of the City of Ladies, or the Book of the Three Virtues*, trans. Sarah Lawson (New York: Penguin

Classics, 2003 [1405]); Anna Julia Cooper's *A Voice from the South* (Xenia, OH: Aldine Printing House, 1892); He-Yin Zhen, "On the Question of Women's Liberation," "On the Revenge of Women," and "The Feminist Manifesto," in *The Birth of Chinese Feminism: Essential Texts in Transnational Theory*, ed. Lydia H. Liu, Rebecca E. Karl, and Dorothy Ko (New York: Columbia University Press, 2013), 53–186.

11. Janet L. Borgerson, *Caring and the Power in Female Leadership: A Philosophical Approach* (Newcastle upon Tyne: Cambridge Scholars Press, 2018).

12. Jaspal Kaur Singh, *Violence and Resistance in Sikh Gendered Identity* (Milton Park, UK: Routledge, 2020).

13. Carol Gilligan, *In a Different Voice: Psychological Theory and Women's Development* (Cambridge, MA: Harvard University Press, 1982); Michelle Walker, "Silence and Reason: Woman's Voice in Philosophy," *Australasian Journal of Philosophy* 71, no. 4: 400–424; Kathryn Lasky, *A Voice of Her Own: The Story of Phillis Wheatley, Slave Poet* (Somerville, MA: Candlewick, 2005); Melissa Silverstein, ed., *In Her Voice: Women Directors Talk Directing* (Women and Hollywood, 2013); Miki Raver, *Listen to Her Voice: Women in the Hebrew Bible* (Vancouver: Chronicle Books, 2005); Judy Yung, *Unbound Voices* (Berkeley: University of California Press, 1999); Emily Honig and Gail Hershatter, eds., *Personal Voices: Chinese Women in the 1980s* (Palo Alto, CA: Stanford University Press, 1988); Xinran, *The Good Women of China: Hidden Voices* (New York: Anchor Books, 2003).

14. See Cheryl R. Rodriguez, Dzodzi Tsikata, and Akosua Adomako Ampofo, eds., *Transatlantic Feminisms: Women and Gender Studies in Africa and the Diaspora* (Lanham, MD: Lexington Books, 2015).

15. Jacob Grimm and Wilhelm Grimm, *The Original Folk and Fairy Tales of the Brothers Grimm: The Complete First Edition*, trans. Jack Zipes (Princeton, NJ: Princeton University Press, 2016 [1812–1815]). The Queen in the original 1812 version was Snow White's biological mother, but this was too much for audiences to bear, so she was rewritten as a stepmother.

16. Chandramohan Sathyanathan, "On the Slave Bible," included here by permission of the poet.

17. Deloria, *Custer Died for Your Sins*, 8.

18. Coulthard focused on Fanon's *Black Skin, White Masks*. For Patrick Wolfe's writings, see his "Settler Colonialism and the Elimination of the Native," *Journal of Genocide Research* 8, no. 4 (2006): 387–409, and *Traces of History: Elementary Structures of Race* (London: Verso, 2016). See also Sandy Grande, ed., *Red Pedagogy: Native American Social and Political Thought* (Lanham: Rowman and Littlefield, 2004).

19. Robert Hughes, *The Fatal Shore: The Epic of Australia's Founding* (New York: Vintage, 1986).

20. Specifically, "the death project." See Julia Suárez-Krabbe, *Race, Rights and Rebels: Alternatives to Human Rights and Development from the Global South*

(London: Rowman and Littlefield International, 2014), passim, but see the first chapter, "Bad Faith and the Death Project," where she defines it as a set of attitudes and systematic organization of a world dedicated to the elimination of other forms of life.

21. In addition to Deloria's analysis in *Custer Died for Your Sins*, see Du Bois, *Black Reconstruction in America, 1860–1880*; and Oliver Cromwell Cox, *Race: A Study in Social Dynamics* (New York: Monthly Review Press, 2000), the fiftieth-anniversary annotated edition of his classic *Caste, Class, and Race*.

22. Chandramohan Sathyanathan, original unpublished version of "My Language," quoted here by permission from the author.

23. The earlier argument is from Frantz Fanon, *Peau noire, masques blancs* (Paris: Éditions du Seuil, 1952), and the later one is from *L'an V de la révolution algérienne* (Paris: Maspero, 1959).

24. Fanon, *Peau noire, masques blancs*, chapter 6.

25. Fanon, *Peau noire, masques blancs*, last sentence of the text.

26. For elaboration of this argument, see Lewis R. Gordon, *What Fanon Said* (New York: Fordham University Press, 2015). See also Lewis R. Gordon, "Decolonizing Frankenstein," *The Common Reader: A Journal of the Essay*, no. 10 (Fall 2018): 37–47, where I offer a similar argument through placing Mary Shelley's famous novel in conversation with Fanon's thought.

27. See Frantz Fanon, *Les damnés de la terre* (Paris: Éditions Gallimard, 1991 [1961]). This work is most known in English as *The Wretched of the Earth*. I prefer to call it *The Damned of the Earth* since that title not only is literal but also highlights the actual argument of the text.

28. Steve Chapman, "Why Do Whites Oppose the NFL Protest?," *Chicago Tribune*, September 6, 2017, https://www.chicagotribune.com/columns/steve-chapman/ct-perspec-whites-nfl-anthem-protests-20170927-story.html (accessed February 21, 2021).

29. This idea comes from Jane Anna Gordon building on W.E.B. Du Bois's and Paget Henry's thought on potentiated second sight in her essay "The Gift of Double Consciousness: Some Obstacles to Grasping the Contributions of the Colonized," in *Postcolonialism and Political Theory*, ed. Nalini Persram (Lanham, MD: Lexington Books, 2007), 143–61. She expands on this concept in her theory of creolization in *Creolizing Political Theory*.

30. I offer more analysis of this experience of oppression in writings ranging from *Bad Faith and Antiblack Racism* to *Existentia Africana* and *Disciplinary Decadence*. For commentary and creative elaboration, see danielle davis, ed., *Black Existentialism: Essays on the Transformative Thought of Lewis R. Gordon* (London: Rowman and Littlefield International, 2019).

31. James Davis III, "Law, Prison, and Double-Double Consciousness: A Phenomenological View of the Black Prisoner's Experience," *Yale Law Journal* 128 (2018–2019), https://www.yalelawjournal.org/forum/double-double-consciousness (accessed February 21, 2021).

32. Steve Bantu Biko, *I Write What I Like: Selected Writings* (Chicago: University of Chicago Press, 2002 [1978]).

9. BLACK CONSCIOUSNESS IS POLITICAL

1. See, for example, Temma Kaplan, *Democracy: A World History* (Oxford: Oxford University Press, 2015).
2. Frantz Fanon, *Les damnés de la terre* [The damned of the earth] (Paris: Éditions Gallimard, 1991 [1961]), 217; and Benjamin R. Barber, *Cool Cities: Urban Sovereignty and the Fix for Global Warming* (New Haven, CT: Yale University Press, 2017).
3. Derefe Kimarley Chevannes offers elaboration of these issues in "Creolizing Political Speech: Toward Black Existential Articulations," *Review of Education, Pedagogy, and Cultural Studies* 40, no. 1 (2018): 5–15, and "The Philosophical Project of Political Speech," *Black Issues in Philosophy* (blog), American Philosophical Association, August 21, 2018, https://blog.apaonline.org/2018/08/21/black-issues-in-philosophy-the-philosophical-project-of-political-speech/ (accessed February 21, 2021).
4. See, for example, Joel Mendelson, "Disney World Is Anything but Magical for Its Employees," *Jobs with Justice*, December 5, 2017, https://www.jwj.org/disney-world-is-anything-but-magical-for-its-employees (accessed February 21, 2021); and Henry A. Giroux and Grace Pollock, *The Mouse That Roared: Disney and the Loss of Innocence*, 2nd ed. (Lanham, MD: Rowman and Littlefield, 2010).
5. This incident is now infamous and well reported across the globe. See Katie Rogers, "Protestors Dispersed with Tear Gas So Trump Could Pose at Church," *The New York Times*, June 1, 2020, https://www.nytimes.com/2020/06/01/us/politics/trump-st-johns-church-bible.html (accessed February 21, 2021).
6. Associated Press, "Report: Feds Considered Using 'Heat Ray' on DC Protesters," *The Washington Post*, September 16, 2020, https://www.washingtonpost.com/world/national-security/report-feds-considered-using-heat-ray-on-dc-protesters/2020/09/16/74bc499a-f892-11ea-85f7-5941188a98cd_story.html (accessed February 21, 2021). See also Tim Elfrink, "Safety and Ethics Worries Sidelined a 'Heat Ray' for Years. The Feds Asked About Using It on Protesters," *The Washington Post*, September 17, 2020, https://www.washingtonpost.com/nation/2020/09/17/heat-ray-protesters-trump-dc/ (accessed February 21, 2021).
7. See Adriaan de Buck and Alan H. Gardiner, eds., *The Ancient Egyptian Coffin Texts*, c. 2181 B.C.E.–2055 B.C.E., University of Chicago Oriental Institute Publications, vol. 67 (Chicago: University of Chicago Press, 1951).
8. Sigmund Freud, *Civilization and Its Discontents*, trans. James Strachey (New York: W. W. Norton, 1989), 76.
9. Corey D. B. Walker, "'Is America Possible?': Protest, Pandemic, and Planetary Possibility," *Black Issues in Philosophy* (blog), American Philosophical Association, July 7, 2020, https://blog.apaonline.org/2020/07/07/is-america-possible-protest-pandemic-and-planetary-possibility/ (accessed February 21, 2021).
10. Documentation of this phenomenon is manifold, but see, for example, L. A.

Kauffman, "We Are Living Through a Golden Age of Protest," *The Guardian*, May 6, 2018, https://www.theguardian.com/commentisfree/2018/may/06/protest -trump-direct-action-activism (accessed February 21, 2021). The year 2020 made this article also prophetic.

11. "Goal-setting" is Marilyn Nissim-Sabat's formulation in her essay "A Phenomenological and Psychodynamic Reflection on Freedom and Oppression Following the Guiding Thread of Lewis R. Gordon's Existential Phenomenology of Oppression," in danielle davis, ed., *Black Existentialism* (London: Rowman and Littlefield International, 2019), 149–66.

12. See Greg A. Graham, *Democratic Political Tragedy in the Postcolony: The Tragedy of Postcoloniality in Michael Manley's Jamaica and Nelson Mandela's South Africa* (New York: Routledge, 2017).

13. James Boggs, *The American Revolution: Pages from a Negro Worker's Notebook*, 2nd ed. (New York: Monthly Review Press, 2009 [1963]), 90.

14. Karl Jaspers, *Die Schuldfrage: Von der politischen Haftung Deutschlands* (München: Piper Verlag GmbH, 1965 [1947]). The subtitle is "On the Political Liability of Germany."

15. Karl Jaspers, *The Question of German Guilt*, trans. E. B. Ashton (New York: Fordham University Press, 2000 [1947]).

16. See, for example, J. Q. Whitman, *Hitler's American Model: The United States and the Making of Nazi Race Law* (Princeton, NJ: Princeton University Press, 2017). Madison Grant's *The Passing of the Great Race: or, The Racial Basis of European History* (New York: Scribner's Sons, 1916) was especially influential on Nazi eugenics.

17. Iris Marion Young, "Responsibility and Global Labor Justice," *Journal of Political Philosophy* 12, no. 4 (2004): 365–88.

18. Young, "Responsibility and Global Labor Justice," 377.

19. Iris Marion Young, *Responsibility for Justice* (New York: Oxford University Press, 2011), 180–81.

20. Frederick Douglass, *My Bondage and My Freedom* (New York: Penguin Classics, 2003 [1855]), and *The Life and Times of Frederick Douglass* (Radford, VA: Wilder Publications, 2008 [1881]).

21. For some of these accounts, see C.L.R. James, *The Black Jacobins: Toussaint L'Ouverture and the San Domingo Revolution* (New York: Vintage, 1989); Angela Y. Davis, *Women, Race, and Class* (New York: Vintage, 1983); Hilary McD. Beckles, *Natural Rebels: A Social History of Enslaved Women in Barbados* (New Brunswick, NJ: Rutgers University Press, 1989); Hilary McD. Beckles, *Britain's Black Debt: Reparations for Caribbean Slavery and Native Genocide* (Kingston, Jamaica: University of the West Indies Press, 2013); Lamonte Aidoo, *Slavery Unseen: Sex, Power, and Violence in Brazilian History* (Durham, NC: Duke University Press, 2019); and Herbert G. Gutman, *The Black Family in Slavery and Freedom: 1750–1925* (New York: Pantheon Books, 1976).

22. José Ortega y Gasset, *The Revolt of the Masses* (New York: W. W. Norton, 1994 [1929]).

23. Angela Y. Davis, "Unfinished Lecture on Liberation—II," in *Angela Davis: A Primary Reader*, ed. Joy Ann James (Oxford: Blackwell Publishers, 1998), 53–60.

24. For elaboration of this bad-faith "need," see Lewis R. Gordon, "Exoticism," chapter 16 in *Bad Faith and Antiblack Racism* (Atlantic Highlands, NJ: Humanities International Press, 1995), 117–23.

25. James Boggs, "Liberalism, Marxism, and Black Political Power," in *Pages from a Black Radical's Notebook: A James Boggs Reader*, ed. Stephen M. Ward (Detroit: Wayne State University Press, 2011), 159. The criticisms are of Louis Lomax, *The Negro Revolt* (New York: Harper and Brothers, 1962).

26. For the skeptics, see, for example, World Bank, "Poverty," https://www.worldbank .org/en/topic/poverty/overview (accessed February 21, 2021); Tanvi Masra, "The Working Class That Wasn't," *CityLab*, December 11, 2017, https://www.citylab .com/equity/2017/12/who-is-working-class-in-3-infographics/547559/ (accessed February 21, 2021); Tamara Draut, "Understanding the Working Class," *Dēmos*, April 16, 2018, https://www.demos.org/research/understanding-working -class#Who-Calls-Themselves-Working-Class? (accessed February 21, 2021).

27. Boggs, "Liberalism, Marxism, and Black Political Power," 160.

10. BLACK CONSCIOUSNESS IN WAKANDA

1. These conspiracy claims of powerful Jews controlling blacks and other people of color in the interest of destroying the white race, or at least white might, are worldwide. Sources are many, but for critical discussions, see Andrew F. Wilson, "#whitegenocide, the Alt-right and Conspiracy Theory: How Secrecy and Suspicion Contributed to the Mainstreaming of Hate," *Secrecy and Society* 1, no. 2 (2018), especially 15 and 25. See also the Anti-Defamation League's report "White Supremacists' Anti-Semitic and Anti-Immigrant Sentiments Often Intersect," October 27, 2018, https://www.adl.org/blog/white-supremacists-anti -semitic-and-anti-immigrant-sentiments-often-intersect (accessed February 21, 2021).

2. See, for example, Melanie Kaye/Kantrowitz, *The Color of Jews: Racial Politics and Radical Diasporism*, annotated edition (Bloomington: Indiana University Press, 2007). See also Lewis R. Gordon, "Rarely Kosher: Studying Jews of Color in North America," *American Jewish History* 100, no. 1 (2016): 105–16.

3. See Shaye J. D. Cohen, *The Beginning of Jewishness: Boundaries, Varieties, Uncertainties* (Berkeley: University of California Press, 1999); Charles Finch III, *Echoes of the Old Darkland: Themes from the African Eden* (Decatur, GA: Khenti, 1991); and Sigmund Freud, *Moses and Monotheism*, trans. Katherine Jones (New York: Vintage, 1955 [1939]).

4. Kwasi Wiredu, *Cultural Universals and Particulars* (Bloomington: Indiana University Press, 1996).

5. Drucilla Cornell, *Defending Ideals: War, Democracy, and Political Struggle* (New York: Routledge, 2004).

6. Chris Lebron, "'Black Panther' Is Not the Movie We Deserve," *Boston Review*, Feb-

ruary 17, 2018, http://bostonreview.net/race/christopher-lebron-black-panther (accessed February 21, 2021).

7. Sudip Sen, "The Panther and the Monkey Chant," *African Identities* 16, no. 3 (2018): 231–33.

8. See Mikhail Lyubansky, "The Racial Politics of Black Panther," *Psychology Today*, February 20, 2018, https://www.psychologytoday.com/us/blog/between-the -lines/201802/the-racial-politics-black-panther (accessed February 21, 2021); and Sen, "The Panther and the Monkey Chant."

9. Nkiru Uwechia Nzegwu, *His Majesty Nnaemeka Alfred Ugochukwu Achebe: A Ten-Year Milestone* (Endicott, NY: Africa Resource Press, 2013).

10. Timothy Obiezu, "Group of Chibok Schoolgirls Reportedly Escape Boko Haram Captors," VOA News, January 29, 2021, https://www.voanews.com/africa/group -chibok-schoolgirls-reportedly-escape-boko-haram-captors (accessed February 21, 2021).

11. This phenomenon is well known among scholars of the history of colonization in Africa. See, for example, Walter Rodney, *How Europe Underdeveloped Africa* (Washington, DC: Howard University Press, 1982), especially 355, 409, 424. See also Nkiru Uwechia Nzegwu, *Family Matters: Feminist Concepts in African Philosophy of Culture* (Albany: State University of New York Press, 2006), 68, 72–75, 80–85; and Moses A. Awinsong, "The Colonial and Post-Colonial Transformation of African Chieftaincy: A Historiography," *Historia* 26 (2017): 121–28.

12. See Asfa-Wossen Asserate, *King of Kings: The Triumph and Tragedy of Emperor Haile Selassie I of Ethiopia*, trans. Peter Lewis (London: Haus Publishing, 2017); and, of course, from the emperor himself, Haile Selassie, *My Life and Ethiopia's Progress: The Autobiography of Emperor Haile Selassie I*, 2 vols. (Chicago: Frontlines Publishers, 1997–1999).

13. Frantz Fanon, *Alienation and Freedom*, trans. Steven Corcoran (London: Bloomsbury Academic, 2018), 283.

14. Frantz Fanon, *Les damnés de la terre* [The damned of the earth] (Paris: Éditions Gallimard, 1991 [1961]), 253.

15. Lyubansky, "The Racial Politics of Black Panther."

16. This question of what we should be learning from Africa has a long line of reflection from Black intellectuals such as W.E.B. Du Bois, Anténor Firmin, and Cheikh Anta Diop, as well as intellectuals of European Jewish descent such as Franz Boas through to Jean Comaroff and John Comaroff. For discussion, see, for example, Lewis R. Gordon, *Freedom, Justice, and Decolonization* (New York: Routledge, 2021); and Jean Comaroff and John L. Comaroff, *Theory from the South: Or, How Euro-America Is Evolving Toward Africa* (New York: Routledge, 2012).

17. Mira Jacobs, "Infinity War Director Confirms Shuri Is the Smartest MCU Character," CBR.com, August 14, 2018, https://www.cbr.com/infinity-war-director -confirms-shuri-smartest-mcu-character/ (accessed February 21, 2021).

18. Richard Wright, *Native Son* (New York: Harper Perennial Modern Classics, 2005 [1904]). For discussions elaborating on these themes, see Jane Anna Gor-

don and Cyrus Ernesto Zirakzadeh, eds., *The Politics of Richard Wright: Perspectives on Resistance* (Lexington: University Press of Kentucky, 2019).

19. Frantz Fanon, *Peau noire, masques blancs* (Paris: Éditions du Seuil, 1952), 117.

20. César Ross, "The Role of Africa in the Foreign Policy of China," in *Geopolitics and Decolonization: Perspectives from the Global South*, ed. Fernanda Frizzo Bragato and Lewis R. Gordon (London: Rowman and Littlefield International, 2018), 227–41.

21. V. T. Rajshekar, *Dalit: The Black Untouchables of India*, 3rd ed. (Atlanta, GA: Clarity Press, 2009), 43.

11. BLUE

1. Amiri Baraka, *Blues People: Negro Music in White America* (New York: William and Morrow, 1963).

2. Ralph Ellison, *Invisible Man* (New York: Vintage, 1990 [1952]).

3. Frantz Fanon, *Les damnés de la terre* [The damned of the earth] (Paris: Éditions Gallimard, 1991 [1961]), 300.

4. Debra Devi, "Why Is the Blues Called 'the Blues'?," *Huffington Post Arts and Culture*, January 4, 2013, http://www.huffingtonpost.com/debra-devi/blues -music-history_b_2399330.html (accessed February 21, 2021).

5. Catherine E. McKinley, *Indigo: In Search of the Color That Seduced the World* (New York: Bloomsbury, 2011).

6. Frantz Fanon, "Racism and Culture," in *Pour la révolution africaine: Écrits politiques* (Paris: François Maspero, 1964), 41–42 (my translation).

7. Fanon, "Racism and Culture," 38–39 (my translation).

8. Søren Kierkegaard, *Either/Or*, vol. 1, trans. David F. Swenson and Lillian Marvin Swenson, with revisions and a foreword by Howard A. Johnson (Princeton, NJ: Princeton University Press, 1959), 19.

9. Ralph Ellison, *Shadow and Act* (New York: Vintage, 1964), 78–79.

10. Fanon, *Les damnés de la terre*, 291 (my translation).

11. Stephon Alexander, *The Jazz of Physics: The Secret Link Between Music and the Structure of the Universe* (New York: Basic Books, 2016). See also Robin D. G. Kelley's study of one of the giants of bebop: *Thelonious Monk: The Life and Times of an American Original* (New York: Free Press, 2010).

12. Mabogo Percy More, "Philosophy and Jazz," chapter 7 in *Looking Through Philosophy in Black: Memoirs* (London: Rowman and Littlefield International, 2018), 135–58.

13. Lewis R. Gordon, "The Problem of Maturity in Hip Hop," *Review of Education, Pedagogy, and Cultural Studies* 27, no. 4 (October–December 2005): 367–89. I had also written on hip hop's postmodern elements in "Sketches of Jazz," chapter 13 in *Her Majesty's Other Children*, back in the late 1990s. See also Devon Johnson, *Black Nihilism and Antiblack Racism* (Lanham, MD: Rowman and Littlefield, 2021), 152–91.

14. Friedrich Nietzsche, *"The Birth of Tragedy" and Other Writings*, trans. Ronald Speirs (Cambridge, UK: Cambridge University, 1999 [1872]).

15. From Richard A. Jones, *A Hill in Lunenburg: New Poems* (Frederick, MD: American Star Books, 2014), 27.

16. See, for example, Evelyn Brooks Higginbotham, *Righteous Discontent: The Women's Movement in the Black Baptist Church, 1880–1920,* rev. ed. (Cambridge, MA: Harvard University Press, 1994).

17. Carlo Collodi, *Pinocchio,* trans. Geoffrey Brock (New York: New York Review Books Classics, 2009).

18. Apuleius, *The Golden Ass: The Transformations of Lucius,* trans. Robert Graves (New York: Farrar, Straus and Giroux, 2009).

19. See K. Kris Hirst, "The Domestication History of Donkeys (Equus Asinus)," ThoughtCo., May 30, 2019, https://www.thoughtco.com/the-domestication -history-of-donkeys-170660 (accessed February 21, 2021).

20. This was initially speculation on my part, but Danny Glover, the actor who plays this character, confirmed to me in a conversation at the African American History Museum in Detroit that the character is indeed a reference to the African American poet Langston Hughes.

21. See Lewis R. Gordon, "Continues to Rise: Muhammad Ali (1942–2016)," *Viewpoint Magazine,* June 7, 2016, https://viewpointmag.com/2016/06/07/continues -to-rise-muhammad-ali-1942-2016/ (accessed February 21, 2021). Repost also available at *Truthout,* July 17, 2016, https://truthout.org/articles/continues-to -rise-muhammad-ali-1942-2016/ (accessed February 21, 2021).

22. See Dante Alighieri, *The Divine Comedy of Dante Alighieri,* vol. 1, *Inferno,* trans. Allen Mandelbaum (New York: Bantam Books, 1980).

23. Brian Locke, *Racial Stigma on the Hollywood Screen* (New York: Palgrave, 2009).

24. Keisha Blain, *Set the World on Fire: Black Nationalist Women and the Global Struggle for Freedom* (Philadelphia: University of Pennsylvania Press, 2018).

25. See Jane Anna Gordon, *Statelessness and Contemporary Enslavement* (New York: Routledge, 2020); and Douglass A. Blackmon, *Slavery by Another Name: The Re-Enslavement of Black Americans from the Civil War to World War II* (New York: Anchor, 2009 [2008]).

26. Rowan Ricardo Phillips, *When Blackness Rhymes with Blackness* (Urbana, IL: Dalkey Archive Press, 2010).

27. Alicia Garza, interviewed by L. A. Kauffman, "A Love Note to Our Folks: Alicia Garza on the Organizing of #BlackLivesMatter," *n+1,* January 15, 2015, https:// nplusonemag.com/online-only/online-only/a-love-note-to-our-folks/ (accessed February 21, 2021). See also the following memoirs of the movement: Alicia Garza, *The Purpose of Power: How We Come Together When We Fall Apart* (New York: One World, 2020); and Patrisse Khan-Cullors and Asha Bandele, *When They Call You a Terrorist: A Black Lives Matter Memoir* (New York: St. Martin's Griffin, 2018).

28. Garza, *The Purpose of Power,* 111.

12. VALUED

1. See Frederick Douglass, *Narrative of the Life of Frederick Douglass, an American Slave* (Boston: Anti-Slavery Office, 1845), *My Bondage and My Freedom* (New

York: Miller, Orton, and Mulligan, 1855), and *The Life and Times of Frederick Douglass* (Radford, VA: Wilder Publications, 2008 [1881]).

2. The literature is vast, but the most infamous is Daniel Patrick Moynihan's *The Negro Family in America: A Case for National Action* (Washington, DC: Government Printing Office, 1965). Responses were many. Among the most poignant and historically accurate is Herbert G. Gutman's *The Black Family in Slavery and Freedom: 1750–1925* (New York: Pantheon Books, 1976); and for a classic theoretical critique, see Hortense J. Spillers's "Mama's Baby, Papa's Maybe: An American Grammar Book," originally published in 1987 and included in her collection *Black, White, and in Color: Essays on American Literature and Culture* (Chicago: University of Chicago Press, 2003), 203–29.

3. I have already discussed this phenomenon of white and often derelict fatherhood in chapter 5 and chapter 7. For comprehensive studies across North America, the Caribbean and Central America, and South America, see Jane Dailey, *White Fright: The Sexual Panic at the Heart of America's Racist History* (New York: Basic Books, 2020); Hilary McD. Beckles, *Natural Rebels: A Social History of Enslaved Women in Barbados* (New Brunswick, NJ: Rutgers University Press, 1989); Tanya Katerí Hernández, *Racial Subordination in Latin America: The Role of the State, Customary Law, and the New Civil Rights Response* (Cambridge, UK: Cambridge University Press, 2014); and Lamonte Aidoo, *Slavery Unseen: Sex, Power, and Violence in Brazilian History* (Durham, NC: Duke University Press, 2019).

4. Douglass, *The Life and Times of Frederick Douglass*, 16.

5. Simone Weil, "The Love of God and Affliction," in *The Simone Weil Reader*, ed. George A. Panichas (Kingston, RI: Moyer Bell, 1985), 446.

6. James Boggs, *The American Revolution: Pages from a Negro Worker's Notebook*, 2nd ed. (New York: Monthly Review Press, 2009 [1963]), 12.

ACKNOWLEDGMENTS

This book was written under difficult circumstances. I thank the kind community of family and friends who took time to read through drafts and gave me feedback along the way. They include several of my current and former students: Stephon Alexander, Phil Barron, Derefe Kimarley Chevannes, Gregory Doukas, Douglas Ficek, Matthew B. Holmes, Josué López, Dana Miranda, Tom Meagher, Stephanie Mercado-Irizarry, Michael Monahan, Steve Nuñez, Darian Spearman, Sandra Stephens, and Taylor Tate.

Colleagues and beloved friends, all astute readers, include Alexandra Bernstein-Naples, John Carney, Drucilla Cornell, Sayan Dey, Sukhdeep Ghuman, Oscar Guardiola-Rivera, Patricia Huntington, Richard Jones, Samantha Sulaiman Kostmayer, Rozena Maart, Mary Malley, Mabogo More, Nancy Naples, Marilyn Nissim-Sabat, Wandia Njoya, Michael Paradiso-Michau, Gina Rourke, Gary Schwartz, Rosemere Ferreira da Silva, Jaspal Kaur Singh, Jason Stanley, and Sherry Zane.

I also thank Richard Jones and Chandramohan Sathyanathan for permission to quote verses from their poems and James Davis for permission to quote from his article.

My mother-in-law, Jean Comaroff, and father-in-law, John Comaroff, dedicated much time to reading the text carefully and offering very helpful feedback. So, too, did my cousin Claudia Gastrow. My children—Mathieu, Jennifer, Sula, and Elijah—offered their perspectives on some of the chapters. My wife, Jane Anna Gordon, read through early drafts, for which I give thanks, as she is also my primary interlocutor and the person who, when I open my eyes each morning, makes me happy to be alive.

I also thank Eric Chinski for proposing the project; Deborah Ghim, Julia Ringo, M. P. Klier, and Eric for their valuable editorial recommendations; and Josephine Greywoode for a delightful conversation on the book over lunch in London.

And finally, I thank the ancestors to whom this book is dedicated. Their spirit shines through many of these pages, even where they are not mentioned. The love they offered the world continues through the love they brought to the lives of many.

INDEX

Aaron (ancient Hebrew priest), 227
Aaron, Hank, v
Abd-al-Rahmân, 79
Abel, Colin, v
Abya Yala, 56–57, 76, 77, 81, 134
Abyssinians (reggae group), 202
Achebe, Chinua, 209
Aegisthus, 205
Aeschylus, 205
affirmative action, 130
Africa, 46, 51, 73, 76–78, 90–93, 101,
    105, 110, 132–34, 138, 141–42, 147,
    167–69, 174–92, 204, 225; anti-colonial
    struggles in, 15
African American History Museum
    (Detroit), 225n20
African Americans, 27, 135, 144, 167–68,
    172, 190, 197, 205, 225
Africana people/African diaspora, 132,
    176, 182, 186, 190–91, 241n14
Africans, 56–57, 79, 93, 136–37, 141,
    147, 168, 173, 177, 186, 191, 196,
    198
Afro-Brazilians, 202
Afrofuturity, 184
Afro-Jews, 50, 168
Afro-Latin Americans/Afro-Latinx, 130,
    167
Afro-Muslims, 77–80, 117
afrosomatophilia, 36
Agamemnon, 205

agency, 64, 76, 84, 121, 143, 189, 205, 216,
    225
agriculture, 92, 211
Agrippa, Henry Cornelius, 236
Ahmed, Sara, 246n20
Aidoo, Lamonte, 233n9, 236n12, 245n15,
    251n21, 256n3
AIDS (acquired immunodeficiency
    syndrome), 49
Ainu people, 97
Aja, 52
Akan, 52
Aker (the god), 226
albinos, 55
Alcestis, 134
alcoholism, 45, 48, 197, 200
aletheia, 170
Alexander, Michelle, 243, 247
Alexander, Stephon, 202, 254, 257
Ali, Muhammad, 212, 255n21
allegory, 76, 169, 170, 183, 184, 224
Alper, Joe, 240n7
Americas, 56, 93, 98, 134
Amharic, 77, 80, 176
Amin, Samir, v
anarchy, 184
Andalusia, 77, 80
Anglo-Saxons, 57
animals, 41–42, 52, 66, 69, 78, 215, 233n2;
    love of, 41; wild, 42, 138
animal studies, 233–34n2

A NOTE ABOUT THE AUTHOR

Lewis R. Gordon is an Afro-Jewish philosopher, political thinker, educator, and musician. He is the head of the philosophy department at the University of Connecticut, Storrs. He has received accolades for his numerous influential books and articles, many of which have been reprinted and translated around the world. He is the honorary president of the Global Center for Advanced Studies and a former president of the Caribbean Philosophical Association, for which he now serves as the chairperson of awards and global collaborations.